WCVB-TV BOSTON

WCVB-TV BOSTON

How We Built the
Greatest Television Station
In America

Robert M. Bennett
with Dennis Richard

WCVB-TV Boston © 2013 Robert M. Bennett

Trade Paperback ISBN: 978-1-939447-11-1
Ebook ISBN: 978-1-939447-12-8

Printed in the United States of America

For Marjie, Kelly, Casey, and Brandon

Contents

Foreword

I ONCE TOLD Bob Bennett that if he ever made something out of a television station he was going to be working at in Boston, I would be very interested in buying that station if it was ever offered for sale. Apparently, as he was making his way out the door to take his new job at Boston Broadcasters, Inc., my words registered with him. Many years later, when he and his team had built WCVB-TV into one of America's best television stations, he called me and told me it was for sale. I had been waiting for that call because I knew that if anyone could build a station from the ground up, and make it a station of unbelievable recognition and success, that person would be Bob Bennett.

Bob's work at Metromedia is legendary. I first met him in 1963, when Metromedia was buying KTTV-Los Angeles. Bob was a sales manager at the time and I remember quite vividly when we met. After we had made our purchase, I was making my way around the room greeting the new Metromedia employees and introducing myself, when someone came over to me, yanked on my tie, and said, "Mr. Kluge, that's the ugliest tie I have ever seen." I broke out laughing at the joke and then, for the first time, met the man who was to help me shape the future of Metromedia. I think he was quite taken aback at his statement about my tie, and soon realized it might not have been the best way for him to make an introduction to his new boss, but I took it in a good-natured way and we became friends.

Bob's first assignment was to be the General Manager of WTTG-TV in Washington, D.C. In the late 50s, I bought a controlling interest in the DuMont Television Network, and thus acquired the New York City and Washington, D.C. DuMont stations. We changed the name of the company in 1961, to Metromedia Broadcasting, Inc, and when the time came in 1966 to choose a GM for WTTG-TV, I chose Bob. Even though he had come out of sales and had no real-world experience as a general manager, I knew there was something special about him, so we sent him to Washington.

He faced a tough assignment at that time. Other stations were already entrenched in the market: NBC had an owned and operated station, as did CBS, which was owned by the *Washington Post,* and there was also an ABC affiliate. Bob and his team did extraordinary things with the station, and by the end of the first year, WTTG had made seventy percent of all profit in the market. He took a station that was losing in the ratings, and made it a model for emulation by other stations. He seemed to have the uncanny ability to create popular local television programming, which would be the hall-mark of his career.

Based on the success he had at WTTG, we then sent Bob to New York's WNEW-TV to be the GM. While there, he once again showed his tremendous local programming talent and made the station a winner. He was the first broadcaster to create an all-minority news-cast and to create local programming that touched a nerve in the New York market.

In the early 1970s, he was offered a job with a company in Bos-ton that had been embroiled in a long and bitter battle to acquire a license to run a television station. At the time he was hired as the GM, the company did not formally own the license. But I knew that if they did acquire that license, it was going to take a man like Bob Bennett to make that station a success.

They eventually acquired the license, and that station became WCVB-TV Boston, one of the most highly awarded and talked-about stations in television history. It also became the number one ABC affiliate in the country. *The New York Times* declared that WCVB was a "television station with a different vision." That dif-ferent vision belonged to Bob Bennett, so when he called me and told me that the station was for sale, I went right up to Boston and bought it. We had come full circle in some ways, because after I bought the station, I offered Bob the position of President of Metro-media Broadcasting, Inc., and he took it. We went on to do great things at Metromedia, including taking the company private in what was then the highest leveraged buyout in U.S. history. I was fortunate to have great partners around me, which included Bob, Stuart Subotnick, and George Duncan.

My philosophy for all of my life has been the pursuit of excellence. Throughout Bob's career, he has joined me in that lofty pursuit. Bob Bennett is a truly unique individual and a legend in television broadcasting. He is the recipient of many awards, including the coveted *Broadcasting & Cable Magazine*'s Hall of Fame Award. He is an extraordinary person and a man of enormous understanding, insight, and talent. There was never a job for Metromedia that he could not get done. Bob is a builder. People would gravitate toward him and were always eager to join his team. I always believed that one of the major reasons for Bob's success was his ability to motivate people. He was hailed as "the man most responsible for balancing the profit motive with a concern for quality programming."

I never met a person at Metromedia who would not work his or her heart out just to please him. From all of this came the extraordinary career of a man who has helped shape the business of television. They don't make people like him anymore.

—John W. Kluge

Preface

I FIRST MET Bob Bennett in 1995 in Los Angeles, when a friend of mine suggested that I meet him. This friend went on to tell me that he felt strongly about getting the two of us together because, as he put it, "You and Bob speak the same language." I did not know who Bob Bennett was at the time, nor did I know what language we had in common, but I took his telephone number and called to introduce myself. Bob agreed to meet me, and our first meeting was very congenial. We asked one another questions as to who we were, what we did, and what projects we were working on. I remember him telling me that he was financing three full-length films all at once out of his own pocket, and that he owned a film library. He spoke very little about his background in television, and he never really explained to me what his previous accomplishments were. I didn't realize at the time that he was the man behind one of the most respected and honored television stations in the country, WCVB-TV Boston.

Even though I grew up in Boston, I had not heard of Bob Bennett. He came to Boston in 1971 to become General Manager of WCVB-TV, and it was not too long afterwards that I moved to New York City. Under the leadership of one man, WCVB-TV was about to offer some very new and exciting original local programming. The new WCVB-TV was to become a television station that responded to the needs of local viewers, yet showed such originality that other station managers across the country were forced to sit up and take notice, even if they didn't want to. The person who was leading that charge was Bob Bennett. In many ways, Bob forever changed the face of local television and made it into something original, exciting, and very much tied in with the local community. As a previous WCVB-TV sales executive put it to me, "Local programming was in our DNA."

If you really wanted to find out what was going on in Boston, and for that matter in New England, you turned your channel to WCVB-TV. Bob's unique slant on original local programming struck a meaningful chord with viewers. He had already done similar things when he was General Manager in Washington, D.C., at WTTG-TV, and then in New York as General Manager of WNEW-TV, but it was in Boston where he perfected and set the stage for what local television was to become, and what he was to become—the pioneer of local broadcasting. He made a programming commitment to the community that garnered such devotion and loyalty from viewers that the station's ratings were sky high over and over again.

In many ways, Bob Bennett was the man behind John Kluge, who helped build Metromedia into the powerhouse that it once was. John was in some ways low profile and almost invisible. Bob was the voice of Metromedia. It was his job to speak directly to Wall Street.

Today, Bob Bennett is not a household name, nor is he remembered to any great degree by the younger generation working in the broadcast world. In some ways he believes that his legacy is folded up somewhere in time and forgotten—that he was a product of another time and another generation. But he has vowed to stay current, and today he works with a group of innovative people on the launching of a global, live, Web-based, business-to-business video news network.

This is the book about a man who came from Altoona, Pennsylvania, and by sheer luck and hard work, carved out a career in the broadcast business as one of the most celebrated broadcasters ever. This is a book about the celebration of his accomplishments, his thoughts and reflections on his life, and the shared memories of his close friends and colleagues. Many remember him as a "lion" in the broadcast world. He thinks of himself as an enabler. "I like to give people a chance to do their jobs and to do them well," he has said on many occasions. He is highly competitive and does not like to lose at anything. He loves the television business and has a great passion for it.

During his career, he had the foresight and the constant urge to try something different and to surround himself with the best possible people he could find. His career weaved in and out of three major television markets, and he has left behind an impressive list of accomplishments that people today are still trying to emulate. He is known for his warm personality and for his ability to get people to believe in themselves and to do the best possible job they can do. There is a certain sense of magic and popularity about him that inspires people to live up to his standards. In many ways, they want to succeed because of him.

In trying to gain a true understanding of people's interpretations of Bob, I have usually started my interviews with one very basic question: "In your mind, what is it about Bob Bennett that has made him able to achieve such great success in his life?" The answer always came back the same: "Bob Bennett is the very rare individual who has the ability to make you feel that when he is talking to you, you are the only person in the world and that you are his equal." Everyone I came in contact with told me he is the most likeable person they have ever met.

In many ways, the Bob Bennett who pioneered local programming back then could not exist in today's corporate world where individual personalities mean very little, if anything at all. He was fortunate to have been around in a time that was truly the Golden Age of Television, and thankful to have had the opportunity to work with such people as John Kluge. In relation to WCVB-TV, he considers himself fortunate to have had a group of investors, board members, and owners who thought their major job was to bring quality television programming to their viewers, not just to make a lot of money. It was in this world that Bob Bennett lived and thrived.

He has been rewarded by the television industry in many ways and is the recipient of many coveted awards that include the following: Broadcasting Cable Hall of Fame, National Television Academy Management Hall of Fame, 1985 NAPTE President's Award, MDA Paragon Award, New England Broadcasting Hall of Fame, Emmy Award for Outstanding Leadership and Innovation, ABC Leadership Award, NAPTE International President's Award, Variety Club Heart and Charity Award, Peabody Award and the 2005 National Association of Broadcasters Pioneer Award, as well as Bryant College and Stone Hill College both having bestowed upon him honorary doctorate awards.

Bob Bennett is truly a remarkable and unique individual. The television world he was a part of was responsive first to the problems, needs, and interests of its viewers, and second to its profits. In many ways, that world does not exist anymore. The digital age is now upon us and he is making sure there is a role in it for him. He is a man with a great passion for television and we are all grateful recipients of his life's work.

—Dennis Richard
Los Angeles, CA

Introduction

I NEVER THOUGHT a book about me, or any of the successes I have had over the years, would be of great interest to the general reader. I have always thought about writing my story, but for many reasons, never got around to it. I have never really looked at my own personal accomplishments as being of enough historical significance that I should tell the world about them. I do know one thing: I was always very fortunate to have gifted and talented people around me. All of us seemed to have the feeling that there was nothing in the television world that we could not accomplish. What we did not know at the time was that we were making television history.

WCVB-TV in Boston is the place where I really made my mark. The opportunity came from a chance telephone call to join a broadcast group that was engaged in a fight to gain control of a television license that the FCC had put up for bid. Something inside me told me this might be my chance to hit a home run, so I went for it. I must have been a real gambler back then. While I was only involved in this day-to-day battle for a short period of time since my arrival in Boston in 1971, it had already been a raging bitter 25-year war that had hundreds of briefs, petitions, filings, challenges, and multiple appearances before the FCC and the Court of Appeals. There were at least four million dollars in expenses to both parties involved and approximately one million dollars in expenses to tax payers. It was the story that broke the hearts and souls of some, dashed the hopes of others and ultimately made forty-five people millionaires by the time the station was sold to Metromedia.

Today, WCVB-TV is a television success story that has been, by all measures, difficult to rival by any other television station in the country. Some say that Boston and New England came together as a region because of WCVB-TV. The station has won many coveted awards for excellence in live local television programming, including the George Foster Peabody Award. In 1981, the station won eighteen of forty-seven Emmy Awards and the *New York Times* called us one of (if not) the finest television station in the country. WCVB-TV has consistently received high ratings for its exceptional news coverage and is regarded as one of the nation's best commercial television stations. There was one point in the station's history that we produced over sixty hours of local weekly programming, which was twice the amount of any other ABC affiliate.

The way in which people watch television today and what they watch has radically changed. I am involved with a group of people who are focused on the creation of a global video news network to be distributed over the Internet. While this global video news network is still in its infancy, it has the same look and feel of any of the news presentations on one of the three major networks or any of the cable news networks; its news reports are scheduled to come in from news bureaus globally to its news hubs in London and New York. These news feeds will then be distributed on computer screens around the world and then archived on their company's website for future viewing. With live streaming video, the viewer has the immediacy of watching as it is happening; and with archived video, there is the whole idea of video on demand, the "when and where I want to watch it" idea that is so prevalent today. Viewers of this news network can go on to the company's website to see the news feeds. I am involved with this group as the Chairman of the Board and our company is building a business-to-business global news network for the financial services industry.

All of this is designed and structured to take advantage of the shift in the way media is now produced, consumed, and sold. We are living in the Digital World which gives us content any time, night or day, directly to our current location. As broadband penetration deepens worldwide, those who are in traditional media are forced to change the way they do business. Old media is out and new media is in. Today, everybody needs a digital strategy to succeed.

Faster connections mean greater growth in broadband penetration. Greater broadband penetration means that more people,
young and old, are watching video when and where they want to
watch it, which means one does not have to turn on the television
set anymore just to watch a program. The growth of digital content
consumption has challenged existing business models in the entertainment industry. With the use of the Internet, you can build value
by aggregating a lucrative global online audience and create effi-
cient, high-margin advertising and sponsorship revenue streams.
You can also build a digital content library and license digital content to consumers live, on demand, and across multiple platforms
from IP to mobile.

Programmers of today have tremendous challenges. The digital consumer is somewhat elusive and is searching for content that
is specific to them, so it is quite a task to try to program to this
massive universe of people. Upstart video networks have surfaced,
with each trying to attract digital consumers who represent a young
demographic for which advertisers have always been searching.

This audience is a sophisticated global audience that exerts
control over when, where, and how they consume media, which
throws a monkey wrench into the traditional ways of old media.
And because of the capabilities on the Internet, all consumer behavior from clicks to clickthroughs can be tracked and analyzed, giving advertisers and programmers further information on which to
study and base their ideas.

In the case of the web-based video news network that I am associated with, the origin of their news feeds, or for that matter, the
studios they use, can essentially be anywhere in the world they
want them to be. This rapidly changing digital technology offers
the ability to record from anywhere in the world right through the
Internet. No satellite is needed. For example, a live webcast can be
produced in a small closet in China, and viewers around the world
can be watching it streaming on their computer screens in a matter of seconds, with very little noticeable delay. And the cameras
needed today to make a web video will fit in your pocket. All of this
is low cost, compared to the cost structures in place for old media,
and certainly a million miles away from the broadcast business I
grew up in.

When I started out in television, you had to have a big studio with big cameras, long, thick cables, primitive (by today's standards) recording equipment and plenty of people running around. We weren't huddled around a small screen with a keyboard attached to it on a desk planning the full buildout of a television network. It was just the opposite: we had to build a big building, fill it with equipment, clear markets and run like hell to sell advertising. We weren't running around back then using the word viral, and everything that we did seemed to have a technology that was more at a standstill than in motion.

I started my career in the age of test patterns. Anybody remember test patterns on television screens? They were television test signals typically broadcast at times when a transmitter was not active and no program was being broadcast. They were also known as Test Cards, as they had a set of lineup patterns that enabled television cameras and receivers to be adjusted to show the picture correctly. In some cases, even today, Test Cards are still being used at television production studios. That was my world. Today we turn on the computer and the marvel of live video is playing right in front of us. The computer screen has taken the place, some would argue, of the television screen, or are they now becoming one?

When I started out in television, we were using the most up-to-date technology available at that time, something called kinescopes, which began as telerecording devices in Britain by using a 16 mm or 35 mm movie camera mounted in front of a video monitor and synchronized to the monitor's scanning rate. Kinescopes back then were the only way to preserve live television broadcasts prior to the introduction of videotape in 1956. The Television Museums in Beverly Hills and New York City have kinescopes for viewing of network programs such as the DuMont Television Network. If you want to see something primitive, go look at a kinescope. This was the available technology back then, and these kinescopes were sent by plane to the west coast after shows were broadcast on the east coast. Today, people record a video on their cell phone in one country and send it to someone else's cell phone in another country for instantaneous viewing. Everything is instant and very available to you when and where you want it. You don't have to check TV Guide anymore to see what you can watch.

But is this still television? It sure has the same look and feel to it. As I look back, I realize that the television world that I started in was filled with very primitive technology by today's standards, but we made it work and we had fun doing it. We didn't really have much to work with in the way of equipment back then but we had a lot of enthusiasm for a new medium that was sweeping across the country. So what has really changed in today's world of television? We're still rushing forward. We're still making programs and people are still watching them and there's still a great deal of enthusiasm out there among writers, actors, producers, and industry executives.

I'm pleased to still be in the game, making programming that means something to someone. In addition to working on programming for the financial services industry, I am very involved with Bennett Worldwide Productions. Television keeps moving and so do I.

I'm honored to have been recognized by many in the industry for my accomplishments along with many others who have had an impact. I'm very glad to be part of today's new Digital Age and I continue to shake my head in wonder as this new kind of global news network is being built on a desktop.

I want to thank my family, friends, and colleagues in the television industry who have made it a point to remind me that what I did along with others in local television, and the story of WCVB-TV in particular, is of enough importance for me to write this book and for you, the reader, to find it interesting.

To me, television is still the kind of miracle that we should never take for granted. It is hard to believe that long ago, before the Internet, streaming video, cellular phones with video capabilities, YouTube, Facebook, Twitter and many of the other distribution methods that are with us today, there was once a new and emerging medium called television. I am very fortunate to have been a part of it all. I guess a magic dust of some kind was sprinkled on me. For that I am forever grateful.

—Robert M. Bennett
Newport Beach, CA

Beginnings

A Kid from Altoona, PA

I WAS BORN at Mercy Hospital in Pittsburg, PA, on April 17, 1927, and shortly thereafter went to live with my grandparents in the Juniata section of Altoona. The Altoona of back then was a thriving manufacturing and railroad center. The Pennsylvania Railroad made its home there and had a very large manufacturing facility that built locomotives, freight cars, passenger cars, and railroad equipment. Railroad construction yards were all over the place and seemed to stretch on forever. Everybody seemed to work for the railroad. I can still remember the noise and the smell of that old world.

The Native American tribe known as the Iroquois Confederacy originally inhabited Altoona, with the first western settlers arriving sometime in the 1700s. In 1849, the Pennsylvania Railroad was chartered and quickly began developing Altoona as the staging area for the construction of the rail line. By 1925, 14,000 of the 17,000 industrial workers in the area were employees of the railroad. In addition to the railroad, Altoona was also home to its fair share of silk, meatpacking, and clothing businesses. The city of Altoona grew to support the shops and the railroad workforce, which in turn, grew to support the railroad. Immigrants from all over Europe moved to Altoona to take advantage of well-paying jobs. Altoona's population more than doubled from 39,000 in 1900, to 82,000 in its peak year in 1930.

In the Altoona where I grew up, everybody knew everybody

within a ten-block radius. It was a time when the rules of the day were to be good to people and respect your neighbors. My mother, Elma Charlotte Bennett, was working for the Stouffer restaurant chain in Pittsburgh at the time that I was born. I grew up with my grandfather, Harry Bennett, and my grandmother, Rebecca Carney Bennett, in Altoona. When I went to live with them, my grandfather was already retired from the railroad. My mother continued to live in Pittsburgh and, in 1937, met and married Dr. Leonard Arons, who was a general practitioner.

My earliest memory is that of walking down the street with my grandfather. He was the most incredible man I have ever met. I was just fascinated by him. As we walked down the street, everyone would wave and say hello to us. My grandfather worked for the railroad as the Master Mechanic. He was born in Canada, came to the States as a young man, and started working for the railroad as a machinist for seven cents an hour. He barely had a fifth grade education, but he worked his way up through the railroad ranks from machinist to assistant foreman and then foreman, and then all the way to being in charge of all of the railroad workers. He was of English and Irish extraction and had four sons, Raymond, Emery, William, and Burt by his first wife, and then my mother and her brother Wallace with my grandmother, his second wife. His son Emery was one of the founders of the railroad labor union. This, of course, made for an interesting situation, since my grandfather was a tried and true railroad man and, as I mentioned, the Master Mechanic for the railroad. Here was his son now running the labor union and causing all kinds of trouble by breaking into the railroads and trying to disrupt the flow of railroad business.

To finally put an end to the growing trouble the union presented, my grandfather called a meeting of all of the union men to meet at the top of a mountain. As my grandfather described it to me, there were fires burning and people chanting and yelling for the establishment of the union. My grandfather drove up to that mountaintop and confronted the angry union people. He was about sixty-five years old at the time and gray-haired. As he walked through, the crowds parted to let him by. His son Emory was already at the top of the hill preaching the union mantra, "Let's get the railroad! Let's go on strike." And all of a sudden silence came over the crowd as my grandfather walked up to the platform and just simply slapped his son in the face. The crowd was stunned. I'm sure Emory was stunned. He then turned and talked to the crowd and gave them a piece of his mind. As for the results of that mountain top meeting, the union did not strike. It was not until many years later that they finally unionized.

My grandfather always struck me as a religious man, but it always embarrassed me that neither my grandfather nor grand-mother ever went to church. He would always insist that I go to Sunday school, which I did on a frequent basis. I seemed to be cov-ering most religions back then, since I attended a variety of Sunday schools: Lutheran, Episcopalian, and Catholic. Finally, this nagging question had built up so much inside of me that one day I got up the courage to ask him, "Grandpa, why don't you go to church? Why do you insist that I go to church and not you?" He sat me down and gave me his answer. He simply said, "Bobby, the only thing you need to remember as you go through life is the Golden Rule. If there is a heaven, you'll get there. And when you get there, I'll be waiting for you." I'm sure he's up there right now waiting for me, and I have never forgotten the Golden Rule.

I've always tried to live by the basic principles he taught me. Even today, I am terribly afraid of hurting anyone. If I feel that I have in any way, and on occasion I have (which happens to all of us), I will feel troubled to the point of losing sleep. If I feel that someone dislikes me, even if I don't know the reason why, I want to correct it. I've always thought, given these kinds of emotional feelings, that I would never succeed in business, since I did not have an iron will that just stampedes its way into the world. But I'm not like that. In time, I learned to use these emotions to my advantage by reach-ing out and establishing connections with people. I have always felt that it was better to treat people with respect, no matter what the circumstances are.

Harry Bennett died when he was eighty-six. At that time, the railroad business was moving to Chicago. It was the start of World War II, and the demand shifted from steam locomotives to the more cost-efficient and reliable diesel and electric locomotives that were being built in Chicago. After World War II, the era of the railroad ended. The nation was developing interstate highways and the ways that goods were being shipped was changing.

I still worship the memory of my grandfather. In the Altoona where I was raised, people sat on porches in the summer, and as my grandfather would walk by, they would wave and I'm sure talk about him. On his birthday, many people in the town, especially the people who worked for him, would come out to celebrate.

Years later, I was going through an old railroad book and found a story about Harry Bennett and the Pennsylvania Railroad. It seems that when my grandfather was the Master Mechanic for the railroad, he bet the railroad's president that he could build twenty locomotives in sixty days. Something like that had never been done before. Up until that time, it took four months to build twenty locomotives, so what my grandfather was proposing would have been quite an accomplishment, if not an impossible one. And he did it. He ended up putting on three work shifts and he won his bet. Today, this would not seem like much, but back then, in the early days of railroading, this was something big.

Some time ago I received a poem in the mail dedicated to my grandfather. I take it out from time to time and read it.

Old Man
By Robert Fleming Lantz, "Poet Laureate" of the Altoona Works
Dedicated to W.H. Bennett, Master Mechanic

Old Man never had so much to say
When he made his rounds through the shop.
A nod of the head or a curt "Hello"
Was usually all you got,
But if he caught you soldiering
Or trying to run a bluff
His keen gray eyes would reduce your size
Then...what he said was enough!

Old Man wasn't the driving kind
But he knew what his men could do
He knew if he set a certain task,
That somehow they'd carry it through...
For back of that grim immobile face
And that voice of authority,
These men had found a heart profound
In its depth of sympathy.

Old Man may never have won a prize
In a modern efficiency school,
But he knew that a man is something more
Than a wheel, a cog, or a tool.
So he mourned with us when we suffered loss
And smiled when our hearts were glad.
In sorrows or joys, we were always "his boys"
And he gave the best he had.

Old Man, though your hair is silvered o'er
And our paths are drifting apart,
We know that you still retain a place
For "your boys" in your rugged heart.
May your future years be the best of all,
And may all your dreams come true;
For "the boys," you bet, will not forget
Old Man, who was "white" clean through.

My mother was a very special person. She was eighteen when I was born and I always looked upon her as a sister. She was fun and we always did a lot of things together. I became a real part of her life. She liked it that way and so did I. She always had a very youthful outlook on life and it was contagious. In some ways, it was my grandmother who really played the mother role in my life. I met my birth father only once, some years later. We had lunch and I was able to tell him about all of my early accomplishments in television and that I was not looking for anything from him. I was very proud of myself at that lunch.

My mother's kid brother was named after the president of the Pennsylvania Railroad, Richard Attebury, so his name was Wallace Richard Attebury Bennett. The president of the railroad was a very important figure back then so it was fitting that they would name Wallace after this man, especially since my grandfather was the Master Mechanic.

Unfortunately, Wallace went into the hospital for a tonsil operation and the doctors suggested they should take out his adenoids while he was there. When they did that they clipped an optic nerve by accident, which made one of his eyes look off to the side. He had a very difficult time trying to overcome that and, since there were no operations back then to repair the damage, he had to deal with it. The kids in the neighborhood were merciless in their teasing of Wallace. As a result, he became very distant and depressed and soon was borderline retarded, since he was not able to live a normal life. Other than the kids, everyone loved Wally Bennett. He was fun to be around. He and I shared a brotherly kind of bond.

I went to public school in Altoona, starting first at Noble Grade School for six years and then to Keith Junior High School.

Bud Shaffer, a friend, writes:
"As kids, we played in a ball field a few blocks from Bob's home. It was owned by a Dr. Brubaker and the field was called Brubaker Field. If we needed money for a baseball, a bat, gloves, etc., Dr. Brubaker would generously provide money for us to buy them. We always sent Bob up to his house to seek donations, because he always came back with the goods!

In those days we'd spend most of our time in Memorial Park, swimming, playing basketball, and playing cards, usually pinochle. One rainy afternoon, Bob decided we should go to a friend's house whose parents were out of town. We decided we would invite a few girls in the neighborhood and we ended up playing strip poker. The game was rudely interrupted before anyone was totally naked because the parents returned home unexpectedly. Bob was always egging us on to do something that would usually result in us getting in some kind of trouble."

I remained in public schools until I moved to Pittsburgh in 1940. At the time, I was living with my mother and stepfather. It was a very interesting year. We lived in a place called Squirrel Hill, which was made up of about ninety-nine percent middle to high-income Jewish families. I was enrolled at Alderdice, a kind of junior high and high school combined. On the other side of Squirrel Hill was an area called Greenfield, which was one of the roughest areas in Pittsburgh and was made up primarily of Polish, Italian, and Black steelworkers. There was a long-running sports competitiveness between Squirrel Hill and Greenfield, but the mountain separated everyone to some degree, so the two sides never really had much occasion to mix with one another. But that summer, just prior to my arrival, the high school and junior high school combination burned down in

Greenfield and they had to bus all of the kids to Squirrel Hill. And here I was, just fresh in from Altoona, eager to meet new friends, with no idea what I was in store for.

Well, needless to say, race riots soon broke out so frequently that the state police were called in on a regular basis. It got so bad there that the school principal was beaten up at a school gathering at Kenny Wood Park just because he was carrying tickets to a sporting event that some of the students wanted. He later died. The whole place was in a state of police emergency and here I was, the eager kid from Altoona just moving into town.

In the midst of all this chaos, I attended Taylor Alderdice School and was given books and a locker. I didn't know a soul. One day as I was putting my books in my locker, this guy came up to me and grabbed my books out of my hands and threw them down to the floor and started kicking them. I looked at him and got ready to fight. Then I looked around and saw four or five of his friends coming up behind him. This was not the time to start anything, but I was mad. This went on for three or four days, in which he would continue to take my books and kick them. One day, I swung at him, and somehow my punched missed. He came back at me and connected and I went down like a sack of potatoes. All of his buddies joined in and started kicking me. So I did the first thing that came to mind after that fight: I stopped going to school. My stepfather would drop me off in front of the school and for two or three weeks I would skip out the back door and just go to the movies or just walk around. I was scared to death of going back to school. Walking around town seemed like a much better and safer idea at the time.

Finally, the school called, and wanted to know why I was not in class. My stepfather came down on me, so it wasn't long before I was back at school again getting into daily fist fights. I always seemed to come home with a cut lip or black eye. I didn't want to hurt my stepfather's feelings, so I never told him why I was always in so many scrapes at school. I never told my mother the truth either because I was afraid she would tell him. So as a result, every night my stepfather would send me to bed thinking I was a roughneck who needed someone to keep me in line.

Mitzi McCall, friend, writes:

"Bobby's mother, Elma, and my mother were best friends. In some ways, he always considered me his bratty little sister. On a vacation one summer to Atlantic City, we were playing around on the beach and I remember kicking sand in his face, which used to make him very mad. I told my mother that Bobby was kicking sand in my face and when his mother heard the story, she grounded him for the day. He still holds that resentment 71 years later."

Before Squirrel Hill, I was always a good student, not a great one. I always attended and enjoyed school. As my school fist fights and brawls continued, my stepfather would threaten me with military school if I didn't stop. I never really thought he'd make good on his threat, but one day he did just that. He announced he was sending me to Staunton Military Academy in Virginia. The year was 1941, and I was not at all thrilled about going.

Life at Staunton Military Academy

MY MOTHER DROVE me down to Staunton Military Academy in September of 1941, when I was at the ripe age of fourteen. She felt military school was going to be good for me. My stepfather felt this would be reform school for me, and I thought they were both crazy. I was betting for sure that I was heading for a terrible experience. Ironically, it turned out to be the best four years of my life. I liked the place as soon as I arrived. The success in life that I have achieved in dealing with people and gaining control of my drive and ambition I believe I owe directly to my four years at Staunton Military Academy.

From the moment I arrived, I realized that Staunton was all about serious competition. You were either the best at something and if you were not, you strove to be better. This was not a place for coming in second place. Strangely though, I was ready for military school. Something inside me made me rise to the task. I was ready for challenges and I was ready to take on the world—even though I was still only a fourteen-year-old skinny kid.

In December of 1941, the war broke out, and being at a military school, our lives were greatly affected. When I look back now, I realize that I was at the right place at the right time. During those four years I met some incredible people and I am happy to say that I am still close with some of them today. Staunton was no walk in the park. It was tough. It could take a lot out of you and some guys couldn't take it. But none of this seemed to bother me.

What they put cadets through back then in military school might be construed today as being extremely degrading. I cannot say if the life of a cadet is the same today, but back then you really had to walk a straight line. The officers had sabers, and if you stepped out of line, you were in for swift retribution. If they didn't hit you with a broom, they would hit you with a saber. They would just walk into your room, inspect the place, and if they found your room was not clean, they would say, "Okay, this deserves one swat. That deserves two swats." If one guy got hit, his roommate got hit. You would have to stand side-by-side, lean over and grab your ankles and get hit in the buttocks with the end of the saber. Not my kind of fun. Needless to say, you kept your room clean and your shoes shined. You made damn sure you were in bed on time and punctual to class, and there was no tolerance for any kind of smart-ass behavior.

We soon realized that punishment from the school officers was one form; punishment from our fellow cadets for screwing up could be much worse. They could lash out with their own torturous kind of punishment if they had to. And they did if you didn't keep your act together.

At Staunton I was a skinny kid with a big mouth. It was important for me to get a letter so I went out for boxing and boxed for all four years. I was All State Boxing Champion for four years and I was tops in all four different weight categories. I seemed to have the soul of a fighter and I was throwing strong punches. Staunton was teaching me all about self-discipline, academics, military thinking, and strategy.

We fought the Naval Academy and West Point. The first year I went out for boxing, I weighed almost 130 pounds. I was in training and when the first match was coming up, I told the coach that I wanted to fight bantam, which was 120 pounds. He told me I was not eligible since I weighed too much. I think I lost the 10 pounds in two or three days and fought bantamweight that year.

When I entered Staunton I never thought of myself as a boxer. The only exposure I had ever had to boxing was when I was much younger in Pittsburgh when my stepfather would go to fights as the ring doctor. Many times there were not a lot of seats left, so if there was a celebrity in town, they would tell him to go and sit where Doc Aron's son is sitting; "just put him on your lap," they would say. I think I sat on a lot of famous laps back then, including John Henry Lewis, Joe Lewis, Buddy Baer, Abe Simon, and Billy Conn.

I grew to like boxing and I had my share of boxing heroes. My biggest hero at the time was Joe Taylor, Staunton's boxing coach. He was the light heavyweight champion of the Army for about four years in a row during World War I.

During my senior year, our boxing team had been training hard for a big fight with West Point. For some reason, whenever I go anywhere on a trip or on a vacation, even today, I usually get sick. I must have something programmed into my system that sets this off. Here I was—captain of the team, boosting moral, training night and day and as soon as I got on the train, I felt a tug in my throat. I thought to myself: oh boy, here it comes. With me, I just never get a common sore throat; I always get strep throat. People would think I had the mumps because my glands would swell up so bad. By the time we arrived at West Point, I was running a high fever.

The coach said to me, "Bobby, you don't look good. Go over to the infirmary and get checked out." I did and I ended up spending the night there.

The next morning the doctor told me, "I don't want you to fight. Go tell the coach you're coming down with something and you can't fight. But you can leave." I got dressed and went to see the coach. He wanted to know if everything was alright with me and I told him, "Yes, no problem. The doctor says I can fight." So I fought the captain of their team, a guy by the name of Hezard. I did win that fight, but I'm sure I had no business even being in the ring at the time, feeling the way I was feeling.

In those days we used to wear woolen jerseys, so I put this jersey on and for some unknown reason began scratching and itching. I thought it must have been my nerves because I was somewhat nervous fighting in front of the nine hundred expected cadets who were attending the event. We used to fight by weight, so the lighter guys would fight first and then the heavyweights would come on. There were four or five guys ahead of me and I was scratching and itching and wringing wet in this woolen jersey. Finally my fight came up and I fought a good battle. I knocked the guy out in the second round and I was exhilarated. I came back to the locker room, took a shower, and to my surprise saw these little red splotches all over me. I thought I must have been allergic to the woolen jersey.

As a special treat for winning, the coach took up us to New York to Billy Rose's Diamond Horseshoe for a celebration and we spent the night at the Edison Hotel. While we were at the Diamond Horseshoe I got up from the table to go to the men's room and I suddenly fainted. It scared the hell out of everybody so they took me back to the hotel, where we were staying. The doctor came in and said that I had Scarlet Fever and that I would have to leave right away or the whole place would have to be in quarantine. My fellow teammates quickly put me in a private train car and sent me back to my grandmother in Pennsylvania. The doctor said that no one could really tell for sure if I had scarlet fever until maybe six weeks or so later, if the soles of my feet and palms of my hands began to peel. I put that thought out of my head. Scarlet Fever? No thanks. Not me.

Soon after that I went back to school and missed one fight. I was told under no circumstances to do anything strenuous that could affect my heart. Our last boxing event was in Washington, D.C., and I wanted to make that fight so badly that I told the coach I was fine and didn't have Scarlet Fever. I fought in the fight and won. A couple of weeks later, I went out for baseball and I was looking at my feet and hands, and sure enough, they were peeling. I had Scarlet Fever. Nonetheless, I became captain of the team and played shortstop and first base.

I was also president of the senior class and head of the Cotillion Club that put on dances. We brought in big bands like Les Brown and Woody Herman. That was as close to show business as I could get back then and I was thrilled about it.

Through my Staunton years I had many roommates, but on my last year there, I had a very large room with four roommates. One of my roommates was a guy named Roger Brown, who had been a close friend of mine over the years. We had similar interests and were very competitive in everything we did, especially with girls.

Roger Brown, Roommate at Staunton:

"Bob and I were roommates our senior year at Staunton and were competitive at everything. At graduation I was awarded the Best Athlete Trophy for football, boxing, and track (co-captain) and this irked him to no end. He thought he was the one entitled to that trophy since he was then captain of the boxing and baseball teams. He was not happy. However, giving credit where credit is due, Bob was a fabulous boxer in his time. He won three fights his senior year in less than three seconds of the first rounds and was state champion in two different weight

categories, 145 and 155 pounds, and he accomplished this on skinny legs only a mother could love. Back then, we both had acne problems and we would make fun of each other's face. Bob brought this to a peak when he posted a quarantine notice on the door, warning cadets of my extreme acne problem. I was mortified needless to say, but to this day, we are still very competitive against one another. Throughout his career, he knew it would drive me crazy if he sent me any positive PR regarding his career and accomplishments, which he seemed to always do to me. One day I was so fed up with all this positive press about him, that I called his secretary Maria Morales and requested that I be removed from all his mailing lists because, in my opinion, anyone could look good in the noncompetitive world of television. I soon received a letter from Maria telling me I had been on the "B" list, and that now Bob was going to put me on the "A" list so I would now be receiving massive mailings that would only irk me more."

In some ways, the conditions I experienced back then at military school between 1941 and 1945 will never be the same again. All of the eighteen and over guys were in the service and here we were at fourteen through eighteen years of age in prep school, in a town that had one military school, one all-girl college, and two all-girl prep boarding schools.

Patsy Good, friend, writes:
"I really didn't know Bobby when I was growing up in Juniata. It was wartime and like most kids, my 'uniform awareness' was at a peak level. So when a boy (not much older than I) began showing up on my next door neighbor Sarah Wilson's porch swing sporting a military school uniform, I, of course, became very aware of him (or at least of his uniform). Every time I saw him on Sarah's porch, I would roller-skate over the brick sidewalk, past her house to the corner and back many times, resulting in a few skinned knees and elbows.

I never met that uniformed boy until years later, but my grandfather told me that he was Bobby Bennett and that his grandfather lived in the big brick house on the corner of Broadway and Ninth Avenue.

Time passed, and I grew up and met and married Tony Good, who talked a lot about his good friend Bobby Bennett who was married and living in California. It's funny now, as I think back and remember that same uniformed boy on Sarah's porch."

My mother was a good friend of Bob and Dolores Hope. Dolores was singing under the name of Dolores Reade with the Don Bestor Orchestra, which was the house band at the William Penn Hotel in Pittsburgh. Sometime around 1936, Bob and Dolores moved to Los Angeles and urged my mother to visit them. For the next five to seven years, my mother and stepfather were frequent guests at the Hope's Palm Springs home. When the war came along, my stepfather went into the service and was overseas for several years. Hope was overseas entertaining the troops on a regular basis, which left Dolores alone in a very big house on Moorpark Street in North Hollywood. She asked my mother to move in with her and she did. I spent my summers in Los Angeles and ended up spending a lot of time with the Hopes.

My mother never wanted to impose upon her friendship with the Hopes, but one night she told Bob that I was graduating from military school and that I did not have an appointment at West Point. Might he have any connections? Hope jumped up and called Happy Chandler, who was then either the Governor or the Senator from Kentucky. He asked Chandler if he had a possible appointment for West Point. Shortly thereafter, I received a telephone call from my mother who told me that through Hope's connections I might have a chance at either going to West Point in 1945, or Annapolis in 1946. I didn't really want to go into the Navy, but if I didn't get into West Point I was ready to take what I thought was the next best thing. So I told her my first choice was West Point. A few days later she called me and told me I was in at West Point.

In April of 1945, I had broken my ankle on the very day that President Roosevelt died. Everybody I saw that day was crying so I thought they felt sorry for me because of my ankle. At the time I was romantically involved with a girl named Esther Sperlock, who was from Alabama and a student at Mary Baldwin College. She was very southern and very sexy and used to call me "sugar" all the time; I would just melt.

When Esther and I were separated by distance, we would write fifteen- to twenty-page love letters to one another. One day I received a letter from her in which she stated that said she did not think she could wait the five years it would take me to go through West Point. Upon reading this, I was devastated. I believed strongly that we were in love and we were planning a future together. This shouldn't be happening to me, I kept saying to myself.

Now I had major decisions to make. In those days, if you were in the military, you had a three-year accelerated course during the war instead of four, and then you were transferred overseas immediately for two years, and those were years you were not allowed to be married. It was a very emotional time for me because I was in love and I knew I had a big sacrifice to make. I now had to decide between my interest in a military career and my love for Esther Sperlock.

I decided I could not live without Esther Sperlock, so the next day I wrote a wire to Senator Downey of California, who had given me the West Point appointment and told him that I wanted to relinquish my appointment. Boy, talk about being stupid, young, and in love. I was all of them in one. Within minutes of actually sending that wire, my mail came—and I'm not exaggerating—it could not have been more than minutes—I opened what I thought was another love letter from Esther only this time to find it was an announcement of Esther Sperlock's forthcoming marriage to a colonel in the Air Force. I was devastated. Here she had been telling me she was in love with me and what our future together would be like, and all the time she had a boyfriend.

When my senses finally returned, I quickly tried to get Senator Downey on the telephone, and with some difficulty, finally got through to his office. He came on the phone and I told him that the wire I had sent was a mistake and that I did not want to relinquish my appointment to West Point. I can still remember his icy words, "Sorry Bob, it's too late. We've already notified the first alternate and there is nothing we can do." Then he lectured me about being impetuous. When I told my mother, she was just as devastated as me. It finally sunk in just how stupid I really had been. Now of course, I had to quickly sign up for the draft.

In a lot of ways, Staunton Military Academy prepared me for life. When I enrolled there I was a smart-aleck little skinny kid with a big mouth. After four years I was a very subdued, highly disciplined, and prepared man ready for my life ahead. I was now a person with strong leadership skills that would some day prove to be essential to me. I loved Staunton and I loved the military life.

On V-J Day (Victory in Japan Day), August 14, 1945, I volunteered for the army and was accepted. The war seemed to be coming to an end and here I was now getting ready to start basic training—me, again, with my strep throat.

Life in the Military

SOON I WAS on a troop train from Pittsburgh to Indiantown Gap, Pennsylvania, on my way for induction into the armed forces, and of course, I looked like I had the mumps again. I was very distressed at the time and really felt I had blown my life. What I did not know is that I was given the luckiest break in my life, and I have Esther Sperlock and her "Dear John" letter to thank for it. She may have actually saved my life. Had I gone to West Point at that particular time, my graduating class would have been the class of 1949 and about fifty percent of the 1949 West Point graduating class died in Korea. It was a terrible thing, but I still had the Army ahead of me and I was terribly unhappy, so much so that the first eighteen months of my life in the service is pretty much a blank page.

When I had been in for six months, the officers came around and asked me if I wanted to re-enlist for another year; if I did, they would give me a thirty-day furlough. I reenlisted even though I knew I shouldn't have. I took the thirty days and went to California. My outfit went to Paris.

Now, to get to California I had to fly in an airplane, and I had never flown before. I was scared to death of flying. To this day I am afraid of heights and still not too thrilled about flying. There were no commercial planes in those days so I was going to hitch a ride on an Army plane, instead of taking a week by train to get out to Los Angeles. When I was ready to leave, one of the guys told me to go over to the Army Transport Command and ask for a ride to California. So I went up to the counter and told the officer that I was on leave and that I was going to California and would like to hitch a ride on a plane. He looked at me like I was from outer space and said, "Get the hell out of here kid! You think the Army has nothing better to do than fly GIs all over the world for recreation? Get the hell out of here!" So I walked away and really felt like a fool. Then it dawned on me, I really should start playing some angles here. One way or the other, I was going to get to California.

I waited for the night shift to come in because that brought a different change of officers at the counter. When a new man took his shift at the counter, I walked up to him and started in on a story that even made me shake my head in bewilderment. I told him the following: "I have to get to California and it is a matter of life and death. I just reenlisted so the service could be my career and this terrible thing has happened and I have to get to California. I can't really tell you what it is, but it's horrible."

"All right, I'll tell you what I'll do," he said. "You hang around here. If there is a seat on a plane tonight I'll give it to you. If not, you come back tomorrow night and then the next night and for how-ever long it takes until I have a seat. It could be two nights, it could be a week, but that's the deal. I can't guarantee you a seat, but at least you'll have a shot." So I sat there and went to sleep.

About six o'clock the next morning I woke up and the same guy said to me, "Hey, I've got a seat for you. Get yourself ready." I took a look at the plane which looked like a C-47 and I noticed that it was filled with field grade officers. They were all colonels and gener-als. There were two empty seats on the plane. I climbed in and sat myself down and put on my strap. I was scared to death sitting in an airplane that would soon be taking off. But at this point, I was at least happy that I was leaving and heading to California.

The longer I sat in the plane the more the idea of flying was turn-ing my stomach over. I didn't want those doors to close. Something was telling me to get off the plane. The engine started revving up and the plane started shaking the butterflies around in my stomach. I knew for sure I was going to die. We started to move and then sud-denly this man came on the runway and waved the plane down. We turned around and headed back. I started to think that maybe they knew I had snuck on the plane. I was sure that they were going to take me off and put me in prison. When the plane came to a stop, the same man opened the door and told the pilot to hold the plane because General Eisenhower would be getting on momentarily.

Now remember, in 1945, General Dwight D. Eisenhower was like Napoleon. He was the king. He could walk on water. He won the war for us. You can imagine all the mumbling and whispering that was now going on in the plane. It was as though God was getting on the plane with us.

There was only one empty seat left on the plane and it was right next to me, of course. General Eisenhower was soon going to be sitting right next to Bob Bennett. I was frozen solid with fear. There was a general seated in front of me and I leaned forward and softly said to him: "Sir, as you know, General Eisenhower is getting on the plane and the only empty seat is next to me. I think you two might have more in common, so I'd be very happy to exchange seats with you."

I then stood up to change seats and the general yelled out to me, "Sit down pal! Nobody wants that seat."

I was stunned. What was I going to sit and talk to General Eisenhower about for the six-hour trip to California? If he found out that I was lying about the reason I was on the plane he might try to check me out. I was just sitting there like Jackie Gleason as the Poor Soul getting ready to have a nervous breakdown.

Somewhere between one to thirty minutes went by with no sign of General Eisenhower. There was now dead silence in the airplane. I was wondering if anyone was even breathing. Suddenly this same man who waved the plane down ran out on the runway carrying a giant box. He opened the door and put the box on the plane and said, "Here's the box Admiral Nimitz is sending to General Eisenhower in California. Have a good trip," and closed the door. Boy did my heart rate suddenly return to normal. I was so relieved that Eisenhower wasn't getting on the plane that I forgot about my fear of flying. I made it to California, stayed for thirty days and had a really great time. My only problem was that everybody seemed to be getting out of the Army back then and here I was re-enlisting.

After my thirty days in California were up, I wanted to stay a little longer and my stepfather came up with an idea. Being a doctor, he had certain pull with the hospitals. I had developed a little sty in my eye and he took me over to Pasadena Hospital. As my admitting doctor, he told the nurses there that I had conjunctivitis. He then said to a hospital official he knew, "Look, this is my kid. He has just come back from the service. He's only got a thirty-day furlough. Book him in under conjunctivitis and let me spend a couple of weeks with him." So they booked me into the hospital, and there I was, a very embarrassed healthy man walking around in a white outfit with funny shoes. Others there had lost legs and arms and had very serious medical conditions. For me, I was admitted with fake conjunctivitis, so I knew I had to get out. I managed to leave, and I stretched my furlough into two more weeks.

Finally, I had to go back and I went to Camp Beal in California, which was then a kickoff center for those who were going to Korea or Japan. There were thousands of service people waiting in what looked like a four block line to be sent somewhere. Every day we would go stand in line to get our orders. Up toward the beginning of the line you could hear a guy's voice yelling out, "Smith, Japan;" "Jones, Korea," etc. When I got to the beginning of the line he said to me, "Bennett, Fort Lewis, Washington." Fort Lewis, Washington? I didn't even know where Fort Lewis, Washington, was. Now that I was in the Army, I wanted to go to Japan. I told the guy that everyone else was going to Japan and Korea and that's where I wanted to go. He said to me, "Fort Lewis, Washington, is where you're going, Bennett." And off I went again like a poor soul. The war was now over, and the 2nd Division, which was the most decorated division in World War II, was now stationed in Fort Lewis, Washington. It was an artillery unit and I wound up in the 16th Battery of the 2nd Division.

When I got to Fort Lewis with my funny little bag and my ill-fitting suit, I opened the door to report for duty and I thought the first sergeant was so happy to see me that he was going to kiss me. What I didn't know was that the men of this outfit had been promoted so many times that they only had high ranking noncommissioned officers. This section had something like fifty master sergeants, thirty-seven first sergeants, two staff sergeants, five corporals, and now one private, me. And these guys had just come back from overseas. They were heroes. They had fought a war. They were decorated and here I was, the new private who only had one decoration to his credit, a good conduct ribbon. "I'm reporting for service sir," I told him.

None of these guys wanted to pull K.P., none of them wanted guard duty, and none of them wanted grunt duty of any kind. That's where I came in. They had no one to assign these lower duties to except me, one of the few privates in the division. I pulled K.P. I pulled guard duty. It was like being in prison. It dawned on me quickly that it was time to get out of the Army. Every time I put in for a transfer they said to me, "Wrong, you ain't going anywhere." I did all the work; they just rested. Occasionally, they'd bring prisoners in to do some work, but I was really the guy carrying the load. I had to get out of there.

Finally I went to the Commanding Officer and the Table of Organization and I found out that there was a slot for a noncommissioned athletic officer that had not yet been filled. That job had my name all over it. I walked over to the Battalion Commander and gave him the heaviest stroke he probably ever had in his life. I told him all about my athletic background. I told him that I would develop a well-rounded schedule that would include softball and all kinds of other activities. He said, "Okay," and sent word down the ranks that I was now going to be the new athletic officer. When the first sergeant got the news, he almost cried in front of me—here was his only grunt worker now joining the ranks of all the others who where just sitting around doing nothing. I spent about six months with my room in the pool hall and spent the rest of my time in the Army putting on softball games.

Once again however, and against my wishes this time, I was going to have to return to the boxing ring. The Battalion Commander called me in one day and told me he wanted me to represent the battalion. Our welterweight was a truck driver who had broken his wrist in an accident and couldn't fight. They had gone through their records and found out about my boxing background. I pleaded with the commander and told him, "Thank you for thinking about me, but I'm not interested. I've only got three our four more months left and then I'm out of here. And besides, I'm not in shape to box. I haven't worked out in a long time and I've been smoking too much." The commander looked at me and laughed and said, "Guess what private, get your ass in the ring and start boxing!"

I had to start training and I wasn't in what many would consider the best of shape. My nose had been busted and it had never really healed properly. I was having trouble breathing. I knew I had to get in shape, so I went to the trainer Bob Miles who put me on a rigid training program. When I did get finally get out, I thought I might go into the Golden Gloves. I had visions of boxing in the Olympics. Who knows, maybe I actually might have measured up back then.

In 1947, I went with my mother back to Pittsburgh for a vacation and while we were there, we went to a place called the Bachelor Club, which was owned by Jimmy Greenfield. He was somewhat of a notorious character and the father-in-law of the boxer Billy Conn, one of the greatest fighters of all time. Billy was known, among other things, for the great battle he fought with Joe Lewis. Billy fought Joe hard and it looked like he had the title in his hand. After the twelfth round, his manager came to his corner and told him he'd give him back half his bet on the fight if he'd knock Joe out. Billy went back in the ring intent on knocking Joe Lewis out, only it was Billy who got knocked out. Joe knocked him out cold. It was a very famous fight.

Billy Conn was the light heavyweight champ of the world and a very good friend of my mother and father. Billy's problem at the time was that Jimmy Greenfield did not want his daughter marrying a fighter. Unbeknownst to Jimmy, Billy had already married his daughter. Jimmy was so mad when he found out they were married, that he ran over to Billy's house and tried to beat him up. Some time later, Billy had a major argument with his father-in-law and for a while stayed with us in our apartment in Pittsburgh.

Back at the Bachelor's club in Pittsburgh with my mother, one of my mother's friends walked up and kissed me on the cheek, leaving a lipstick mark. Then Billy walked up and the two of us went off to sit at a separate table where we could talk privately. He started telling me about his boxing career, when this guy walked in right past Billy and rudely brushed up against his elbow. I could see that the two of them exchanged angry glances.

"Who's the guy? It looked like he was going to knock you on your ass," I said to him.

Billy was aggravated. "That guy is a nobody."

"A nobody? Who is he?"

For some evil reason, of which I am uncertain, I kept edging Billy on. I was fueling the anger that I could see was raging inside of him.

"You know Billy; you're not in great shape anymore. Looks like you put on a few extra pounds. What would they say if the great Billy Conn got knocked on his ass by some Mr. Nobody? What would they say about that? Your reputation is at stake here Billy."

With that last line, Billy sunk down into his thoughts, gulped down his two massive steak sandwiches and started gritting his teeth like a mad dog. I was beginning to realize I had gone too far.

Billy jumped up and followed the guy into the game room. I followed him. Our friend Mr. Nobody was sitting at a table. Billy marched up to him and, as he was getting ready to throw a punch, Mr. Nobody pulled a gun out. Everybody in the room scattered except Billy, who just stood there and refused to back down. There was a lot of noise and confusion which brought my mother into the room. She sensed something wasn't right, especially when she saw Billy standing in front of Mr. Nobody and me there with lipstick on my cheek. My mother assumed that there was a fight over a woman and more bloodshed was on the way, so she ran and stood right in front of me. When she did this, she saw the gun and fainted. Suddenly, everybody was worried about the woman on the floor and rushed to her aid. Mr. Nobody quickly took off out the back door.

As I look back on it now, I certainly went way too far in pushing Billy. There could have been blood all over the place and I would have been responsible for it.

Life in California

WHEN I FINALLY got out of the service, I headed straight for California and decided that show business might be in my blood. Hollywood, here I come! I never saw myself as a director or producer, but I knew that somewhere out there in Hollywoodland there might be a place for me. The fact that my mother and stepfather were already living in Los Angeles certainly made it easier. My stepfather opened his medical office on the Sunset Strip, which back then was the place to be. Through the relationship my stepfather had with Bob Hope, he never had a shortage of celebrity patients. Some names that come to mind are Robert Young, Jerry Colonna, and James Dunn.

This was a very interesting period for a young man to be in California. Shortly after my arrival, I matriculated at UCLA, and to help put myself through school, I opened up a small insurance office in the back of my stepfather's office. I used to hustle all his patients for insurance. I'd be sitting there doing my homework and they'd ask me what I was doing. I'd tell them that I was working my way through college. I would continue my conversation with them and before long it would lead to the fact that I was selling insurance and that they might have a need to be insured. I'd ask them if they knew who their insurance agent was and nobody seemed to ever remember their agent's name. This would, of course, open the door for me to write their insurance for them. Why not give a young college kid a try? I got so good at it that I used to write three to five insurance policies a week. I was probably making five hundred dollars a month, which came in handy back then. Since I had no real expenses, I was living pretty well off my insurance sales job. I also sold used cars and then went to work for the circulation department of the *Los Angeles Times*. I even worked one summer for Edgar Bergen.

In the fall of 1948, I was at UCLA, and somehow I heard that Edgar Bergen was looking for a chauffeur. I thought it was a one-weekend job, but it ended up lasting about five weeks. My job was to carry Charlie McCarthy in a box to wherever Bergen was appearing. It was fun. I had no preconditions as to what I was going to get paid, but I really didn't worry about it at the time. Bergen was very rich and I worked very hard and drove him everywhere. I was supposed to be going to school at the time, but I was not going to class and was falling way behind in my schoolwork. Finally, I went in to see Bergen about my check and I had allowed myself to think that I was going to get at least one thousand dollars for a whole month's work, which would have equated to about $250 a week, which, back then, was a lot of money. However, to my surprise, the check Burgin handed me was for $250. I looked at it and I couldn't believe it.

I asked him straight out, "Edgar, is this the right number?"

He looked at me in disbelief.

"Why Bob, isn't it alright?"

"No, Edgar it is not," I told him in an angry voice. "What are you paying me here, thirty cents an hour? It looks like you need this money more than I do," I shouted to him as I threw the check back at him and walked out the door.

That afternoon, I received a call from his office and they apologized. They didn't want me to be upset so I went back over the office and this time the check was for about three hundred dollars. I still wasn't happy about the amount, but I took it. I then found out sometime later that Edgar Bergen was one of the cheapest guys in Hollywood. Everyone thought it was Jack Benny who held that title, but Edgar Bergen took it to a new level. But, I was learning all about Hollywood, and I was very happy to be living in Los Angeles.

Jack Duffield, friend, writes

"Around the time I met Bob I was working at a haberdashery on Sunset Boulevard. Bob and I became good friends and we soon rented a room together in North Hollywood. To say that we were poor is somewhat of an understatement. We were beyond poor, but somehow we managed to survive. To be able to pay the rent

and eat, Bob and I sold aluminum siding together and it was the one thing in our lives that both of us were not successful at. We went through our training together and we were soon out on the street knocking on doors trying to make sales. One day he would do the knocking and then the next day I would do the knocking.

On one of his days to knock, the door opened and a guy came out holding a baby. One of the biggest fears that Bob has is a fear of Dobermans, German Shepherds, and Chows. Of course behind the guy holding the baby, a Chow walked out and started circling Bob's legs and growling. The look of death came over his face. He was stone cold with fear, not moving, and no words were coming out of his mouth. His face turned white. I couldn't help but just stand there and laugh. I don't think he spoke to me for a week, he was so mad.

We only lasted about a week on that job because we felt guilty trying to hustle aluminum siding to little old ladies."

One time, I was traveling back from Altoona to Los Angeles, and with me was the actor Jimmy Dunn. In those days there were no nonstop flights from Altoona to Los Angeles, so we had to make a stop in Chicago. While we were getting ready to leave Chicago, I was sitting in the plane with Jimmy in the section where the seats were facing one another, when in walked the film star Hedy Lamarr, who at the time was considered by many to be the most beautiful woman in show business. She and Jimmy knew one another so she sat down next to me and began talking to Jimmy. Midway through the flight, she told me that she always has trouble sleeping on airplanes since the seats are upright, and asked if it would be possible for her to rest her head on my lap. I quickly grabbed a pillow, placed it on my lap, and she placed her head down on the pillow and fell asleep. I couldn't believe what was happening. I was in heaven. When we landed, I told Hedy that I was to meet a friend of mine named Jack Duffield, and wondered whether she would be good enough to hold me by the arm while we walked off the plane. When we landed, Jack was watching us deplane as Hedy was holding me by the arm walking with me. When we got up in front of Jack, she said to me, "Don't forget to call me, Bob." Jack's face fell on the floor. Later, when he was able to muster the strength to ask me what that was all about,

I told him, "Jack, some things in life you just can't discuss." To this very day, I have never told him the whole story.

Somewhere around this time I met a person by the name of George Fisher, who was then on the CBS radio network in the afternoons. He did a gossip show and it was very well liked. He was a patient of my stepfather and also a friend of my mother's. One day my stepfather said to him, "George, why don't you get Bobby a job as an usher at CBS Radio and then maybe he'll like radio and go into that." On my behalf, George talked to the Head Usher at CBS, a guy by the name of Barr Sheets, who was then head of guest relations at CBS. Barr told me he'd consider me when the next opening came up.

Not long thereafter, an usher job opened up and he hired me. I used to get one dollar a show. One week I'd work as many as fifteen shows. It wasn't much money, but I supplemented it on the side by selling tickets to Lux Radio Theatre to people who wanted to get in. Occasionally, we would have the chance to pocket some Lux tickets that came our way. Cecil B. DeMille was the producer and narrator of Lux Radio Theatre, so it was a big draw back then.

My Own Little Marjie

I WAS INTERESTED in a very attractive young woman named Marjie Albright who was working the switchboard at CBS. Marjie was from South Dakota and I must say, a woman who really caught my interest. She had, and still has, a very sparkling personality. I was very drawn to her right from the start. I used to make excuses just to go and visit her at the switchboard.

At the time, CBS was looking to name a series staring Gale Storm and somehow after meeting Marjie Albright, they named the show, *My Little Margie*, which premiered on CBS as the summer replacement for *I Love Lucy* on June 16, 1952. *My Little Margie* was an American sitcom set in New York City that featured Gale Storm as the twenty-one-year-old Margie Albright, along with former silent film star Charles Farrell as her widowed father, Vern Albright. The show alternated between CBS and NBC from 1952 to 1955. The series was canceled in 1955, and today can be found in syndication.

Dale Sheets, my friend, writes:
"I first met Bob in 1948 at CBS Radio in Hollywood. My brother, Barr Sheets, was in charge of hiring the ushers for all CBS Radio Shows and he had just hired Bob. At that time, I was Head Usher so that meant I was Bob's boss. That didn't make him too happy because I was younger than he was. It was my job to assign the ushers to their posts. We had to show up one hour before each show, fresh-faced and in jacket and tie, shoes shined to a mirror finish and line people up outside the studio. This meant two ushers had to be outside in the hot California sun.

On occasion, Bob and another usher, Kenny McManus, would have had a late night on the town the night before an afternoon show. When they showed up already somewhat wilted, I would assign them to the line (in the hot sun). It was also necessary to have an additional two ushers stand by each side of the stage during the show in order to keep the audience from going onstage after the show. Yes, Bob and Kenny got both of those assignments. All for $1 per show! In spite of all this, Bob and I became best friends.

When I left CBS, I moved to the Time Mirror Newspaper *in the Circulation Department on the Complaint Desk. Shortly after that move, I received a call from Bob asking me if they had any openings. I told him the desk next to me was open. He applied and got the job. What a great experience it was back then for both of us. We gave the circulation manager a tough time. He was seated at his desk in the center of the room, surrounded by other people at desks like ours. We shot rubber bands at him, instantly returning to our phones the moment the bands struck him with pencils at the ready. He never did figure out who was shooting those rubber bands."*

George Fisher's Gossip Show

NOT LONG AFTER my usher job, George Fisher offered me a job at fifty-five dollars per week. The job sounded good on the surface and I was happy to take it. I soon found out that old George didn't have it in his schedule or in his mind to pay me on a regular weekly basis. His idea of paying me was more like every three weeks, or every four weeks, or whenever he got around to it, which didn't make my cash flow situation very comfortable.

One of my job duties while working on George's gossip show was to visit the publicity department of each studio on a daily basis. One day I would be at MGM, the next day at Fox, then at Paramount and so on. It was great fun. After a while I was able to spot which stories were fake stories and which stories were real. Sometimes I was invited on the set of a movie while it was being filmed because they wanted to make sure I took their story and gave it to George. I was also given the chance to interview various movie stars and write about them, even though I really wasn't a good writer. George would always rewrite everything in his own style anyway.

One of the best things about George's job was that he would go out every night to dinner with celebrities and plug their stories. He was always mentioning restaurants on his show. Many places used to let him dine for free just for the advertising he was supplying. Sometimes, we would go to dinner and it was great fun because they always made a fuss over him. We'd go to places like the Macombo or Ciros or the Trocadero, all of which are closed today, but back then, they were the places to be seen.

George did have one big problem: he was a terrible drinker and a nasty drunk. He would get into a fight just about every night. It seemed there was always somebody trying to take a swing at him. He was fascinated with my boxing background, and I think he felt secure that anytime he got into a beef, he had a boxer with him. George's other big problem was that he couldn't fight his way out of a paper bag; so many times I would have to stand in the middle and deflect some guy's punch, or actually take the guy on. I was always coming home with ripped clothes. I finally told George that I had had enough and that I wasn't his bodyguard. I told him I was just trying to get into show business. I said I wanted out and he promised me he would not do it anymore, and for about two weeks, he kept his promise.

One day, at the end of one of his programs, the telephone rang and I picked it up.

"Is Ham Fisher there?" said a rough voice from the other end of the line.

"Ham Fisher? You mean George Fisher?" I asked.

"Ya, that's it. George Fisher. Put him on the phone."

So I handed the telephone to George and he listened for a few moments and then started yelling and screaming at the guy.

"Ya, well let me tell you something, I said it because it's true! Well, I don't care. When I put out a story I check it before so I know what the hell I'm talking about. And I happen to know for a fact that it's true. Alright wise guy, I'll come over there right now. Where are you? I'll be over there in half an hour."

He hung up the phone and looked at me and I could see that he was nervously biting his lip.

"Who was that guy?" I asked.

"Nobody. Don't worry about it."

George did not look happy.

"Tell you what Bob; I want you to come with me."

"Hey George, I just want to remind you about that promise you made to me."

"Bob you have nothing to worry about. Trust me."

I wanted to make sure that there was nothing to worry about so I asked Marjie to join us. I figured if a woman came along, there wouldn't be any fist fighting. I never actually told her the reason we were going and I'm glad I didn't. She agreed to join us and we went to the building, up the elevator, down the hall, and were soon knocking on some guy's door. George kept reassuring me that there would not be any trouble, but if a problem did break out, he was sure I could handle it.

The door suddenly jolted open and to my surprise Max Baer was standing there in his shorts, all two hundred and eighty pounds of him. He was the biggest man I had ever seen. Baer wanted to know which one of us was George Fisher and I quickly pointed to George. He leaned over and picked George up and held him over his head, turned, and then walked into the apartment and gently put him down on the couch. I thought George was down to his last moments on earth; for sure, Max Baer was getting ready to kill him. George was frozen stiff on the couch looking at me and probably wondering why I hadn't thrown any punches at Baer yet. At this point, I just wanted to grab Marjie and get the hell out of there. Baer looked at our terrified faces and broke out laughing. He was known for his sense of humor and was really an all around great guy. But, I didn't know any of this at the time. I think George saw himself being thrown right out the window.

I thought it might be a good idea to change the subject, so I brought up boxing to Baer and he went for it. We ended up talking until 4 a.m., with more people coming and going and all kinds of stories being told. It was one of the greatest moments of my life. When it was over and we walked out to the elevator, I turned and said to Fisher, "George, I remember when Joe Louis got $238,000 for fighting Max Baer. If you think I was going to go up against Max Baer for the meager $55 you pay me every other week, you're a sick person. I don't want to work for you anymore. I quit." I never again worked for George Fisher.

All of this was during the golden days of radio and there were some big names doing a few great programs. At this time, Paley had just raided NBC and a lot of people moved to CBS, except Bob Hope. Suddenly, CBS was a giant in the industry. In Los Angeles, KNX radio was where it was happening with stars like Steve Allen, who was doing a popular nighttime program. It was one of the most exciting times in the history of radio. Television really didn't get started until around 1948–1949. Those prior years of 1944–1948 were so powerful in the radio business that I knew I wanted to be part of it.

Marjie Bennett writes:

"After Bob and I had been going out for a while, we were talking together at CBS and he said to me, 'Marjie, look out the window.' I did so and saw this great big Packard automobile standing outside which he paid about $35 for. He had bought it for me and I didn't even have a driver's license at the time. I didn't have the heart to tell him that I didn't like the car. It was so big you had to jump up on the running board just to get in it. He ended up selling it at a loss, but I'm sure he wishes he still had that car."

On one occasion, as Marjie and I were talking at the switchboard, I looked out the window and saw a guy drive by in an old junk heap of a car. I asked Marjie who that was and she told me it was one of the writers on Lux Radio Theatre. Another car soon drove by but only this time it was a big fancy new one. I asked Marjie again who that guy was.

"Oh, that's a salesman, Bob."

"A salesman?" I said to her. "Let me get this straight, you're telling me the writers drive the junk heaps, and the salesmen drive the high-priced cars?"

"That's it," she told me.

I looked at her as the following words were coming right out of my mouth: "I want to be a salesman."

It had hit me like a bolt of lightening. Of course, becoming a salesman right there and then would have probably been one chance in ten thousand, but at least I finally knew what I wanted to be.

The Age of Television

WHAT I DIDN'T know at the time was how fast the age of television was coming upon us. Commercial television broadcasting did not begin until 1947. Before 1947, the number of television sets in the U.S. probably numbered in the thousands; today, of course, it numbers in the millions. The fastest produced product on the market back then was black and white television sets. And by 1955, over half of all U.S. homes had one.

Early television was very primitive, with baseball games being covered by just a single channel. Early newscasts were known as "chalk talks" where a news man would move a pointer across a map to show geographic locations; close-up talking heads were the order of the day and visuals of any kind were in very short supply. Actors going through the motions of a television show would melt under very hot lights. Most programs back then were done live with any number of problems happening during a broadcast.

By 1948–1949, anyone who lived within the range of the growing number of television stations could watch new programs such as *The Texaco Star Theatre* and a children's program called *Howdy Doody*. In 1948, NBC had a fifteen-minute news cast with Douglas Edwards and *Camel News Caravan* with John Cameron Swayze. Most of the formats of news, situation comedies, variety shows, and dramas were borrowed from radio format, and the number of television sets rose from 6,000 in 1946, to over 12 million by 1951. In 1950, the *Jack Benny Show* appeared, based on its previous radio format.

Television was indeed an industry on the move and I wanted to be part of it.

My Sales Career Takes Off

BY 1950, I needed somewhere between fifteen to eighteen more credits to graduate from UCLA where I had been a part-time student since 1948. The radio bug had bitten me and I really didn't care much for college studies. In retrospect, it was not to bright of me to have quit college, but I thought that as my business career advanced, I would someday return to school.

Marjie and I were married at the Forest Lawn Cemetery in Glendale. Not many people know it, but it is one of the most beautiful places for a wedding. Ronald Reagan and Jane Wyman were married there. We had about 150 people at our wedding and a lot of great memories.

We soon moved into a small apartment on Elm Street in Burbank. When Marjie started as a CBS switchboard operator, she made $55 a week. Now as a secretary, she made $90 a week. That was more money than I was making at the time. We didn't have much, but we were in love and we stretched to make ends meet. Our weekly budget for meat was $10, and whenever we could, we went out to enjoy the nightlife.

Marjie Bennett writes:
"When we moved into our apartment on Elm Street in Burbank, we had very little money and no furniture. We decided to have a Halloween party for the people at KTTV-TV. We took in a wooden patio table from outside and used it for our decoration table. A lot of people showed up that night and one woman remarked to me, "Oh how nice, you moved all of your furniture

outside so we can have a Halloween party."

Mitzi McCall and Charlie Brill, friends, write:
"Way back when the Bennetts were newlyweds and struggling, they invited us to dinner at their modest home in Burbank. Marjie is a world-class cook and that evening had prepared a beautiful prime rib. Everyone was in the den when we saw through the corners of our eyes our dog dragging the expensive prime rib across the floor. Even though the Bennetts were gracious and forgiving over the incident, it sure put a damper on the evening."

One month after we were married, my mother died and the circumstances surrounding her death were very traumatic. I had not heard from her in two or three days and I thought that was rather unusual since we were always in close contact. Edna Dunn, who was a friend of the family, called me and asked me if I had recently seen or been in contact with my mother. I told her no and she suggested I should maybe go over to her house and check on her.

I drove over and opened the door to the house and walked in calling her name. There was no answer, so I walked around the house and then went upstairs where I found my mother dead on the floor. I was in such a state of shock that I was frozen, but somehow I managed to call the police. She had died of natural causes but it was a great and utter shock to Marjie and me. She had no symptoms of any kind and no recent illnesses that anyone could point to. She was only forty-one years old when she died.

My mother was my dearest friend and was very important to me. She was an outstanding woman in many ways. I only wish we could have been together more during her short life. The times we spent together were fabulous. She was always funny and optimistic. She was the life of the party and many people sought out her company. She was beautiful in the way Ginger Rogers was beautiful. She lit up any room and was always the center of attention. People liked to talk to her and she liked to talk to them. I have many vivid memories of dancing with my mother when I was about eighteen years old. My grandparents adored my mother. Needless to say, my mother's death was a very tragic moment for all of us.

Marjie and my mother were the best of friends and always got along well, especially since they shared a mutual love of sports. My wife is a big Lakers fan. During baseball season in Pittsburgh, my mother always had box seats. I would come down on the streetcar from school and meet her at the games. She and baseball in Pittsburgh became one. This was so much the case, that for three or four seasons in a row, my mother's picture was always on the front page of the newspaper with the announcement, "Baseball Season Opens Today." We always knew a lot of baseball players and I considered myself one lucky kid. They were great days for me with lots of wonderful memories.

Bud Shaffer, friend, writes:
"I remember one very special time when Bob and his folks were living in Pittsburgh; his family went to New York City for the week. Bob's grandmother and I went by train to visit with Bob. His grandmother was a really great lady and was always very nice to me. The highlight of the week was when Bob and I went to Forbes Field to see the Pittsburgh Pirates play. Bob's folks had a private box at the field and I thought it was really something very special to be able to be in Forbes Field watching my favorite team play. Bob was grinning from ear to ear. He was such a great host and enjoyed showing us around as much as he could.

"Bobby," She Used to Say

I WILL ALWAYS remember the one thing above all that my mother taught me: "Bobby," she used to say, "There is something I always want you to remember. When you are talking to someone, always look that person directly in the eye and make them feel as though you are only talking to them and that they are the most important person in the world. They will respect you for it and never forget you." I must admit, that is something that I have always remembered and utilized in my career, and it works. People remember and respect you for it.

I like to think that what she taught me has had a tremendously positive effect on me. I believe I can trace my own success to my relationship with my mother and the many things she taught me. I have a lot of her qualities in me and I have always felt myself fortunate about that.

With great sadness, I took my mother's body back to Altoona because my grandmother wanted her daughter to be buried near her. While I was there I received a call from my mother's next-door neighbor who asked me if I knew what was going on with my mother's house. I told her I didn't know what she was talking about and asked if she could be more specific. She told me that the house had been sold and that all of my mother's belongings were now out in the street. I couldn't figure out why this was happening. It didn't make sense to me why the house had been sold without my knowledge. I was certain that mother would have wanted me to have some percentage of the sale of the house. I called up my stepfather who told me that he had sold the house and most of her belongings. He said I had nothing coming to me. I didn't know what to make of this.

When I returned to Los Angeles I noticed that my stepfather was very distant toward me and acted like a person I had never met before. My friends advised me to hire a lawyer, which was something I really didn't want to do, but I finally relented and hired one. A court day was set and while we were in court, I looked over at my stepfather. He looked just like a broken down man. He was all hunched over and had a pasty white color. I began to feel sorry for him. I decided I could not go through with this and told my lawyer to call the lawsuit off.

"Bob, you can't call this off. Not now; we're in court."

"I can call it off and I'm going to do just that."

"But we're standing in front of the judge. You can't call this off!" he pleaded with me.

"Call off the law suit!" and with those final remarks, I walked out of the courtroom.

Later my stepfather moved to Australia and I did not see him for a while. As his career was going downward, my career and life were going upward, and fast.

On January 16, 1953, Marjie and I celebrated the birth of our daughter Kelly and on March 9, 1956, we welcomed our son Casey into the world. I was a father now. It was the best and one of the strongest emotions I have ever felt. As parents, Marjie and I were very devoted to our children and sought in every way to make our family as strong as possible. We soon bought a house in Sherman Oaks, CA, and Casey and Kelly were enrolled in the local school.

Life in the Golden Age
of Television

Time to Get into Television, KTTV Los Angeles

BARR SHEETS, THE fellow who had hired me as an usher, had a brother by the name of Dale Sheets, who to this day is one of my oldest and dearest friends. Dale is a few years younger than me, and, at that time, he was an assistant head usher making about $35 a week, as compared to being a regular usher who was taking home about $15 a week. Dale soon moved up and became the film buyer for KTTV, and he wanted me to get into television with him. At that time, I really wasn't that interested in television. Radio was still on my mind and I felt television was too new and not yet stable enough. I had still not finished school, but he suggested I take a semester off and see if I liked it. I took him up on his offer.

Dale Sheets, friend, writes:
"After I left Times Mirror, *I went to work for KTTV in Los Angeles. At that time it was owned by the* Times Mirror *and CBS. One day I received a call from Bob asking if I knew of any openings at the station. A sales job was open. He applied again and he got the job. That was Bob's first position in television broadcasting—at $37.50 per week. From there, as we all know, he became the best in the broadcasting business, and it couldn't have happened to a better human being. My wife Joan and I consider Bob and Marjie to be our best friends, and that friendship has lasted over 60 years."*

As soon as I set foot in the world of television, I loved it. It was for me and I instantly knew it. I soon interviewed again for the position of Assistant Service Manager and got the job. When I started at KTTV, a guy by the name of Val Conte had just been promoted to Sales Service Manager and I would be working with Val at a starting salary of $55 per week. Ironically, Val's salary was $65 and the secretary's was $75. *How was this even possible?* I made a note to myself that there was something definitely not right with this picture. My thought was that I better stay at this job for only a short time and move on fast. What kind of place is this if the secretary is making more money than the boss?

Working at KTTV at the time were account executives Jim Aubrey, Bob Wood, Dick O'Leary, Chuck Young and Les Norins. All of these guys were older than me. I was about twenty-four, and they were all around twenty-nine to thirty-one and making a lot of money. The natural progression was for Val to become a salesman and for me to take his spot, but I could quickly see that Val really liked his sales service job and had no intention of moving on to another position. It seemed the only way my career was going to move forward was for me to go around Val, or over him, or to somehow get miraculously promoted.

The sales manager was Bill Whiting and someone I hardly ever saw during the work week. I wasn't even making $3,000 a year, and the sales guys were making somewhere between $20,000 to $30,000 a year. I was hungry and I wanted a job with a salary like that. In fact, it seemed that everyone in the world would like to have one of those jobs. On the weekends I was selling cars to make ends meet, but I was really focused on my sales career and how to move up the ladder.

What I really wanted was Jim Aubrey's job. The rumor going around was that Jim would be leaving soon for the CBS sales manager's job, so I knew I had to make some kind of move and fast. Of course, my chance of landing Jim's job was like somebody suddenly saying, "I want to be the coach of the Oakland Raiders." It was never going to happen. At least, that was what I believed at the time.

Making the Pitch of My Life

I KNEW BILL Whiting's secretary, so I was very nice to her and asked her to make an appointment with him for me. She asked me what it was about, and I told her I wanted to pitch him for a job. She just sort of giggled, which drove me a little more nuts for Aubrey's job. She made the appointment, and I went in to see Bill. I had prepared myself for a week and had psyched myself up to a point where I could have jumped over the building that day.

I went in, closed the door behind me, and I'm sure he didn't even know who I was or what I was doing there. He probably figured some kid in the building must have walked through the wrong door. I did a twenty-minute number on him, building to crescendos and ending with the pounding of my fist on his desk. I then pointed my finger at him and said, "You, Bill Whiting, will always be remembered negatively if you don't hire me. You will be remembered as the guy who had the opportunity to hire Bob Bennett as a salesman and didn't do it. You now have the chance to make a decision as to how you want to be remembered. Do you want to be remembered for the rest of your life as the guy who hired me or the guy who let me walk out the door? Nobody can sell more than me. I promise you."

I felt like I was out of control, but this was my one and only time to make my case so I was going to make it. I actually had tears in my eyes. He was sitting in his great big green chair and hadn't said a word for twenty minutes. He looked like the Sphinx with no emotion. I had no idea if what I was saying was getting through or if he really just wanted to throw me out of there as quickly as he could.

My presentation finally came to end and I stopped talking and wiped my eyes. He was still and silent, and then finally said to me, "Okay, you start on Monday."

I was so elated I wanted to jump over the desk and kiss him. I knew one thing from experience, once you get the order, shut up and get out. I turned and said to him, "Thank you, you'll never be sorry for this Mr. Whiting," and started to walk out.

I got to the door and all of a sudden he said to me, "Hey kid, come back here." I stopped dead in my tracks and figured he'd changed his mind. I turned and started walking back and he said to me, "What's your name again?"

"Bob Bennett," I told him.

"Okay, Bob Bennett, you start on Monday."

No one in the station could believe what I had done. Here I was, the youngest kid on the block, just twenty-four years old, and I was now going to start pretty high up the ladder in sales. I remember starting my new sales job with as much enthusiasm as anyone can generate in a human being. I went off like a rocket. My first sale was to an automobile dealer. I sold him a movie on Friday night. I went down into the toy section of Los Angeles and convinced them to start advertising. One sale lead to another sale, and my whole career started to move forward. In my first year I made $12,000; the year before that I had made just $2,700. The next year I made $25,000, and I was now driving one of those fancy new cars. I thought I'd died and gone to heaven. The more enthusiasm I could muster, the more sales I made.

Bob Wood was selling at KTTV and was probably the best sales-man I have ever met. He had the great ability to sell himself first, and he had a fantastic sense of humor. He would walk into a room and the room would just light up. He very quickly became the most talked about sales guy in Los Angeles. He was respected, well-researched and very bright and filled with self-confidence. He was a sales legend. For him, there was no difference if he was addressing the CEO of some big company, or some salesman on a car lot. For both, he had the same kind of dialogue, and his dialogue was very convincing.

I had trouble being as well-rounded as Bob Wood. I had my own sales methods that I developed, and they worked for me. I liked to believe that I enjoyed a good reputation in the marketplace. What was important to me then was not how much money I earned, but that I was the top salesman in the place. I had to be the top biller and I got up every morning with that goal in mind.

Dick O'Leary, Television Executive, writes:

"We have to begin by putting everything in perspective by first understanding the conditions of the time and the cast of characters that were involved. When Word War II ended, everyone came back from the service to get on with their lives—jobs, marriage, family, etc. And then some of us looked up and there was this new frontier known as television—no organizational lines to get in and no old ways of doing things. Like in war, it was an opportunity to participate in a wide-open, exciting, and sometimes fearful, unknown world. And a bunch of young guys, whiskey drinking, heavy smoking, responsibility seeking, used-to-the-unknown, adventure-seeking ways of life were somehow drawn to this new and exciting arena.

Once we were all in, I can't remember anyone ever wanting to opt out. We were all in for the rest of our working lives, and together we somehow won this war. We were a blessed bunch of talented, hard-working, and unknowingly ambitious people. We relished it! And Los Angeles was the perfect playing field: seven TV stations, three networks, and four independent stations. All the other 200-some television markets had three or four stations in total. The Los Angeles makeup of so many stations created a unique situation and a fierce and challenging environment: seven stations competing for audience and advertising dollars where the rest of the markets only had to split the TV pie three or four ways. There's nothing like playing in the toughest field to develop the toughest participants. And then, to work for an independent, non-network station was really a challenge for all of us. No measurable audience, no network programming, and no real programming at all, except what we could come up with ourselves. KTTV Channel 11 was one of those stations. And thus begins the saga of Bob Bennett and myself, among others. Bob and I started at KTTV in the same week in 1951. We both started at the lowest rank possible—Bob in sales service, me in merchandising. His humble job was to handle the almost overwhelming tasks and headaches associated with television commercials. Imagine, sixteen hours a day, seven days a week on the air, twelve minutes of commercial time, plus program promotion and a public-service announcement in every single station break, with each break containing ten-, twenty-, and sixty-second film spots. That's thousands of little spools of film that had to be coordinated with all of the advertiser's ad agencies and the film studios, film laboratories and all of the other sources of these materials. Each little film roll had to be gotten from the source, scheduled on the air, removed from the spool, and put together for sending over the air. And that's not factoring in the chaos and the logistics of scratched and broken and otherwise unusable film. This process had to be reversed, and every single piece of film had to be put back on the spools and returned to their sources all over the country. What a to-do list that was. Good luck! And don't get sick and don't spend too much time at lunch and keep your bathroom breaks to a minimum.

My job, exciting as it was, was to go out to all of the super markets, drug stores, department stores, and any other places where an advertiser's products were sold, and to then sell these stores on giving our advertisers special attention in their outlets. By today's standards, I hold an honorary Master's Degree in building End-Aisle displays for stacking our advertiser's products into seductive and eye-catching towers with signs displayed that the product was "On Sale" as had been seen on KTTV Channel 11. Needless to say, these were both rather humbling positions for two future Masters of the Television Universe. But how could we dare complain when we were making the breathtaking salaries of $55 per week. And that was for every week of the year—all 52 of them.

One day, I realized that Bob was destined for great things. Somehow, he could accomplish his excruciatingly detailed tasks like no other person could. He was actually finding the time for more things to do. Not possible, I thought. Eureka! He found a solution that changed how an entire industry did its day-to-day business. He had realized that the other side of this logistically demanding equation was as deep in doo-doo as he was. And so, he took the entrepreneurial, visionary, and self-starting step of calling the people responsible at all of the advertising agencies involved and convinced them that they did not want to get back all of the twisted, scratched, and broken films on all those little spools that they had to check on for integrity and then store. Not just the spools from Los Angeles TV stations, but from every station in every one of the 200 television markets in the U.S. and Canada. Of course they did not want all that hassle. Think of the man-hours and resultant dollars saved. On these principles of insight, strategic vision, and action are such remarkable careers built. From the beginning, I realized what a masterful breakthrough Bob had conceived and executed. I held him in the highest esteem. I also came to see him as a good person (i.e., a man who possessed goodness from within): highly intelligent, creative, action oriented, charismatic, and an inspiring leader of men and women. This has led me to a lifelong sense of admiration and respect.

As I look back and remember it all, the business offices of KTTV were on the second floor. The functions handled on this floor were the offices of the General Manager, the General and National Sales Manager, the Program Manager, the Promotion Manager, the Sales Services Department and the six-man Sales Department, and crunched in there somewhere was me, the Merchandising Gofer. That was thirteen people. Of those thirteen, one went on to work at the White House before becoming the Ambassador to Ireland; one became an owner of KTVU-TV San Francisco; one started his own television programming distribution firm and gained exclusive USA rights to sell all the BBC programs to all of the television stations, including the PBS stations; two became future Presidents of CBS television network; one became President of MGM studios; four became General Managers of network television stations in major markets; one also became President of the ABC-owned television stations and President of ABC International (me); and one became Bob Bennett. Most of them remained friends and industry colleagues over the years. Most of them lived happily ever after, and all eventually made more than $55 a week. One of them even has a huge yacht in his front dock to prove it!"

Chuck Velona, friend, writes:

"I first met Bob when I worked at KTTV for Val Conte as National Sales Coordinator. I had been working previously for Chuck Young who was then the National Sales Manager. I then went to work for Bob as an assistant under Chuck Martin and Tom Maney. We always had a sales meeting on Tuesday nights, and afterwards we would all go to dinner where we would always end up playing Liar's Poker for the tab. With me being the youngest, they delighted in sticking me with the bill. In 1968, I purchased Bob's home in Royal Woods in Sherman Oaks. It was a beautiful two-story home with four bedrooms and a pool. He made me pay the then-ridiculous price of $52,000! Now we laugh about today's value of the house, which is well in excess of $1 million.

In 1979, I was made VP, General Manager of KHJ-TV, and I always like to rub it in to Bob that I was the youngest GM in LA-TV history. On the day of the announcement, the first congratulatory call I received was from Bob, who told me to make sure I didn't screw it up. Bob and I have always had our jovial moments together—egging one another on, but I have always respected his opinion.

In 1988, my wife was facing a personal problem of great magnitude. Bob wrote her a letter when she was in the hospital that said, 'We never know in life when tragedies will happen to us. I want you to think about all of the people who love you and are willing to help you.' We have never forgotten that heartfelt gesture, and my wife Michelle still has the letter today. We can never thank him enough, and he knows how dearly we love him."

John Vrba, General Sales Manager, KTTV Channel 11, Los Angeles, writes:

"I recall Bob being hired as an assistant in the traffic department where he had come from KNX Radio. KTTV had taken on a week of on-location shooting at the LA County Fair. To help pay the cost of those live remotes, we came up with the idea of selling participations to the various exhibitors. Bob had said he would like to get into sales, so he and another new guy were assigned the job of going to the Fairgrounds in advance and

getting orders from exhibitors. Needless to say, Bob rose to the task, and with his natural gift of gab, he brought in what we considered to be new 'found' money."

Arnie Mills, a friend, writes:

"My first recollection of Bob was of him squirting me with a water pistol as he chased me down the hall of Channel 11. Years later, when my wife was diagnosed by doctors with heart disease, Bob was very instrumental in getting her in to see some of the best heart doctors that UCLA had to offer. It was a very difficult time for my family, but Bob was there for us. Those UCLA doctors prolonged her life for many years, and I still remember him handing me the key to his condo on Wilshire Blvd, saying, 'Arnie, take this key and use my apartment any time you need to be close to your wife and the hospital.' I will never forget how he was there for my wife and for my family."

Joe Seidman, Sales Executive, KTTV, 1959–61, writes:

"In 1959, I was working in radio and Bob had asked me to join the KTTV sales staff and get into television. I had mixed feelings at first because I loved radio and I loved the way the business of radio was conducted. I soon found out that television was a very different world and as a result, I only lasted two years in television before I decided to leave and open up my own advertising agency.

The business of radio was simple. I liked that. It was a smaller world and a place where everyone knew one another, deals were done on handshakes, contracts were written weeks later, and spots aired as soon as possible. Whatever was available in inventory in the radio business you could buy, and as a result, people became dependent on a word-of-mouth system they could count on. When I got into the rough and tumble world of television advertising, it was foreign to me. Essentially, the national rep firms wanted primetime television for their clients like Proctor & Gamble, so they came up with an ingenious system they called the Preemptable Rate Card—which meant that anything was fair game—spots were always in a state of flux and dependent on which national advertisers wanted to spend more money for prime time at any given point in time.

You could buy a local spot for $1,000, but if a national advertiser made a national buy in prime time, you would probably lose your local spot. This caused many heated arguments among the five KTTV salesmen at the time.

Since KTTV was the top independent station in the Los Angeles market, we were in demand from national rep firms and their advertisers. Prime time was everything to them, and they were prepared to do whatever it took to insure their clients had the penetration. When enough local people were burned, the arguments started. A local advertiser would opt for a local spot for say $1,000, but when burned one too many times, they would then reluctantly come up with the $2,000 for the guaranteed prime time spot, whereby, at least they were sure their spot would air.

When I came to KTTV nobody told me exactly how this all worked. I sold my first sale and it was then preempted. My client was furious. And then it happened to me again and again. I found this untenable because I had brought many clients over from radio, and they didn't like this structure. Radio was always simple: you bought what you paid for, you only paid one price, and it aired when they were told it would air. Radio did have discounts for length of time purchased, but you really paid for what you bought.

Finally, I decided working in television sales was not for me, so I left KTTV and started my own advertising agency. I did continue to place clients at KTTV now that I knew how the system worked. The national guys wanted prime time and they just wanted to trample and preempt all the little local guys, and they had the muscle to do it. Every station wanted the national rep firms selling their inventory, and KTTV was no exception. Boy, did Bob Bennett do a lot of dancing back there and calm down a lot of arguments between the sales guys."

By the time 1958 came around, I was thirty-one years old and making about $50,000 a year. That was a lot of money, but if you worked hard and hustled for it, you could do it.

Television started to become popular around this time. It was mushrooming all around us, but we were all kind of naïve about it. All we knew is that we had a job to do, and it was a regular kind of job, not something wonderful and new. We were too busy working to realize that the dawn of a new and exciting medium was upon us.

When you look at it from a historical perspective, a long time before television, motion pictures were generating all the excitement buzz and entertainment. Television wasn't superimposed over motion pictures. In fact, at the time, the television business was not looked upon as any kind of exciting business at all. That distinction of excitement was reserved for the motion picture business. The movie business looked down at the television business and wanted nothing to do with it. The movies had the stars like Clark Gable and Spencer Tracy. The television business had stars like Dude Martin. Who the heck ever heard of Dude Martin?

Strangely though, as television continued to grow and gain a presence in homes across the country, more and more people began to notice its importance, especially in the area of news. But for those of us who were working in television, we were just too busy working to really notice in what direction television was really moving. We did know one thing: the more advertising we sold, the more money we made.

Barry Bergsman, Sales Assistant, KTTV 1962, writes:
"I first met Bob when he was the Local Sales Manager at KTTV. I had recently moved to Los Angeles after college and a stint at patriotism and had been befriended by Joe Seideman, then an Account Executive at the station. Joe wanted to hire me as his assistant, but this required the approval of the boss as there was a hiring freeze going on at the time. The boss, of course, was Bob Bennett, and there he was, sitting behind his important desk, welcoming, charming, and selling me on the notion that it was me who was very lucky to have the opportunity to shuffle fixed, preemptable, and sort-of-preemptable time buys for Joe for a mere $65 a week—with the promise of a raise all the way up to $75 in short order. Well, Mr. Bennett never gave me that raise but a friendship did materialize that has lasted for over fifty years.
I left KTTV for CBS a short while later, and then Bob left Los Angeles, and he commenced his rise to fame, fortune, and humility. There are few people with the significant accomplishments he has achieved in the broadcasting world and

who are as universally liked and respected as he is. As an aside, extensive therapy has finally gotten me to a state of forgiveness for him not having given me the raise he had promised."

The Joe Pine Show

KTTV HAD A show called *The Joe Pine Show*, and it was very successful. Joe Pine was a crazy kind of television host who could turn a seemingly pleasant interview into a blistering attack on his unsuspecting guests in a moment's notice. His interview could be going along nicely and then all of a sudden, from out of nowhere, he would turn on his guests with a barrage of vindictive and bitter questions, essentially attacking and insulting them. Not only were the guests shocked by Joe's antics, so were his viewers. But it seemed the more the viewers were shocked, the more they tuned in to watch *The Joe Pine Show*, and the higher the ratings went. His show was pulling a 25 rating on a Saturday night, which was amazing.

About three weeks into the start of the *The Joe Pine Show*, I was at the Oscar Meyerhof Advertising Agency in Beverly Hills making a sales presentation. One of their clients was Wrigley Gum. I was sitting in the waiting room when Oscar Meyerhof himself came in and asked me who was I there to see. I told him and he asked me to come along with him. I followed him into a room where he introduced me to several agency people. It turned out that Oscar Meyerhof himself was trying to promote something, and he had been booked on *The Joe Pine Show*.

About a week later I was at home watching television, and *The Joe Pine Show* came on. Oscar Meyerhof was on the set with Pine and was about to be interviewed. Everything started off all right. Meyerhof was taking the position that the government should hire advertising agencies to represent them overseas. Pine was going along with his interview in a reasonably polite way, and then all of a sudden he turned vicious.

"Let me ask you a question, Mr. Meyerhof," Joe Pine said to him. "What gives you the right to portray the United States of America overseas when your shop is nothing but an ad agency that sells gum and soap?"

Pine started to beat Meyerhof up, and it was tough. I was melting in my chair. Meyerhof turned to him and said, "I don't have to take this from you," and stormed off the set. That night, Joe Pine had the highest rated show in all of Los Angeles.

Another time Joe Pine had on a guy who had ten wives, and I think all ten of them were up on the set with him. Pine was conducting his interview and as the cameras were rolling, from out of the audience and raging with anger, the father of wife number ten suddenly jumped onto the set and knocked Pine off his chair. Pine went flying and then could not get up because he lost one of his legs in World War II. Absolute mayhem engulfed that television set. And once again, Joe Pine had the highest rated show in Los Angeles. *The Joe Pine Show* was certainly an early pioneer in talk show television and helped set the stage for future shows that would appear many, many years later, such as the *Morton Downey Show, Maury Povich* among others.

The television business knew one thing: it had to fill time. At KTTV, we must have produced over two hundred television shows in ten years.

Kelly Bennett writes

"In 1964, the Beatles were going to be playing at the Hollywood Bowl, and I was frantic to get tickets. There were none to be found. It seemed that all of my girlfriends had tickets, but I must have waited too long and they were all sold out overnight. I asked my father if he had any ideas about how we could get tickets, and he told me he had never heard of the Beatles but would see what he could do. Anxious days passed with no word from my father until one day he came up to me and said, 'Kelly, we're going to see the Beatles.' I was overjoyed. 'And we have front row seats,' he said to me. I couldn't believe what I was hearing.

On the night of the concert, as my family and I made our way up to the front of the stage, I was the envy of all my girlfriends.

That was my dad. Always there for me and always making some kind of magic happen."

In television's early days, the only thing stations had for filler were just old movies. It was not like today where there is so much content around. Back then, the motion picture people were fighting the idea of television every step of the way. If you could sit back and watch a movie in the comfort of your home, you did not have to venture into a movie theatre and buy tickets. The movie industry did not like the idea of watching movies in your home. They wanted you in the movie theatres and buying tickets—lots of tickets—so they were not about to turn over their film libraries to television. It wasn't until about 1956 when MGM finally changed their minds and sold their pre-1948 library to television. This was an enormous deal back then. Every television station wanted a piece of that film library. KTTV was so hungry for it that they sold twenty-five percent of the station to MGM in order to buy that library. That's how important it was. If I remember correctly, KTTV paid approximately $4 million for the library and MGM paid KTTV about $2 million for a twenty-five percent interest in the station. Other than the MGM library, one might have occasionally found some feature films, but it was nothing of any substance.

As a result, the networks were frantically producing programs for network affiliates. That left the independents with nothing. If you were an independent station you had to fill your day from eight in the morning until one in the morning. That was a lot of programming time to fill. You had no choice but to start producing your own content, which meant that all kinds of crazy programming ideas were being tried back then, some good, and many bad. Lawrence Welk came out of that, and his show was produced in a studio across the street from KTTV. Other programs were *Frosty Frolics* and *City At Night*. We did a program called *Success Story*, in which we would go out live at 7:30 on Tuesday nights and go into a place like a fish plant and follow the steps a fish took from the time it entered the plant to the time it came out in a can. Some programs were fifteen minutes in length, others were thirty minutes, and some an hour long.

Television scheduling was not as rigid back then as it is today. Everything today is timed right to the second. Back then there was no real manual to go by so we invented it as we went along. Everyone was in a mad dash to see what would work and get ratings. I suppose that part of television today has not changed. There was really a mad scramble back then to find programming, and the competition was fierce.

KTTV ran on clock time and was also the originator of the live sporting event way before the networks were doing it. We tied up UCLA and USC and we'd bring out those games live. We started the *L.A. Open* and we originated *Sports Spectacular*, which was conceived by a man named Bob Breckner, who was General Manager of KTTV. Breckner believed in live events taking place on Sunday afternoons. We'd cut live from a bowling alley and go to a golf tournament, then to a tennis tournament, then on to a baseball game, and then end the show at a track meet. This was all really amazing and innovative stuff for a bunch of television people who really didn't have much in the way of equipment and very few people on hand to do these kinds of things. Everything was low budget or whatever budget we could find. We knew one thing: we needed programming to keep the station going.

After a while, the networks starting coming in and doing sports events and we started to lose the sports bidding war since they were in the position to out bid us. KTTV did however, as an independent station, put together a network of stations for *The Bing Crosby Tournament*. We put it together, sold it to individual stations, and then fed it to them. One of our advertisers was 3M.

KTTV also started *The Miss Universe Contest*. We made that into not one show, but into ten or twelve shows throughout the course of a week. We would meet the girls as they came off the airplane and we would film them and that would be one show segment. Then for the next show, we would take them all to lunch and we would interview them and then film them walking around the pool. Then there would be a big dinner to film where they would present gifts from all over the world to the mayor of Long Beach. Finally, we would go into the final night and tape that. It became a series of shows over a ten-day period. Viewers loved it. On the final night of *The Miss Universe Contest*, I think it achieved a 70 share in Los Angeles alone. It became so big that the networks quickly took it over and it became a network show. It was amazing that the little independent KTTV originated that. We also produced a program called *The*

International Beauty Contest, but it never achieved the success that *The Miss Universe Contest* did.

Needless to say, it was a very exciting time to be in Los Angeles, even though I was only starting to realize it. Klaus Lansberg started KTLA and between the two stations, I think more live television and more locally produced television had been done there than ever before. The affiliated stations were running whatever their affiliated network ran, but none of them were really producing local original programming.

For a time, *The Gary Moore Show* was very popular, which was kind of a typical show done by a network live on the east coast, and then a kinescope would be sent out to the west coast for running about three or four hours after the east coast broadcast. Jack Parr was doing daytime shows, and Johnny Carson was doing morning shows. There were some soaps, but not any where near the number we have today.

And in Walks John Kluge

AT THIS POINT, television was becoming a big part of my life. I knew that once I had gotten into sales, it could possibly lead me into someday being a general manager of a television station. As soon as I started selling, I remember telling myself that I wanted to be good at this. I wanted to be a sales manager. And I knew that once you become a sales manager, you might have a chance at being a general manager someday. It seemed that all of the general managers had risen out of sales positions, and I wanted to become the general manager for KTTV at some point in my life, even if it took me to the age of fifty before I ever achieved it. I held onto this dream for a long time until one day I received news in 1963 that shattered it. A guy by the name of John Kluge from back east announced that he was buying KTTV from the *Los Angeles Times* and was going to place the station into his Metromedia Group of stations.

John Kluge started in the food business and then entered the radio business when he bought his first station in Silver Springs, Maryland for $150,000. He started buying FM stations before they were popular and over time, FM became the preferred medium for popular music. By the mid-1950s, he had acquired a minority interest in what were then the remaining assets of the DuMont Television Group. John proved over time that a group of independent television stations could makes millions of dollars. Early on, he saw the great possibilities with independent stations. His programming strategy was simply to rerun old network situation comedies and low budget movies. In time, Metromedia would grow into the largest independent television business in the United States. John had the heart of a gambler, very keen insight, and always seemed to make money on just about anything he ever did.

At its height, Metromedia had television stations in the country's top markets, which included New York, Los Angeles, Chicago, Dallas, Boston, Houston, and Washington, D.C. In the 1960s, Metromedia entered the outdoor billboard advertising business and has owned restaurants and other assets like the Ice Capades, the Harlem Globe Trotters, music and publishing companies, television production and syndication units, and a highly profitable direct mail business. In some ways, he was the least-known media mogul in the business, but certainly one of its most powerful.

In 1986, John sold the Metromedia television stations to the 20th Century Fox film studio for $2 billion. Those Metromedia stations later became the core stations for what is now known as the Fox Television Network. In 1987, *Forbes Magazine* placed John at the top of its "Richest Men in America" list, where he stayed for three years.

At the time of this pending sale of KTTV to Kluge and Metromedia, Dick Moore, the general manager, was trying to convince the *Times,* who owned KTTV at the time, not to sell to John, but to rather purchase additional stations in Seattle, San Francisco, Portland, Sacramento, San Diego, and Los Angeles. None of these stations were making a profit, and incidentally, neither had KTTV up until 1963. That year we made about $3,000,000 in profit and only because we had produced one hundred and sixty-five one-hour episodes called *Divorce Court*, the rights of which we later sold to Storer Broadcasting for syndication. That was a lot of money back then and probably one of the first syndication deals on record.

The Times really didn't see the potential for broadcasting. It was foreign to them. They were newspaper people, and they had a corporate policy which stated that everything they owned or invested in had to show a profit of at least 20%. If not, they didn't want any part of it. We all knew they weren't happy with the station, but we never really thought they'd sell it. There were probably a number of us who could have gone out and made arrangements to borrow money from banks or put together investor groups to buy the station outright. I could have even gone to Bob Hope to measure his level of interest.

So as the story goes, from out of the east coast came John Kluge who walked into the publisher of the *LA Times* and said, "I want to buy your station. What do you want for it?"

They said to him, "Ten million, three hundred thousand dollars." (I don't remember the exact price, but it was somewhere around $10.3 million.)

And he said, "Fine with me. Let's do it."

The real estate alone was worth about four million, so the station was really being sold for about six million, which was really not a good deal for the *LA Times* to be getting themselves into. But they wanted out. They were newspaper people.

So here we were, many of us who had worked at KTTV for twelve to fifteen years, now working for some guy named John Kluge and something called Metromedia.

The first time I met John Kluge was at a meeting after he had bought KTTV. We were all kind of standing in a line and he was walking down the line introducing himself, and as he passed by me, I reached out (I don't know what possessed me to do this) and yanked on his tie and said, "Mr. Kluge, that's the ugliest tie I have ever seen." Startled, he looked at me, laughed, and then yanked my tie and told me how ugly mine was. I didn't know it at the time but John was known for his sense of humor and practical joking. Good thing, or I'm sure he would have fired me on the spot.

Over the next year, I worked diligently at KTTV and expanded my sales and marketing efforts and became a very high grossing salesman. I became friends with Bennett Korn who was President of Metromedia Television, who helped move the station forward.

One day Al Krivin, who was the President of Metromedia Broadcasting, came to me and said he wanted me to be the general manager for WTTG in Washington, D.C.

"Get your bags packed and go to Washington," he yelled.

I told Marjie, and we started packing.

Arthur Anderson, friend, writes:
"Just before Bob was moving to Washington, D.C. to take over a job as general manager for a television station, I invited him to invest in an industrial building near Los Angeles International Airport. About that time he had about $20,000 in savings and my family and I had been investing in real estate. We invited Bob to invest with us. In fact, he was the only outside person

we have ever invited to invest with us. He gladly said yes, and I told him I wanted to take him out to see the building. To my surprise, he said, 'Art, what do I want to see a building for? If you say it's a good enough investment, then that's fine for me. I just want to be your partner.' He then left for Washington, D.C., and went on to making television history. It's been over 50 years now, and we are still the best of friends."

Running My First Television Station, WTTG in Washington, D.C.

IN MARCH OF 1966, at the age of 40, I flew to Washington, D.C., to take the job as the new general manager of WTTG-TV. I was somewhat nervous since it was my first shot at running a television station, but somewhere in the back of my mind, there was a part of me that told me I was ready for the job. Marjie, Casey, and Kelly stayed behind and joined me later when school was out.

When I landed at the airport, I rented a car and went directly to John Kennedy's grave. Kennedy had always been a fascinating personality for me, and I wanted to go and pay my respects. I arrived at his grave around dusk as a very dark drizzly mist was sweeping down over the graveyard. I walked up to his grave and stood staring at the eternal flame blowing in the wind. I was mesmerized. As that yellow and red flame twisted in the air, all of the magic of the Kennedy years began running through my mind. Darkness was descending and suddenly I started to get very homesick. I now realized that I was far away from home and all by myself.

I left Kennedy's gravesite and drove to the Lincoln Memorial and stood there looking up in amazement at that great marble statue. I thought that Abe was welcoming me to Washington, and I started to cry. In fact, the more I looked at him the more my eyes were watering. I heard a voice moving close to me so I held back the tears and walked away. I soon stood at the highest step of the Lincoln Memorial looking out over the great distance at all of the lights, the moving cars and people rushing about, and then it all suddenly hit me: I was really now in Washington, D.C. and tomorrow morning I would be the general manager of a television station. I started to shake. I knew it was now time to prepare myself mentally for the job ahead of me—and to convince myself that I was ready.

WTTG-TV traces its history back to 1945 when Dr. Allen B. DuMont founded W3XWT, which was the second experimental station in the nation's capital. NBC owned the other experimental station, which was W3XNB. Later in 1945, the DuMont laboratories began a series of experimental coaxial cable hookups between W3XWT and its other station WABD in New York City. These hookups were the beginning of the DuMont Television Network, which was the world's first licensed commercial television network. On January 3, 1947, W3XWT received a commercial license, which was at the time, the first in the nation's capital, as WTTG. The station was named for Thomas T. (Oliver) Goldsmith, a close friend and associate of Dr. DuMont. In 1956, DuMont ended network operations, and WTTG and WABD were spun off as the DuMont Broadcasting Corporation. In 1958, John Kluge bought controlling interest in DuMont Broadcasting Corporation and became the company's chairman. In 1961, he changed the name of the company to Metromedia and interestingly enough, Thomas T. Goldsmith sat on its board for over twenty-five years. Today WTTG is an owned and operated station of the Fox Broadcasting Company.

Even though I didn't have any real-world experience running a television station, my confidence level seemed to be on the rise. I just had to make sure that I was not overly confident because I wasn't sure what exactly was ahead of me. I also felt that my years in Los Angeles with Chuck Young, who was National Sales Manager of KTTV and Bob Breckner, General Manager of KTTV, played large roles in preparing me as a station manager. I had learned a great deal about station management from both of them. There was also some stability in the fact that with WTTG, I knew I had a station that was good and reasonably well-respected in the Washington market. I thought it was interesting that WTTG had higher rating numbers for its programs than KTTV in Los Angeles.

At the time of my arrival, the Washington market had four VHF stations; one NBC owned and operated, an ABC affiliate, a CBS station owned by the *Washington Post* and WTTG as an independent.

Who's Going to Cut the Grass?

MARJIE AND I bought a house for $93,000 in Potomac Falls, Maryland, that was on a three-acre lot. In fact, all of the houses in the vicinity looked like they were on three-acre lots, which meant there would be a lot of grass for me to cut. Coming from Los Angeles as we did, we had always had a Japanese gardener. I asked the real estate agent if she could recommend a Japanese gardener.

"What do you mean a Japanese gardener?" she asked me in disbelief.

"Well, who's going to cut the grass?"

"You are."

"Me? Well then I guess I'll have to go out and get one of those lawn mowers you push."

"A lawn mower you push? Bob, you're going to need a lawn tractor you can ride on to cut this much grass," she said to me. So I went out and bought a lawn tractor I could ride on and had great fun on weekends cutting the grass.

To our surprise, most of our friends from California we had told to come and visit us in Washington did. It seemed that the first year we lived there our home was maybe empty about three weeks out of the whole year. Casey and Kelly adapted to Washington life well, but for Casey the move from the West Coast to the East Coast was a major culture shock. I remember him running around with a skateboard, which was common enough on the West Coast, only for him to find bewildered faces from the kids in Potomac Falls who had never seen a skateboard before. We had two beautiful Collie dogs. Kelly enrolled in junior high, and Casey was in middle school.

I do remember that the move from California to Washington, D.C., was not an easy move for Kelly and Casey. Marjie did not adapt quickly since she had left close friends and family back in Los Angeles. In time, she accepted the change. Kelly and Casey made school friends, and we became a Potomac Falls, Maryland family. I bought Casey a little motor scooter so he could ride all over the three acres of newly cut grass. I was thrilled about the move to Washington and ready for something different. Having grown up in Altoona, the winters did not bother me. My stepfather came to visit us at the time, and I remember him saying to me that he was very proud of my accomplishments. My relationship with him at the time was improving, and I was very happy to see him.

On my first day of work, I felt like I had a big knot in my throat. My feelings kept bouncing back and forth between trepidation and self-confidence. As I walked in the front door for the first time, I kept saying to myself, *Oh my God, what if I screw this up?* I was lucky, because I liked everyone immediately, and we quickly got down to business. I spent a lot of time talking to the staff, going over station financials, studying the station's sales and marketing practices, and coming to grips with the station's programming schedule. I wanted to understand exactly where the station was, both in revenue and programming, and then see how I could make things better. I spent a lot of time with the sales people to make sure I understood their sales strategies, their problems, and their challenges. I also carved out time to study what our competition was doing and what they were charging for television spots. I wanted the staff to understand that I was there to help them do their jobs and to make WTTG a better television station.

Once I had a thorough understanding of the station, I realized that the first thing we needed to do was to put a state-of-the-art news operation into place. WTTG's idea of a state-of-the-art newscast was using slides from an announcer's booth. Here we were in the number one news market in the country, Washington, D.C., and WTTG was using slides from an announcer's booth. I couldn't believe it. I began creating a news gathering team and a topnotch on-camera group that would generate a first rate newscast segment. Before long, WTTG was producing high-quality news segments daily and giving our competition a run for their money.

However, there were challenges. My new office had no windows.

I don't like rooms without windows; I never have. What I did not know was that John Kluge had an interest in modern cubistic artwork and had hired some guy whose only job was to buy artwork for the Metromedia properties. So as I sat at my desk for the first time, somewhat uncomfortably, trying to settle into my new surroundings, I looked up on the wall and staring back at me was the strangest painting I had ever seen in my life. It was a painting of what appeared to be a person; only this person had two faces, eight eyes, and a contorted nose. I was getting dizzy just looking at it. It drove me crazy. I kept trying to look away, but my eyes always seemed to drift back to it. I knew right away that this office wasn't big enough for me and that painting. I called up somebody in the building and asked him to come and take this piece of confusing artwork out of my office. A few minutes later this guy walked in and informed me that no artwork could be removed from any of the walls in any Metromedia building, unless the person who actually bought this two faced, eight eyed, contorted nose painting came and took it down himself. I couldn't believe what I was hearing. We called the Metromedia art guy and he never called back. So for several weeks I had a daily staring battle with the painting. I eventually got it out but it was not easy.

Soon I got word that the press wanted WTTG to hold a press conference so they could have a chance at interviewing the new general manager. Television was the Hollywood of Washington, and always received big play in the press. Now the press wanted to meet me to see if I had a vision for the station. From the tone of their first few questions, I could tell immediately that they didn't really feel that anything of interest was going to come out of my mouth. Questions being hurled at me were: So what are you going to do that's important and different? What changes are you going to make at the station? Are you going to change the station lineup? How do you know that viewers in the Washington market will like the changes that you want to make? I answered their questions as honestly and politely as I could, and then I told them that I was going to make a lot of changes at the station and that these changes were going to improve WTTG's programming schedule. I told them that that a television station has a responsibility to the community and that a station must be responsive of the needs of that community. My personal goal was to produce as much original local programming as possible; and this local programming would be positioned to both entertain and inform people.

I wanted our viewers to look at our station as though we were part of their families. As I spoke to the press, I noticed that they kept shuffling back and forth in their seats and seemed to have smirks on their faces and a kind of "Oh yeah, right," attitude. I went on to tell them that WTTG was going to produce programming and special segments that had never been done in the Washington market before. The shuffling in their seats continued, but now at least they began to scribble on their note pads.

I continued with my presentation and told them, "WTTG is going to do a one-hour live newscast at ten o'clock five nights a week." There was silence in the room. I knew they did not believe what I was saying and that they felt that WTTG could never pull off a live newscast five nights a week.

"What else are you going to do?" a woman reporter yelled out at me.

"We've got plans to do a live afternoon show, something similar to the *Today Show*, with news segments between 12:00 to 12:30, and from there we will move to a panel of people and invited guests with remotes from all over Washington."

"Do you have the staff to pull something like that off?" was the next question.

"Yes we do," I blurted out with a great deal of confidence.

I was now looking out at blank faces. Again they started scribbling on their note pads. I'm sure they thought I was dreaming. When their articles appeared the next day in the newspapers, to my surprise, they were all very positive about our new programming ideas and me as general manager.

I was very satisfied about the press conference and the message that we seemed to have successfully conveyed to the press. Staff morale was high at the station and everyone was fresh with ideas for original local programming. My real problem was not that I couldn't put in motion and complete all of the promises I had made to the press; it was that I had not yet gotten around to asking permission from my boss Al Krivin to spend the money needed to deliver on those promises. I finally went to him and, after some reluctance on his part, got the budgets I needed.

Andy Ockershausen, VP/GM, WMAL Radio, Washington,

D.C. (1966–1969), writes:

"Bob came into Washington with no connections to the east, but he brought with him a tremendous amount of passion for television. I met him because he replaced my friend at Channel 5, and we became good friends and remain so today. I still joke with him that I was very happy to introduce my Washington contacts to him because he had an unlimited expense account, which he used whenever he needed to put deals together for his station. He was unique insomuch that he brought the West Coast, Los Angeles culture to Washington. In many ways he took Washington by surprise.

Back then, Washington was a sleepy kind of small media town with the only real news being generated from the government. Bob changed all that. He made the station a focal point for local programming. Bob's experience was West Coast, and it showed. Out west they were doing all kind of things the Washington stations were not even aware of. He brought with him a fresh sense of new ideas and West Coast marketing ideas that he put in place and in many ways revolutionized the D.C. market. Many of these ideas were later copied across the country, which is a testament to him as to how far ahead of everyone he really was.

For example, Bob thought up the idea of having automobile dealers do their own advertising on television. This was not being done in the Washington market. He rounded up car dealers, brought them into the studio, taped them and gave them free airtime for a month so they could test the positive reaction they were getting. The response was astonishing, and every other station in Washington followed him immediately. I have to believe that advertising revenue immediately went up at every television station in Washington because Bob Bennett came to town. When he put on news from ten to eleven p.m., every other station followed. Nobody had ever done news at 10 p.m. To me, Bob was, and is, a dynamic guy full of ideas and not afraid to try them out.

His three-hour a day program, Panorama, was a hit, and was copied both in Washington and in other markets. He brought professional basketball to Washington when we didn't even have a team. He made a deal with the then Baltimore Bullets for the broadcast rights to show the games in Washington. It was an instant hit. Later the Bullets moved to Washington permanently. He always wanted to serve the community and to make sure that his station was serving the community. He became very influential in Washington and was on a number of boards and involved with many charity events. As I look back, I can't say it enough: Bob had a real passion for television."

When we put a live 10 o'clock newscast in place, our ratings went through the roof. We delivered on our promise and produced the afternoon program that we called *Panorama*, which became a big success.

Quickly, WTTG was making a name for itself in the Washington market. *Panorama* featured Barbara Howar as one of the panelists, and we brought in John Willis from Los Angeles to join her. The show received very high ratings and became the place to be seen if you were a visiting celebrity from out of town or a congressman from the Hill.

Maury Povich was hired as our sports announcer, and he worked very well with Barbara Howar and John Willis. All three of them did a terrific job. You could see the competiveness between the three of them happening on camera. I'm convinced this helped the show's ratings greatly.

Barbara Howar, television personality, writes:
"Back in the 1960s, before women began demanding professional equality, Bob Bennett, then a total stranger, offered me on-air employment at the Washington, D.C., television studio where he was General Manager and also the creator of its popular Ten O'Clock News. *It was a position in which I had zip qualifications for, aside from high-level social connections I had with the political elite; a reputation recently tarnished at that time by a scandalous divorce that left me both infamous and broke. 'There's no such thing as bad publicity,' Bob jovially quipped while outlining the job description for the first-ever female to broadcast nightly commentaries in the Capital city. 'Just opine on subjects you can handle authoritatively,' he added—a restriction which severely limited my topics.*
The debut telecast, was, alas, "The Poor People's Campaign,"

wherein, Martin Luther King's successor, Reverend Ralph Abernathy, camped alongside his impoverished followers in makeshift tents near the Washington Monument. Standing amidst that ragtag crowd of thousands—and wearing a pricey pre-divorce outfit and false eyelashes—I soulfully lamented the income disparity between black and white Americans. Previewing the videotape, Bob merely said to me, 'Ditch the Minnie Mouse eyelashes next time,' which I did, though with no noticeable improvement to my performance on the countless other commentaries that made me cringe to watch. 'You can do this Barbara,' he kept saying to me, whenever I despaired, always adding, 'and be damn good at it, too!'

Totally confident of being right, he then dispatched me to do colorful vignettes at both the 1968 Republican and Democratic Conventions; political confabs I was either so adept or inept at covering that he gave me the obligatory female shot on Panorama, a live weekday talk show wherein I belabored all the issues that outraged me by arguing with the two male hosts: John Willis, an older kneejerk conservative and the young liberal, Maury Povich, who initially resented my working his side of the ideological street, yet became a trusted pal. The internecine bickering between the three of us so elevated the ratings that Bob Bennett had another of his innovative programs become a moneymaking hit. In response to my anxious query as to what the viewers actually thought of me, Bob laughed and said, 'If hate mail is any indicator Barbara, you are a star.'

After endless lectures to behave with 'ladylike dignity,' Bob selected me to anchor Metromedia's live coverage of the Nixon-Agnew Inaugural Ball. He said to me at the time, 'Putting up the satellite bird costs an arm and a leg, and John Kluge and some of the affiliates are already griping about the expense. Some of them even hope this will be your Waterloo. You've got exactly one hour, Barbara, to prove them wrong, so don't blow it.'

Of course, I never knew what Bob's politics were, or why his success roused such envy among his colleagues, particularly his West Coast Metromedia boss, Al Krivin. But it was Bob's career that John Kluge kept advancing.

For me, Bob Bennett was, and remains, a uniquely gifted rainmaker who not only changed my personal life and launched *the professional one, but also became my most loyal friend and cherished mentor. He'd often excuse my on-air bloopers by saying, 'nobody's perfect, Barbara,' but his extraordinary accomplishments prove otherwise."*

Maury Povich, television personality, writes:
"In the summer of 1966, I was working at WWDC Radio, a five-thousand-watt station in Washington, D.C., which was nonetheless a popular music station with a strong news and sports presence. I had graduated from the University of Pennsylvania four years earlier, tried to get into television, and found it difficult because those were the days when the only way you could get on TV was to be in radio first. Around this time Bob Bennett had come to Washington from Los Angeles, with his first GM job being at WTTG-TV. While at WTTG, he came up with the bold idea to start the first prime time newscast at ten o'clock. The town thought he was nuts. Washington, like many cities around the country, was a creature of habit: three network affiliate stations with eleven o'clock newscasts. That was it. Remember, this was long before all-news cable.
I interviewed at WTTG for the sports anchor job, even though I was a news and sports reporter at WWDC. Bob had hired a news director at WTTG named Ed Turner who was from Oklahoma, and he and Bob interviewed me for the job. I didn't know it at the time, but Bob wanted to hire Warner Wolf, another radio guy. Warner was the hot radio sports guy at the time in Washington. For whatever the reason, Bob did not hire him and Warner went on to become a big local sports guy in New York City.
So Bob hired me and I started as the sports anchor at WTTG's Ten O'Clock News. The newscast was groundbreaking for its time period. I was so impressed with Bob Bennett who was this young, good looking, hip West Coaster who brought dash to the all-business government town of Washington, D.C. And what a cheerleader he was. I was terrible opening night. I fumbled my newscast. I was scared to death. I felt awful. I didn't want to face Bob after that broadcast, but there he was, slapping me on the back and convincing me that I had done a great job. He really cheered me up and got me back in the game. I was ready

*to throw it all in. He was very secure within himself, and that is
something very rare for television management.*

*Bob then had another vision: a daytime three-hour news and
information show from noon to three o'clock daily. Back then,
even in the nation's Capitol, there was no news after the* Today
Show, *until the early evening news. Bob thought that since
WTTG had no network obligations, he could produce local
programming anytime he wanted. (I think that's how his later
success at WCVB began.) Bob brought in a friend of his named
John Willis, from Los Angeles; hired a brash young reporter
named Pat Collins from Boston; and then he and Ed Turner
realized that they had no one who grew up in Washington,
D.C. and knew the market. They looked around the newsroom
and there was only one local guy: me. So that's how I was hired
as the third co-host of another groundbreaking Bob Bennett
idea that was to become known as* Panorama. *I debuted on
January 30, 1967, and within a matter of four months, I was
the sportscaster and co-host of a three-hour news talk show in
Washington, D.C, and all because of Bob Bennett.*

*At this time, Bob was having a lot of trouble with a Metromedia
executive by the name of Al Krivin. Al never seemed to be nice
to Bob or was happy with any of the success that Bob was
achieving. I assumed that he was after Bob's job. At the end
of the first year of* Panorama, *Bob and Al had a major clash.
Krivin wanted to cancel* Panorama. *The show wasn't really
profitable at the time, but Bob knew that the show meant a
great deal to the station's lineup because it had earned a great
deal of respect and positive feedback from critics, the public,
and the FCC and government agencies. Everybody loved the
show, except Al Krivin. Bob dug in his heels and fought Krivin
all the way. All through the battle, Krivin demanded that the
show be cancelled. Bob was very frustrated and threw up his
hands and said, "I'm going on vacation."*

*I believe underneath all of this, Krivin was very jealous of
Bob's success with local programming and in some ways felt
threatened by Bob. Al may have thought that Bob's overall plan
was to some day be president of Metromedia. I have to say that
Bob had a lot of courage for a General Manager to stand up
against management like he did to save a show. In the end, Bob*

was right: as the years went on, Panorama *grew in stature and popularity and ran for over twenty years.*

One night Bob came up to me and said, "Maury, by the way, next week you're going to find an additional $200 in your paycheck." Like all talent, I had a contract and at that time it had two years left to go on it. I was in my late twenties, with two kids, making about $35,000 per year. I was surprised and said to Bob, "Why are you doing this?" He turned to me and said, "Because you deserve it." I can't tell you how much that meant to me. Let me think back now about how many times over my forty-year career that management gave me a raise that I wasn't contracted for. Never.

Our friendship grew quickly. We would play golf every Saturday with John Willis and Tom Maney. Bob told me that if I really wanted to learn the business, I could come to his office any time. He said his door would always be open for me to observe sales and promotion meetings. And that's how I learned the television business. Later on, all that served me so well that I went into syndicated programming with Fox, "A Current Affair;" Paramount, The Maury Povich Show; *and Universal,* The Maury Show. *I am the only talent in TV that I know of who goes out on sales calls to stations and advertisers, all because of Bob's graciousness in allowing me to learn the business of television from every level.*

In subsequent years, and crucial to my career, Bob was the most loyal and game-changing friend anyone could ever have. I left Washington in 1977 to see if I could make it elsewhere. By this time, Bob had moved to New York and then struck gold in Boston, not just in terms of making money, but in terms of being able to put his vision of local programming into motion, making Boston's Channel 5, ABC affiliate, one of the most important (if not the most important) ABC station in the country. He was also a very important and strong member of the ABC Affiliate Board. My career continued and I ended up in Chicago at NBC and had some management problems with them. After six months, I left. I was then hired and fired as a news co-anchor in Los Angeles at the CBS owned and operated station. All of a sudden I had gone from this stable news and talk show anchor to this roving anchor trying to go national, city by city.

An opening occurred for an anchor and talk show host in San Francisco in 1978. The GM was Russ Coughlin who was a little skeptical of my sketchy track record in television. I told him to call Bob Bennett. He did so and said to me later, 'In my book, Bob Bennett is the greatest broadcaster in America and he said you would be great, hard working, and loyal to a fault, and that I'd be making a big mistake if I didn't hire you.' Coughlin hired me at a point in my life when there was a good chance that my career was over. I lasted there for three years and then wanted something different. Bob by this time had returned to Metromedia to run their stations and he was thinking about launching a fourth network.

We had a drink together one night some time in 1983, and I told him that I wasn't happy. He said to me, 'Maury, I've got a great idea. Why don't you come home and we can do it all over again. Panorama *and* The Ten O'Clock News *had fallen on hard times and maybe you are just what they need and this will reenergize you.' I couldn't believe what I was hearing. I did it. I went back to Washington and within two years, the* Ten O'Clock News *won an Emmy as the best newscast in Washington.* Panorama *was revitalized. Bob had brought me home.*

Connie Chung and I were married in 1984, and I felt I was on top of the world. Bob had changed my life and it now would never be the same. After Rupert Murdoch bought Metromedia, he came down to Washington and saw that we were the best newscast he had, and in June of 1986, brought me to New York to start A Current Affair, *and for me, the rest is history.*

I owe Bob Bennett a great deal. In my forty-five years in television, he has had the most important influence on me. I've learned the business from him. I learned how to treat people with an undercurrent of respect and how to brighten their lives, without regard for what's in it for me. I have no trace of envy of anyone or anything. Bob taught me how to be modest. I have never known a more honest or modest person. That's how I remember Bob Bennett."

No Better Job in the World
Than Running a TV Station

I BELIEVE THE job of a general manager of a television station is the best job in the world. And it's a well-kept secret. The general manager is in charge of the entire operation. Everyone reports to the GM. There is no better job in the world than running a television station—any television station. You've got a little bit of Hollywood whereby you can direct people, put people on the air have the power to produce original programming. If, to your surprise, this programming doesn't work, you can take it off the air. There is no better job. I have always said that. And when you have scripted, produced, and agonized over everything, you can then back sit and watch your programs, making changes if needed.

Of course, you have to listen to your audience. They will tell you what they want to watch and what they don't want to watch. You have to be responsive and forever measure your audience as they change their likes and dislikes. As a general manager of a television station, you have a social responsibility to the community you program, too. You have to produce needed programming that hits the nerves of viewers. Sometimes you have to experiment. But at all times you have to keep an eye on your competition.

As a general manager and a television programmer, my strong interest has always been in creating the best local programming possible. The best way to reach a viewer is to create programming that touches them and helps them get through their day. You want viewers tuning into your station because they trust you and know you are going to inform them about the immediate world around them. The true success of a television station rests in it ability to create original local television that makes people feel comfortable.

The structure of WTTG was made up of a GM, sales manager, program manager, promotional manager, news director, and sports director. Under them were all of the people who work for those department heads. Most of our programming came from the syndication market, of which Metromedia was then one of the largest buyers. We benefited greatly from Metromedia's aggressive business tactics and were never at a loss for additional programming. But I must say, WTTG was committed to producing original local programming, and we were doing it with a great deal of success.

My Boss, Al Krivin

AS I MENTIONED earlier, my boss was Al Krivin, who was President of Metromedia Broadcasting. Al was stationed in Los Angeles, and it seemed no matter how much I reached out to try and establish a good relationship with him, nothing worked. In fact, I had no relationship with him at all, other than him coming around on a regular basis to meet with me and complain about what I was doing. I soon realized that he was intimidated by me. I always wanted to please him and always went out of my way to keep him in the loop and to inform him about everything I was doing and trying. But he was never happy with anything I did. I believe he felt that since I was in Washington, D.C. and John Kluge had a farm in nearby Virginia, that somehow John and I were getting together on a frequent basis and making plans. There seemed to always be a lot of misinterpretation between Al and me. I had started out liking him, but the more I dealt with him, the more he irritated me. Regardless, I was an executive at Metromedia and I was going to remain loyal, despite this lack of communication between the two of us. I just think he was so bent out of shape about his twisted idea of John Kluge and me communicating on a regular basis, that it always got in the way of our personal communication. The truth of the matter is that during my Washington years, I very rarely, if ever, heard from or spoke to John Kluge. And it was not in my job description to call him.

One thing I could always count on while I was working at WTTG was that Al would always be on my case about something. I could set my watch by it. Unfortunately, this was how it was going to be for many years to come. One time he said to me, "Bob, that damn station better be good, and it better work and not cost us any more money, or it's your ass." Unfortunately for me these kinds of conversations were all too frequent. He would come to Washington on a regular basis, want to go to dinner, and then he'd critique the *Ten O'Clock News*. I never really thought he knew anything about the makings of a newscast or about programming in general, but he was always telling me how to produce something or what not to produce. He was constantly getting on my nerves.

On KNXT-TV in the Los Angeles market, Jerry Dunphy was the co-anchor for the news and Ralph Story had a nightly segment within the news broadcast. Ralph also had an hour show on Saturday night. Both of these guys were terrific at what they did and had high ratings to prove it. From my neighbor, who was the agent who represented both of them, I found out that their contracts were coming up, so I offered them more money if they moved to our station. Our discussions went well, and they both agreed to come over if I could work out the details with their agent and Metromedia. I had to go to Al Krivin for his permission; and of course, he didn't like it.

"We don't need those guys. We're doing fine just the way we are," Krivin said to me.

"Al, you must be out of your mind. I don't understand why you don't see the wisdom in this. Bringing these guys over means we have a good shot at generating the same high ratings as where they are now. What's the problem?"

He smirked and gave me no answer. The real problem was that it was not his idea. That was the real problem. It was a shame because both Dunphy and Story continued at KNX and had fabulous careers. They would have aided in the growth of KTTV, but Al just hadn't been the one who thought up the idea.

As the years went on, Al continued to criticize both the WTTG news and me whenever he came to Washington. "Bob, I think you need to put more fire stories on the ten o'clock newscast," he would say.

"You really think that, Al?"

"Yeah, put more fires into your news and that will jazz it up and you'll get higher ratings."

I looked at him and didn't say a word. An idea struck me. The next day I had the news department edit ten fire stories into one fake WTTG newscast. On Al's next visit to Washington, I would be ready for him. About a month later he called and told me he was in town, so I invited him to come to my office. I also told him that I had taken his advice regarding his idea for our newscast, and I hoped that he would be very happy with what I was going to show him. He arrived that evening just in time to watch the *Ten O'Clock News*. I had him sitting in my office in front of a monitor that was going to play the fake newscast. As it played, he could not believe what he was seeing. Fire after fire, after fire, after fire. He must have thought the whole town was ablaze. He sat there glued to the monitor.

"Now this is how the news should be, Bob. You do that every night and you'll have one hell of a newscast," he said to me with a twisted smile on his face.

As the WTTG years were unfolding I was very happy and pleased with the creative things our staff was doing and the results we were achieving in the ratings. Our newscast continued to refine itself as we went along and *Panorama* took on a life of its own and was now being talked about nationwide. Our thirty-second spots were going for about five to six hundred dollars each and we were signing up new advertisers and sponsors on a regular basis.

Two months after my arrival, I brought Tom Maney from Los Angeles in to be the sales manager for WTTG. Tom was a very talented sales person and a very driven person. We were good friends, so when I talked to him about coming to join me at WTTG, he jumped at the chance. Al was very unhappy about it. He didn't want me to steal anyone from our LA station.

As soon as Tom arrived he got down to business. He was very competitive. I rolled up my sleeves to give him a hand, and together we started knocking on doors and doing a lot of entertaining. To our surprise, we found that the general sales manager of WCOP had not made a sales call to a local advertising agency in eight years. Tom and I used to be there at nine in the morning when they'd open the door. Under Tom's guidance, we were soon selling out about eighty percent of our inventory. At the end of the first year, WTTG had made seventy percent of all of the profits of all the stations in Washington.

I continued to refine our programming schedule. Mark Evans

had been on radio hosting a nationally syndicated show called *Housewife's Protected League* that recommended home products. The show was very popular and everyone loved him. Mark had two shows going on at the time and one of the shows was a political interview prime time show. He was also a good friend of John Kluge. Alan Smith came in from Baltimore and I made him the anchor of the *Ten O'Clock News*, and he did a great job.

I cancelled the WTTG wrestling show, which was the very first television wrestling show in the country. Although it seemed that everyone loved it and watched it, as I was moving WTTG programming more upscale, I did not want the station to be associated with that kind of programming. That decision unfortunately turned into a nightmare. We must have received five thousand calls in protest. The press couldn't believe what I had done. The telephone calls never stopped, so I apologized to everyone and told them not to worry; it would end up on another station.

Living Through an American Race Riot

IN 1968, MAJOR cities throughout the country were going through race riots and Washington, D.C. was no different. It was a very sad and tormenting time for most Americans. Riots were breaking out in many major cities with looting, fighting and torching going on all around. Police were in riot gear with big sticks, hitting people and firing off tear gas. People were throwing rocks and turning over cars. As the riot in Washington picked up steam, I received a telephone call from some guy who was screaming on the other end of the line.

"Let me tell you something mother f---er, we're going to burn your f---ing station down to the ground. If I was you, I'd get the hell out now!"

At this point, I was taking all of this very seriously. I not only had the safety concern for all of my staff who were working in the building, but I had to also make sure that our people reporting out on the streets were also safe. It was one of those real crisis moments when a general manager has to be a leader and a clear thinker. And then, of course, the phone call came from Marjie telling me it was time to come home. I couldn't go home. I let as many people as I could go home, and kept only a core staff to keep the place running. I was in continuous touch with the news staff out on the streets. We provided coverage of the riot, and I am happy to say that no one ever tried to burn down our station. One soothing moment that had a profound affect on the riots was when the soul singer James Brown went on television and told everyone to calm down. It worked.

At the beginning of the second year I received a phone call from

John Kluge, who invited me to his farm for lunch in Virginia. This was a surprise for me since there had never really been any communication between the two of us on any matters. Apparently he wanted to talk to me about something and I was very happy to accept the invitation.

John had this magnificent farm and was a very gracious host. During the lunch he told me that Al Krivin would be retiring soon from Metromedia and that he was going to have to replace him. He then informed me that the person he felt was best qualified for the job was me. I didn't want to be rude to John, or to not show my appreciation for the job offer, but I wasn't too thrilled about taking Al Krivin's place. I never wanted to be a staff person; I wanted to run a television station. I was happy doing what I was doing. I was seeing the positive results of the ideas that I was putting into motion at the station and I wanted to continue. I felt there were many more challenges ahead of me and my main goal was to make WTTG into the number one television station in the Washington market. I told John that if he wanted me to do it I would, but I'd rather not. He understood.

A Telephone Call from Ethel Kennedy

ONE DAY I received a telephone call from Ethel Kennedy. She invited me out to lunch at her home to meet her and Bobby Kennedy, but would not tell me the reason why she was inviting me. I accepted her invitation and drove out to the Kennedy house in Virginia. As I got out of the car, the biggest dog I have ever seen (I think they called him Brutus) came out running after me. I jumped back in my car in fear of my life. I closed the door and sat there with the dog outside looking in at me and barking. Somebody finally came out and put the dog away and I went in the house.

At the table where I was sitting, I found Jack Parr, David Brinkley, Chet Huntley, and a host of other well-known personalities. Bobby Kennedy soon came in and walked over to me and introduced himself. They had been planning a telethon and they wanted me to help them raise $300,000 to finance a recreation center for African-American children. I told them I was not interested in broadcasting just a regular telethon for them on our station, but I would do something better. I told them I would put on more of an entertainment show and that I would run it on Saturday night at 7 p.m. until 1 a.m. in the morning. "You'll have a bigger audience in prime time," I told them. They were very intrigued and enthusiastic. The show took months of preparation and was finally done at a large auditorium in the Washington area.

During this time, I used to receive telephone calls throughout the day from Ethel Kennedy. She would talk to me about various Hollywood stars participating in the show and would ask my advice about production concerns. We had such stars as Skitch Henderson,

Perry Como, Lauren Bacall, and many other well-known names join us for the telethon. We even had two orchestras.

When it aired, the show was an enormous success. Jack Parr came out of retirement to be our host and things could not have gone any better. Averill Harriman opened his house as kind of the greenroom for the guests—who were all later picked up in limousines and brought over to the auditorium.

Jack Parr told me that in all of the years he had worked for NBC, he had never seen such professionalism in the production of a television show. He found it hard to believe that it was a local television station doing the producing and not a major network.

Marjie came to the show, and that evening Ethel Kennedy went over to her and apologized for taking up so much of her husband's time.

That evening we raised six million dollars.

Perry Mason, McHale's Navy and H.L. Hunt

I WANTED TO buy *Perry Mason* and run it on our station. In order to do so I had to have permission from Al Krivin. What I thought was going to be a no-brainer turned into a fight.

"Al, I'd like to buy *Perry Mason* for the station," I told him one day.

"I don't think that's a good idea Bob. That won't work. Why do you want to do that? When would you run it?" he said to me with a great look of disappointment on his face.

"Well, I want to run it at eleven o'clock after the news," I told him.

"I don't see how that's going to work out. Don't do it," he told me.

"I think it will work, Al. I want to buy it."

After that meeting I was able to buy it without telling him and I put it on at eleven o'clock. The line up was the news at ten and *Perry Mason*" at eleven, five nights a week. All at once, *Perry Mason* took off and it was a complete surprise to the Washington market, and soon it was the highest rated show in the country. It was even outdoing the local news at eleven. Soon Al Krivin was arguing with me, as usual. Here was a guy, fighting me all the way on everything I did, yet he was sharing in my success. It never made sense to me.

A guy named Joe Docherty was a friend of Al's, and he was running a station in Providence, Rhode Island, where he was having success at running *Perry Mason* Monday through Friday at five o'clock.

So Al shouts at me on the telephone one day, "I want you to

move *Perry Mason* to five o'clock, Bob, and I don't want to have an argument about it with you."

"Why would I do that, Al, when we're number one in the time period?"

"You do it because I'm telling you to do it, Bob."

The first rule in broadcasting is that if you have something that works, leave it alone. Don't touch it. I was beside myself with anger.

"No, listen to me, Bob; I want you to move 'Man From U.N.C.L.E.' from your five o'clock time to eleven and put *Perry Mason* in at five."

"I thought about it for a moment, and then said, "Well that may very well work, Al, but it isn't going to work, as good as the way I've got it set up now."

"Just do it, Bob!"

He insisted, and I did it. *Perry Mason* did do reasonably well at five but at eleven, we lost half our audience.

Once again, I was in this constant fight with Al. I never really wanted to compete with him; I just wanted to do my job; but he fought me all the way on everything. And at this time I was starting to get a lot of positive publicity from the press on the things we were doing at the station, and that only bothered Al more. I believed I was doing things based on the fact that I was right, and he was wrong.

Just when I thought matters between Al and me had settled down, I was sadly mistaken. Al and I were about to go head to head again, only this time it was over *McHale's Navy*.

"Al, I'd like to buy *McHale's Navy* and air it Monday through Friday at seven o'clock," I told him one day.

"Bad idea. I'm not going to give you any money for that," he said to me.

"Well, I've got to get it, Al. Somebody else is going to buy it if we don't. We could really use it on our station."

About this time a small UHF station appeared in Washington, and we suddenly had some competition for the buying of syndicated shows. It now appeared that even if I had the money to buy syndication shows, it was going to be a little harder to do so.

Al Krivin continued to tell me, "No. I'm not giving you the money for *McHale's Navy*."

So I had to find a way to go around him and I did. I made a deal with Beatrice Food to buy *McHale's Navy*, and I paid them off in spots during the weekend when we had highly rated children's shows and a lot of unsold inventory. So I had no cash outlay, and it looked like a great deal. After it was on I had to tell him how I did it and he was not happy about it. However, all of a sudden *McHale's Navy* became an enormous hit for us at that time. The numbers were so high that the GM local ABC affiliate sued the rating service and said it was impossible that a show in rerun could get higher ratings than in its original run. And that does make sense, but this market was a very unusual market. We just made television history. Everyone was talking about this. And as you can imagine, when our ratings for *McHale's Navy* went through the roof, Al Krivin just went crazy with anger, but this time he had to back off.

H.L. Hunt, who had built the world's largest fortune at the time, wanted to come on our program *Panorama* and be interviewed. He was an eccentric character who had apparently married twice, had fourteen children, and supported three families at one time. He made his fortune in the oil business. I was thrilled to have him on as a guest but told his secretary that I would agree to it only if Mr. Hunt would have lunch with me. He agreed to it.

On the day he came into the studio, I met with him and he told me that our host Maury Povich could ask him any questions except questions about his money and net worth. He did not want to talk about how much he was worth, nor did he want to talk about the rumor that he was the world's richest person. I told Maury not to ask him any questions about his money or his net worth. Maury agreed and then the cameras rolled and Maury welcomed Hunt to the show.

After a few introductory questions, all seemed to be going well until Maury asked the following:

"Is it true, Mr. Hunt, that you're making a million dollars a week?"

Hunt was stunned and then became angry.

"No, that's not true," he told Povich.

"Is it true that you're the richest man in the world?" Povich continued.

"I wouldn't really know," Hunt said.

Hunt dodged the questions about his money and his net worth and finally the show ended. After the show, Hunt came to my office and had lunch. I was not pleased, nor was Hunt, as to the way Povich asked his questions.

To Hunt, I could only say that I was very sorry for the questions he was asked regarding his money.

"Oh, that's alright I guess," he said to me. "The truth of the matter is, I don't know if I'm making one million a week or four million a week," he told me.

The Move To New York City and WNEW-TV

HALFWAY THROUGH 1968, Al called me and told me to move to New York City because Larry Freberg, the General Manager of WNEW was leaving his job.

"It's your job now, Bob. You're the new GM of WNEW, so pack your bags and get the hell up there," he said to me.

I really wasn't ready to leave WTTG. I was having fun, and our accomplishments were enormous. But I knew that if Al told me to go, I had to go. Now, of course, I had to bring the news home to Marjie and the children. That was not going to be easy. When I told her she was not at all happy about moving, but she reluctantly agreed to go. For me this was going to be an enormous step forward. New York City was the number one market in the country, and I was going to be running a television station there. This was a great opportunity.

The staff put together a farewell party for us in Washington. On the day I left WTTG, I felt like I had accomplished a lot and along with my creative staff, established that station as a very strong personality, so much so that today, some thirty years later, it is the number one independent station in America. For me it was a lot more than just a pleasant experience. It had given me confidence to further my qualities as a General Manager of a television station. I felt a great deal more secure about myself and my ideas.

At WTTG, I loved the people I worked with and I think the feeling was mutual. When I got there, no one was exercising any innovation of any kind. I changed and moved many things around. I felt that I gave people the opportunity to do some terrific things and they did them. I was sorry to leave because I had gotten close to a lot of them. While I was there, I wanted to create an atmosphere that encouraged innovation and a strong lineup of original local programming. I think I was successful in doing that, but I was very fortunate to have a lot of talented and gifted people around me.

I still remember that teary-eyed night when I first came to Washington, D.C., and stood and looked up at that great marble statue of Abraham Lincoln. I had come a long way since then-- a long way in the building of my own level of self-confidence. I had a lot to be satisfied about; I was now a real General Manager. However, with New York City now on my radar, I was busy packing my suitcase.

In January of 1969, I went to New York City to be the General Manager of WNEW-TV at a salary of $75,000 per year. As I mentioned, Marjie was not thrilled about another move, but plans were made for the family to join me in six months in New York after Casey and Kelly were out of school. I was very excited about going to New York. If you are in the broadcast business, the best place to be is in the number one market in the country, and that is New York City. New York has it all. The competition is fierce, the people are highly creative, and the world around you is very sophisticated. On my first evening there I moved into a cramped company apartment and prepared myself for the first day on the job.

WNEW-TV traces its history back to 1938, when Dr. Alan B. DuMont was experimenting with his coaxial hookups between Washington and New York. On May 2, 1944, the station received its commercial license as WABD (after DuMont's initials), making it the fourth oldest continuous broadcasting station in the world. The station was originally broadcast on channel 4 and moved to channel 5. By February of 1955, Dr. DuMont realized that he could not continue in network television anymore and shut down operations. He then spun the two stations off into DuMont Broadcasting Corporation, and as mentioned earlier, John Kluge entered the picture and acquired the company.

Sometime soon after 1958, the station had a new set of call letters which were WNEW-TV. To my knowledge, when I walked through that door on the first day of my new job, WNEW was the largest television station in the country, with approximately three hundred people working there.

With my WTTG experience behind me, I was highly confident about being the new general manager of WNEW. The nut that was in my throat on my first day of WTTG was not there for my first day on the job at WNEW. I was anxious to get to work and walked into the place with a great deal of enthusiasm. However, what was in store for me was something completely different than what I had been used to.

Surprise: A Memo Signed by Every Person on the News Staff

ON MY FIRST day of work, I was given a memo signed by every person on the news staff telling me that I should immediately fire an on-camera person by the name of Martin Aben, or they were all going to walk off the job. Now you must remember that most newsrooms back then were liberal. Martin Aben just happened to be a conservative, and a conservative in a liberal newsroom was certainly setting up a situation that could be highly explosive. It always amazed me that when a news story came in over the wire back then, it would suddenly be turned around to fit the political beliefs of the majority of the newsroom people.

To try and balance the WNEW news, the General Manager before me brought in Aben, so by the time I walked in the door, Aben had already successfully offended all of the liberals. There were a lot of very unhappy liberal news people in the place who were now going to challenge me on my first day of work.

So here now on my desk was this memo signed by all of the members of the news staff who wanted Martin Aben out. The memo was really an ultimatum—either Aben goes, or we go. Some challenge for my first day on the job. I crumpled up the memo, threw it in the wastebasket, and asked the news director to give me the last six Martin Aben pieces so I could study them. I looked at them and I liked Aben's work. What really bothered me was the fact that the news department was basically dictating to me how I should handle the situation. That really bothered me. Instead of just meeting me first and explaining their side of the story, they came right out and challenged me. I decided it was time for me to do a little challenging of my own.

I thanked everyone for their memo and then sent one back asking them to join me in a meeting. When the meeting took place I told them that I had looked at Martin Aben's last six pieces and I liked all of them. I told them I liked how Martin balanced off the news. In fact, I was so impressed with Martin's professionalism that I was going to give him his own half-hour show on Saturday night to be called *The Martin Aben Show*. They were all aghast and did not know what to say. I went on to tell them that if there was anyone here in the meeting who would like to resign, they should let me know immediately. Nobody said a word and nobody resigned. Martin Aben's show went on and became successful, and I never heard another word about it.

WNEW was a very different kind of station than WTTG in Washington, which was primitive in comparison. When I arrived at WTTG, it was a television station that had very little going for it other than its market place reputation. WNEW, in comparison, had its act together. It had quite a budget to support a strong programming schedule, a strong management and sales team, and a news team that was one of the best in the business. I learned quickly that this was not a place that I had to immediately tear down to build up again. I had the strange feeling that in some areas of programming, WNEW had borrowed some of the ideas we had done in Washington, one of which was the ten o'clock live news. But still, what I was now dealing with at WNEW was a station that was much more set in its ways. However, I was determined to find something I could do to make it better.

One of the first things I did that was different and unique was the creation of an all African American newscast. WNEW was the first station in the country to do it. I wanted to have a diversity of programming for minorities so we came up with the idea of an all African American newscast that African Americans could relate to. It was produced on the weekend and had all African American writers, producers, directors and staff putting it together. We had over twenty people working on that show, and it was very popular.

John Lindsay had a show on WNEW, and at that time he was the Mayor of New York City. His show appeared on Sunday night at ten, where he would interview guests about topical political issues. There was a rumor going around that Lindsay might rerun for mayor. I told his assistant that if he runs for reelection, I was going to have to cancel his show because I have to give equal time to all of the candidates. His assistant looked at me in disbelief. Cancel the Mayor's show? How could I do that? There must have been eight people running for mayor that year, and I had to make sure that WNEW complied with all FCC regulations. There was no room for error. Those FCC regulations were carved in stone.

Word soon reached Mayor Lindsay that his show might get cancelled. He was not happy about it, so he called and said he wanted to see me. I had to go to Washington that day but he seemed frantic to meet. I told him I'd be back in New York that evening, and we could meet at the station around 10:30. I took the plane back and went to the studio where an anxious John Lindsay was waiting for me. He was in an agitated state and told me he wanted to continue on with his show, and basically came out and just about ordered me not to cancel him. I told him that the last thing I wanted to do was to cancel his show, but I had to comply with all FCC rules. I told him that if he reran for Mayor, I would have to take him off the air. His face turned red with anger. I told him to call his attorney and check with the rules. "I don't make the rules, the FCC does," I told him. He was quiet for a moment, and then looked around, got right up close to my face, and said, "I wonder if this station could stand an inspection from the fire department, Bob." I couldn't believe those words came out of his mouth. He soon left and the very next day announced he was running for reelection. I cancelled his show and never heard from him again.

My friend Jack Duffield was living in Westport, CT at the time and invited us to visit with him. We fell in love with the town and ended up buying a house on Pequot Road, which was the same street he was living on. Kelly and Casey were now in the local schools in Westport. We owned a boat and docked it at the Westport Marina, and on weekends we water skied and went for cruises up and down the Connecticut coast. Of all the towns we lived in, I believe that Kelly and Casey loved Westport, CT, the most.

Kelly Bennett writes:
"I remember that when we lived in Westport, CT, my father

always came home with a briefcase full of evening work that he would read and go through until the late hours. We had a family room, and in the family room there were three television sets. My father, being the consummate television executive that he was, used to have our television sets tuned to three different stations so he could sample what everyone was doing for their eleven o'clock newscasts. One evening, while he was watching these three different newscasts, he noticed that WNEW's news started about thirty or sixty seconds later than the other newscasts. I remember to this day him picking up the phone and dialing WNEW and wanting to know immediately why his news was starting later than the other stations. He never missed a detail."

Meanwhile, life at the station continued. We did more local programming, and I tinkered with the schedule and tried to improve on our newscast. I had political issues to deal with as people at the station lobbied for their own agendas, but for the most part, we were becoming a tightly knit family whose common goal was to run a fine television station.

The Labor Strike That Shook the Walls

THE STATION HAD a labor strike in 1969, and it lasted for one hundred and one days. Several unions in New York, which included engineers, electricians, and staff people, were holding their ground for more money. This affected WNEW greatly since we depended on engineers, electricians, and staff people to keep us running. It was a tough time and it grew into a very vicious strike. We had protesters with signs and bullhorns lined up outside our station screaming at people as they came into work.

When I arrived in the morning for work, I always made it a point to walk through the crowds to show them that I was not intimidated. As I made my way through, I would generally hear them yelling into their bullhorns, "Here he comes now. This guy is the biggest enemy of them all. Watch out for him. He's out to get us." I looked back at all of them and kept a stern face. I felt sorry for them as they stood out there in the cold not making money and trying to bother everyone. For me, I had enough to do just to keep morale up among those who took their own lives into their hands walking into work every morning. I had to keep the station running and the news had to keep going.

We actually had to put up with two demonstrations at the same time. Not far up the street from us was the Italian American Club, which was also demonstrating, only their demonstration was in front of the FBI building. The source of their anger revolved around Italian Unity and what they considered to be harsh and unfair treatment of Italian Americans.

Ninety days into the strike, there was no end in sight. It was a tough time for everyone involved. Animosity from the striking workers who manned their posts outside our office every morning was hitting an all time high. They were getting more aggressive and had started pushing people as they entered the building. Not only was it dangerous and annoying, it was taking our minds off the job of running our television station. The yelling outside the station was getting louder as the days went on. There was a large water tank on the roof of our building that we all thought would be the target of the protesters. If they did something to it, we would be without water and air conditioning and would have to close down the station.

There was this one big striker who was always yelling and screaming the most out of everyone who stood outside. One day as I was walking through the crowd and entering the building, he said something that offended me. I walked over to him and grabbed him by the throat and told him that if he ever said that again I'd knock him on his ass. He was shocked that I had done this and couldn't believe that I turned around and grabbed him. Everybody broke out laughing because I don't think any of them liked this guy. I never heard him yell at me again.

About a hundred yards from the front of our station was our parking garage. Whenever a news truck or station car was pulling up, they would call us as they were rounding the corner so we could quickly open the gates and let them in, before any protester could get through.

Inside the station, we did the best we could to keep things going with our very limited staff. Under normal circumstances, the station had six fulltime air conditioning people. When the strike hit, we had just one guy who agreed to ride out the strike on the inside. Needless to say, this guy became the most important person in the place. We couldn't do enough for him. Everything he wanted he got. No request was too small. This man had to be kept happy. We brought in a cot so he could sleep in the building. Everyday we would order in meals for him from some of the best restaurants in town. Soon we were ordering lunch from 21, Le Cirque, and other famous restaurants. Like I said, no request was too small. Without him we would not have been able to work. We even had his wife and kids in on a regular basis.

I kept John Kluge apprised of all the turmoil on a regular basis, and of course I also had to let Al Krivin know what was going on. Funny thing is—I don't really remember ever seeing Al visiting at the station when the strike was on. I guess he knew when to pick and choose his arrival and departure times.

Sticking My Neck Out
Just to Play a Game of Golf

PRIOR TO THE strike, a golf tournament had been planned, and I received word that it was still going to happen, despite the union strike. Many of the engineers and workers were scheduled to play in the tournament, and since I had been previously invited and was an avid golfer, I decided that I was going to play. I was not going to let striking workers intimidate me. Everybody in the station thought I was crazy. Marjie thought I was out of my mind. Everyone made the point that my life would certainly be in great danger if I played in that golf tournament. I understood their reasoning and concern for me, but why should I have let these protesters intimidate me? I hadn't done any harm to them. So I gathered my golf clubs on the day of the tournament and drove out to the golf club.

Everyone was shocked to see me as I walked into the place. At first, nobody would even talk to me. I could feel the knives in my back as I was walking around. I went out and shot nine holes. Everybody kept to themselves and I enjoyed my game of golf. When it was done, I went inside to get a drink before dinner and sat down by myself. I could see various groups of people huddled together in the clubhouse looking at me and speaking in hushed whispers. One guy finally came over to the table and said to me: "You really have balls, Bennett, coming in here like this."

I said, "Hey, I was invited. In fact, I'm enjoying this drink and I'm going to enjoy my dinner."

He was surprised at my candor and just stood there looking at me. His friends didn't know what was going on since they could not hear our conversation. He suddenly nodded to his friends and told them to come over. Suddenly, the ice was broken, and people started to sit down and talk to me.

Looking For Some New Challenges

WHILE WORKING AT WNEW, I was reasonably happy, but it did not have the kind of challenges that WTTG had, so I was not overly charged up. New York City can overpower you and you can easily feel worn down after a while. Many things at WNEW were now running smoothly. Metromedia continued to provide us with programming and we benefited greatly from their aggressive syndication buys. Our ratings were always very good and our news was now a shining star in our program line up. In New York, the sales game is highly competitive and filled with a lot of bright people who seem to know every little cubbyhole in the city and hundreds of ways to make a sale. Even though the job wasn't as challenging as I would have liked, I was happy that we developed a competitive, solid, and successful sales team and we had the revenue to prove it.

In 1969, I became very interested in Muscular Dystrophy, and I wanted to become a part of this special group of people who were trying to find a cure for this debilitating disease. I went over to meet with Jerry Lewis and then met with Bob Ross, who was the MDA Executive Vice-President. They asked me to join their board, and I felt really good about it. I gave them facilities for free at the station and added television stations across the country to carry the telethon. I am proud to say that I have been on the MDA Board since then, having been President for ten years, Chairman of the Board for two years, and now Chairman of the Executive Committee. MDA is a fabulous organization that has been doing great work for so many people.

We also came up with a unique question to ask parents every

night at ten o'clock. It was quite simply the following: "It's ten o'clock. Do you know where your children are?" As simple a question as this is, it got a lot of parents taking note of where their children were. It was so successful, that I even used it years later when I was at WCVB in Boston.

By the end of the second year, I felt really good about our success at WNEW. However, something was missing in my professional life, and I was not exactly sure what it was. I was making very good money, running a television station in the number one market in the country, my family was well taken care of, and I had a limousine driver to take me around. Not bad for a kid from Altoona, PA, I used to say to myself.

There was one thing, however, that I could always count on: my old friend Al Krivin. He would continue to bother me on a regular basis no matter what I did. He was always coming in to the station complaining about something. His complaints were constant. He was always unhappy with anything I did, and certainly would never acknowledge any of my successes. It seemed the more positive press I was getting, the more steamed up Al Krivin would get.

Enter Now the Boys from Boston

ONE DAY THE telephone rang in my office and on the other end of the line was a man by the name of Leo Beranek who was the President of Boston Broadcasters, Inc. (BBI). Leo and BBI had filed an application in March of 1963 to try and acquire the FCC permit to operate a television station in Boston, which was now WHDH-TV and operated by The Herald Traveler Corporation.

WHDH-TV was granted a construction permit in 1957, and in 1961, it was granted a temporary license, but only for a three-month period with possible renewals. BBI's objective was to take the authority to run that station away from WHDH. WHDH applied for a renewal, but in 1969, the FCC denied them the renewal and awarded BBI the permit. Legal wrangling between the *Herald Traveler* and BBI had been going on for years, but when the Petition for Consideration had been denied the *Herald Traveler*, television history was made. It was the Court of Appeals in November of 1970 that affirmed the renewal. Something like this had never happened before.

Now that BBI had the license, they were going to need a competent person to run that station, and they thought I might be the man for the job. At the time I was talking to Leo Beranek on the telephone, I did not know that the Herald Traveler Corporation and BBI were involved in a very bitter legal battle that was getting worse by the hour. However, I was aware of the WHDH-TV story, and in some ways it had intrigued me. In our conversation, Leo was lively and energetic about BBI's future. They had made a number of promises to the FCC including the one that they were going to provide more local programming than any other commercial station had ever done. He asked if he could come to visit with me in New York, and I told him yes. The idea of doing so much local programming really intrigued me.

A week later, Leo Beranek was in my office along with Bill Poorvu, who was Vice-Chairman of BBI.

"I appreciate your coming down to talk to me Leo, but why would I want to go to Boston? I'm in the number one market in the country and I'm making the most money I have ever made. I'm very happy here. Why would I want to go to Boston?"

"How much of this station do you own Bob?" he asked me.

"I don't own any of it. I have stock options, but I don't have any equity."

"What do you think the value of the station in Boston might be if we get the license?"

For that I had to stop and think a moment.

"I don't know, maybe fifty million," I said.

"Well, what do you suppose five percent of fifty million is?"

"Five percent? Five percent for who?" I asked him.

"Five percent for you, Bob."

I was stunned. I sat back in my chair and looked at him. He stood up and stretched.

"Do you own any part of this television station? What we're talking about is putting five percent ownership of the station in Boston in your name, Bob. That's pretty good, isn't it?"

"Yeah, that is pretty good," I said to him, holding back my growing excitement.

And then I started to really think about it, and that five percent number became solidly fixated in my mind as something I wanted to have. There was silence in the room as we looked at one another.

I have always thought that I was going to be very successful in life. I had no reason to believe it and I knew I was never going to have it handed to me, but something had always told me I was going to hit a home run someday. The more I sat there and thought about that five percent figure, the more I started to see myself swinging that baseball bat and hitting the ball over the fence. Maybe this was my big chance. Maybe I should go for this. Give it a try. What was the worst that could happen? I could always go back and run a television station somewhere if this failed. I told Leo I would give it some thought and that I would fly up to Boston to meet everyone. Something told me this was going to be good for me.

When I flew up to Boston to be interviewed for the job, they had already met with four applicants before me. One of the applicants was Ben West, who told Don Ward, one of BBI's attorneys, that he hoped he didn't get the job as the first GM of the station, because he felt whoever held the position first was not going to last too long. He was more interested in being the second GM of the station than the first.

Leo took me around for introductions, and I immediately liked everyone I met. The people associated with BBI were professionals with academic pedigrees that could fill volumes of *Who's Who?* Some of the members were Oscar Handlin, a Pulitzer Prize-winning author and professor of American History at Harvard; Dr. John H. Knowles, a famous doctor and general director of the Massachusetts General Hospital; Leo Beranek, famed acoustics expert; Charles Marran, president of Spenser Shoe Company; Alan Neuman, producer-director of Bing Crosby Productions; Louis Smith, industrialist and civic leader, Barry Wood, vice president of Metromedia Producers Corporation, and Robert Gardner, anthropologist, filmmaker, and professor at Harvard. This was certainly a stellar list for a broadcast company.

My Job Interview

FOR MY INTERVIEW, I remember being a little nervous when I walked into the room, but I felt really good about my credentials and past accomplishments and about being the right person for the job.

There must have been a hundred thoughts going through my mind that day, and then it finally dawned on me that all of these guys may be bright and may be experts in their fields, but none of them knew anything at all about running a television station. That was my area. What I needed to do in that interview was to show them just how much I knew about running a television station. The interview process went well, and I seemed to have been well liked and got along well with everyone. I was asked a number of questions about how I would run the station if and when we got the license. I answered all of their questions thoughtfully and honestly, and I appeared to have satisfied them. Not long after my interview I was offered the job, and I accepted. I really felt it was a great opportunity for me. Secretly, I was thinking that this could be my big chance.

Leo Beranek, President, Boston Broadcasters, Inc., writes:
"Bill Poorvu and I knew we were going to need a topnotch General Manager of Operations for BBI who was program-oriented, experienced in handling a television sales department, and in the purchasing of syndicated programming. Five candidates came under consideration, and one of them was Bob Bennett, who was in my view, the best choice. Bob was then General Manager of WNEW in New York City and had also

run Channel 5 in Washington, D.C., prior to that. Bill and I first talked to Bob about the job on October 6, 1970. We found him exceedingly bright, eminently qualified, and almost certain to learn quickly in any new situation. BBI's Board of Directors met on January 14, 1971, to make a selection. We interviewed three candidates one day and Bob the next morning. Bob came on strong. He clearly knew how to manage a station. That he had built the news programming on Channel 5 in Washington from No. 4 to No. 1, and had run a first-class operation in New York, convinced us that management and sales were his strength.

Now came decision time. A split on the board emerged. Half wanted Bob and half wanted one of the other three, Fred Walker, who was strong on programming. In a brief comfort break, Bill Andres took me aside and asked me who I really wanted. There was no doubt in my mind, I told him; we need a man with Bob Bennett's experience. Andres believed that the Board ought to give me, the President, whatever I felt was necessary to get the job done. When we reassembled, Bill expressed his feelings with eloquence and, as a result, only one vote out of eight went against Bob."*

(*Excerpt from his book, Riding the Waves *by Leo Beranek)*

William J. Poorvu, Treasurer, Boston Broadcasters, Inc., writes

"When Leo Beranek and I first met Bob Bennett while searching for a General Manager for Boston Broadcasters, Inc., we knew immediately that he was the person we wanted. His experience in local programming at independent stations in Washington and New York, his commercial savvy, and his enthusiasm for life made him the ideal candidate for what we were trying to accomplish. The courtship took a while, and Leo and I thought discussions were going well. After years of working for others, Bob was intrigued by not only the challenge of running a path-finding station, but finally being able to have some equity of his own. Then I received a phone call one day from Bob. He had just gotten out of the water on a beach in Bermuda and told me that he had changed his mind about taking the GM job we had offered him. He had two questions for me: "Why would he leave one of the best television jobs running the

Number 1 independent station in America? And why would he risk moving to an unfamiliar city to be part of a group that hadn't yet received its final license to go on the air? What could I say? I visualized Bob with a drink in his hand, the sun shining, and the beach filled with tanning beauties. I mumbled that I understood what he said and that we would talk when he got back to New York. Although young at the time, I knew never to argue with someone in a bathing suit.

Luckily, when he returned to colder climates, I was able to reopen dialogue and convince him that life on the beach would get boring. I'm not sure he believed that, but I am delighted that it worked out so well for all of us. Recently I was cleaning out some files and came across a confidential Interview Memorandum from that time.

Boston Broadcasters, Inc.
8 Whittier Place
Boston, Massachusetts, 02114

CONFIDENTIAL

Interview Memorandum
From: **William J. Poorvu**
Person: **Robert Bennett**
Date: **October 6, 1970**

Present: **Leo Beranek, William J. Poorvu**

To put it mildly, I was impressed.
Robert Bennett is presently General Manager of WNEW-TV in New York City. Prior to that, he was General Manager of Metromedia Washington Station and General Sales Manager of their Los Angeles station.
Since all of these stations are non-network affiliated, he has had considerable experience in local programming. He is full of ideas, most of which he has implemented, appears hardworking and practical, and has a good understating of the problems and practice of administration.

This was the first interview I've attended where the interviewee not only understood our aims, but had many ideas of how to implement them. His experience is fairly well summarized in the attached resume, but it might be useful to expand a little on it.

In Los Angeles, he asked for the station to be expanded to 24-hours. They agreed, provided he could sell it, which he did to one advertiser. (He got the station to turn over a whole day prior to election free to political candidates.) In Washington, he took over a "roller derby" and "wrestling" station, and, through a more aggressive news operation, turned the station around to a competitive position both in audience and profits. He instituted a daily two-and-a-half hour live show similar to our Family Journal *(medical, legal segments, guests, etc.). He changed the late news to 10 p.m. which, for an independent station, gave them considerable advantage. He started a remote program* Sound Off, *which was intended to give listeners a chance to express themselves. (Sound familiar?)*

In New York City, he made the same switch to 10 p.m. news. He also instituted a weekly minority news program run completely by African Americans, who for the rest of the week are part of the regular news or program departments. He started a program called Solutions, *where people would write to the station about a practical problem, such as "potholes in the streets," "no locks on the apartment" or a "nonworking street light." Most of the complaints would be referred to the appropriate city agency, while five a day would be investigated by a live crew who would document the people and show the solutions, which the city agency would effect. Somehow, there were not many cases where the city was unwilling to cure their problem. He started a practice of taping twelve noncommercial spots a week for agencies with a specific and immediate problem. These spots are then run daily, six times in prime time.*

Bennett, in this past year, went through a long strike with technicians over work rules, which he claims was won by Metromedia. He says he has not gotten an "anti-labor" reputation, but this should be checked. In any case, he says that as a result, he became very familiar with virtually every phase of operation (he ran a camera for the 10 p.m. news) and knows

*what is important to consider in signing a new contract. He did
not want to have to take over existing contracts from WHDH.
His background is sales, and he understands the commercial
side. However, he is also accustomed to make the "direct" pitch
to sell the local special.*

*Personally, he appears interested in politics and sports. His
approach to management seems personal rather than autocratic.
He does not like to the commute from Westport, CT, to New
York City, but feels that as his base salary is now $100,000/year,
there are few places he can go outside of New York City. Our
situation, especially the stock, intrigued him, and he wanted to
hear more.*

*I suggested that Dick Burdick call him, for the two of them to
get together. He was concerned about the interrelationship, both
from an operating standpoint, and from that of status within the
industry. I would recommend following this up very carefully.*

*We should obviously investigate his reputation in the industry
discreetly to find out: 1, if his claims as to what he has done
to stations are valid and 2, whether he was the moving force
personally behind the changes.*

**Donald E. Ward, Esq.,_Partner (1971), Law Firm of Fly,
Shuebruk, Blume & Gaguine, writes:**

*"At the time of the interviews for candidates for General
Manager of WCVB-TV, I had dinner with one of the other GM
candidates who was interviewing for the job. When I asked him
what his impression of the BBI group was, he responded that
he really didn't want to be their first GM, but their second—
obviously confident that the first GM would not last that long
with the collection of super-achievers who were associated
with BBI. Of course, Bob proved him wrong, but at that time, I
thought he certainly had a very good point.*

*As the station was going on the air in 1972, Leo Beranek had
mentioned me to his Bolt--Beranek and Newman computer folks,
who were then considering commercializing what was known
as the ARPANET packet-switching data-communications
technology that they had pioneered. BBN formed a subsidiary
called Telenet Communications Corporation and that became
my principal project and client for eighteen years. Telenet was*

the foundation for what is now the Internet.

I left the law firm in September of 1975, and set out on my own and had little contact with BBI thereafter, but I did follow the tremendous achievements that Bob and WCVB-TV made in the years to come."

The Legal Battle for WHDH-TV

AT THE TIME that I accepted the job, the legal battle for WHDH, which had been going on since 1957, was now reaching new heights of animosity and rage. I had hoped that this battle would now be winding down and that BBI would soon be claiming victory, but unfortunately I could not have been more off the mark. My problem was that I did not know just how bitter the battle actually was and when it might end. I soon found out that the Herald Traveler Corporation was going to fight this right to the end. And I also realized that BBI was in for the long-term as well. This was going to amount to one hell of a dogfight, and it didn't look like it was going to stop any time soon.

I returned to New York and had a meeting with Krivin who wanted me to leave Metromedia immediately. From the moment BBI called, I made continuous reports back to him about my BBI meetings, because I did not want him to think I was doing anything behind his back. I wanted to make sure he knew who I was talking to and what was going on. He was very positive, and I knew why: he wanted me out of Metromedia. The trade press was giving me credit for everything that Metromedia was doing. Al always seemed to be standing in the background and receiving no credit at all. He did not like that. Plus, John Kluge had already told him that he wanted me to take Al's place. Toward the end of my meeting he was his usual nasty self.

"Bob, if you don't want that Boston job, tell them to call me. I'll take it," he said to me. He really wanted me out of Metromedia and as far away as possible. In his mind, Boston was as good a place as any for me to be.

"I want you to go, Bob, and the old man wants you out of here."

I knew he was lying, and I was getting more steamed up. I came back at him.

"I know what you've been doing, Al. You've been trying to get rid of me for the last two years. Nobody has contributed more to this company than me. You see that window there, Al? If you don't get out of here, I'm going to throw you out of it."

"Are you serious, Bob? You wouldn't do something like that. You're crazy," he said to me with fear in his voice.

"Get the hell out of here, Al! I mean it. Get the hell out of here!"

He ran out of the room faster than I've ever seen anyone run.

John and I Say Goodbye

LATER I HAD a final meeting with John Kluge. I knew that he did not want me to leave Metromedia. We sat down in his office, and he was very encouraging about my job offer.

"If they get that station in Boston, and they do all of the things they say they're going to do, that station will be worth a lot of money. I think you're the right guy for the job, Bob. They couldn't have picked anyone better."

He then wanted to know what Krivin had given me as severance pay for my nineteen and half years at Metromedia.

"John, all Al gave me was my accrued vacation pay. That's it. That's all he gave me."

John frowned.

"Bob, I'm going to give you a whole year's salary, and I wish you the best of luck. But I want you to remember something: if that station ever comes up for sale; you let me know because I want to be the first one standing in line to buy it." Later on, those very words were to come back to me. John gave me my one-year's salary, which came in handy since I had to come up with money to protect my stock position in BBI.

I later learned that Al was telling people how stupid I was to leave New York and Metromedia and to go to work for a group that didn't even have a license to run a television station. Al worked until he was 90 years old for Merv Griffin as a consultant. I never saw him again.

As I look back now at WNEW-TV, I realize that it was the most competitive job I had ever had. All of those stations in the New York market were tough competitors, and everything they did made my team have to fight harder. New York was not Washington. In some ways I liked Washington better because it was a smaller market, and I had the chance to really experiment with local programming. WNEW had been embedded for years in their certain way of doing things, and change did not come easy. Plus, New Yorkers have always believed that they are the best at whatever it is they do, and that New York is the best place in the world to live. I am not going to argue with them.

It was time now for me to leave New York. I packed my bags and as usual, went on ahead without the family.

"Here we go again," Marjie said to me, "Only this time, Bob, you're going to go to work for a television station that does not even exist yet. Are you sure you're doing the right thing?"

I kept nodding my head saying yes, but I really had no idea how bad and how shaky the situation was up there. What exactly I was walking into I really didn't know. Up until then, this case had been the longest running regulatory case in U.S. history and it had been a complex series of court decisions, challenges, appeals, and behind-the-scene dealings.

When I agreed to take the job, WHDH-TV's permit renewal was not extended, and was now in the hands of BBI, so there was some comfort in that; however the final outcome of the case was uncertain since it was still under Judicial Review. WHDH, the denied renewal applicant, still had the right to run the station, and they filed a petition to the FCC for reconsideration of their decision. The fireworks were still going on louder than ever, and there I was now sitting in Boston.

WHDH-TV was coming up with whatever they could to discredit BBI, and apparently they had been doing a very good job at it. Even though I had committed myself to the job, and felt good about my decision, there were still so many things that everyone was unsure about. I remember my own thoughts were very muddled. I knew I had a job to do so I stayed focused, but I was very aware that I was betting my bank account on my homerun.

I knew that Boston was in my future—yet one thing was for sure, and it was not a very comforting thought—BBI did not have clear access to that channel—not yet anyway. The Herald Traveler Corporation was still running WHDH-TV.

Under Judicial Review

How Do You Lose A Television License?

IN HIS 1974 book, *The Hundred Million Dollar Lunch*, Sterling Quinlin could not have summed up the story in a better way.

> *"How do you lose a VHF television license in the nation's fifth largest television market, Boston? How do you eliminate one of that city's four major newspapers, the Boston* Herald Traveler? *How do you blow one hundred million dollars? Two thousand jobs? Sixty million dollars in stockholder profits? It ain't easy. That much can be said for certain. It takes a lot of luck, most of it bad. It takes seventeen years of legal wrangling and over two million dollars in legal expenses. It takes a pixilated course by one of the six major regulatory bodies of the federal government, the Federal Communications Commission. It also takes the cooperation of the U.S. Court of Appeals and the Supreme Court of the United States. Not to mention the friendly assistance of the Department of Justice and the Federal Bureau of Investigation. All this can be done, and has been done in the famous Boston case involving the loss of WHDH-TV and the* Herald Traveler—*and the new kid on the block—WCVB-TV. Channel 5."*

At this point in time, BBI had been granted the permit by the FCC—but not the license to operate it. The entire case was still under judicial review, which meant that the license to operate the station was still theoretically up for grabs. The battle between WHDH and BBI took on a life of its own. It was bitter with no prisoners being taken.

WHDH, under the direction of Harold Clancy, President of the *Herald Traveler*, accelerated their gritty tactics of mud slinging and legal tactical maneuvers against BBI. BBI fired back with everything it could muster.

I was beginning to understand that it was quite possible that should matters not go well for BBI—WHDH-TV might very well be successful in having the permit remanded back to them, and that would have left us with nothing. It was starting to sink in just how much I was gambling here and what I had at stake. And I knew one thing for sure: BBI was feeling the pain.

As I look back on that decision now, I must have been a real gambler. If I had really understood all of the pieces and all of the uncertainty that made up this ongoing legal wrangle, I might not have left Metromedia at all. There was a real strong chance that all this could have been for nothing. I had given nineteen-and-a-half years of my life to Metromedia and they were all good years and I had created a solid reputation for myself. I was well-known in the industry and the kind of local programming I was doing was being watched by viewers and studied by my colleagues and my competitors. I was very proud of my accomplishments.

Now in Boston hard at work at building the station, the legal battle intensified, and my uncertainty soon turned to sour pessimism, and my hope about hitting my home run quickly turned to skepticism. I kept saying to myself, well, if it fails, I can always go out and look for a job. And of course, if it did fail, I was going to have to face my family—something I would not have been happy about doing. But I was not ready for failure so I kept looking on the bright side of things.

The Battle Between
Two Strong Opponents

IT IS IMPORTANT here to take a look at the history of the long, drawn-out battle between WHDH-TV and Boston Broadcasters, and the tangled FCC case for the ownership of a television station, in what was then the nation's fifth largest market, Boston.

It all began in 1949, when television was still in its infancy. The Herald Traveler Corporation filed an application with the FCC for a permit to operate a channel in Boston. That permit was granted for an eighteen-month period, allowing WHDH the time to build the station and to apply for a license, which it did in November of 1957. In October of 1962, that license was granted for just a four-month period.

WHDH was originally an ABC affiliate and changed to CBS in 1961. The Herald Traveler Corporation also owned the only Republican newspaper in Boston and WHDH Radio, both FM and AM. Later in 1957, the Commission overruled the FCC decision and awarded the permit for what would become WHDH-TV to the Herald Traveler Corporation.

In 1958, the House Subcommittee on Legislative Oversight was looking into allegations that the FCC's television hearings were being corrupted by ex parte (meaning out of the presence of other parties) contacts with Commissioners by applicants or their representatives. Two Miami cases, and cases in Orlando and Jacksonville, all had such problems, particularly involving Commissioner Richard Mack, a Republican Eisenhower appointee who had been a member of the Florida Public Service Commission. During these Congressional hearings, it was revealed that several such contacts had taken place involving Channel 5 in Boston. The Subcommittee's Report was brought to the attention of the Court of Appeals during the pendency of the appeals from the 1957 FCC Boston Channel 5 Decision, causing the Court to remand the case to the FCC to consider whether its 1957 Decision should be reconsidered and revised.

One of the major issues up before the FCC was the issue of Robert Choate, who was then President of The Herald Traveler Corporation, having lunch with FCC Chairman, George McConnaughey, not only once, but twice, the second time of which he brought along his attorney. An issue in the hearing before the Commission was the comparative weight to be accorded to the combination of the newspaper and the television station. Choate and his lawyer presented McConnaughey with a draft amendment to Congressional legislation which would remove newspaper ownership as a comparative factor. As this dealt with a significant aspect of the case then pending before the Commission, this was considered an improper ex parte discussion. Because of the serious nature of the allegation, all of the ruling bodies had to take notice. A one-on-one lunch with the Chairman of the FCC, while the case was pending, certainly qualified as a serious ex parte situation and this would haunt the case for many years to come. Because of these contacts, The U.S. Court of Appeals remanded the entire proceedings back to the FCC to look into the matter.

The Reopening of the Case

ON DECEMBER 4, 1958, the WHDH-TV case was reopened by the FCC and the remaining bidders at the time were allowed to bid for the permit. Those remaining bidders were WHDH-TV, Greater Boston, and Massachusetts Bay Telecasters. After all of the evidence was presented, Examiner Stern delivered his final decision and left the license in the hands of WHDH.

This strange legal case might have drifted off into the annals of history had it not been for Attorney General William P. Rogers, who noted the ex parte situation of Robert Choate having had lunch on two separate occasions with FCC Chairman George McConnaughey. Ex parte meant that all parties in a court case must be present at the same time and that no one person or group can meet alone with someone like the FCC Chairman. Rogers filed a legal brief and in his brief he stated the following: "The facts of the record show that Robert Choate, president of the Herald Traveler Corporation went beyond the recognized and public process of adjudication on behalf of his application." This was, needless to say, very bad for Robert Choate and very bad for The Herald Traveler Corp.

In 1961, President Kennedy appointed Newton Minow as Chairman of the FCC. The case was going to be taken up again by the full Commission, on exceptions directed to the Stern decision, and all parties now had to file new briefs and appear again.

Oral Argument before the Commission

THE ORAL ARGUMENT before the Commission happened in July of 1962, and the Commission, by a vote of 4 to 1, (with two abstaining) voted to grant only an additional four-month license to WHDH-TV, which under the Commission's Act provided that the license be conferred only for the right to continue to operate the facility until the application to renew the license was fully denied. This four-month license was to demonstrate the FCC's disapproval of the ex parte contacts, and to facilitate an early introduction of new competing applicants. WHDH-TV was not happy about this, which now meant that their permit was set to expire on January 26, 1963, and they had to file for its renewal in just two months.

On November 25, 1962, WHDH filed for renewal, which now meant that the Case would continue, and for the first time, new applicants were invited to file for applications. Responding to this invitation were Charles River Civic Television and Greater Boston II and a new company called Boston Broadcasters, Inc. (BBI).

The Infamous Hearing

THIS NEW HEARING was set to be heard in front of Herbert Sharfman in October of 1963, and was delayed until June of 1964. Sharfman was known for his eloquent writings and sometimes confusing decisions.

On June 27, 1964, in the Post Office Building in Washington, D.C., the hearing began with the following docket lineup: WHDH-TV, Greater Boston II, Charles River, and Boston Broadcasters, Inc. Attorneys from all sides presented their cases which ensued in strong confrontations. The hearing ended thirteen months later on July 16, 1965. Sharfman then disappeared with all of the briefs and testimony and emerged on August 10, 1966 with the following decision: He granted the license renewal to WHDH-TV for the regular period of three years.

The attorney for Boston Broadcasters was Benito (Benny) Gaguine of the Washington law firm of Fly, Shuebruk, Blume, and Gaguine. Benny's firm was adroit at FCC matters and felt that the next step would be to go to Oral Argument. Benny's assistant was Don Ward, who was highly intelligent and possessed strong writing skills and a deep understanding of FCC issues. Benny would be the one making the oral argument.

However, some in the BBI camp by this time felt they had had enough. They were tired of the bitter battle, the drain on funds, and were very unsure of any success they might have should they continue to press on. However, when it was put up to a vote, it was decided by the majority to continue on and appeal Sharfman's decision to the full Commission. BBI filed for Oral Argument and the other parties did the same, which was done in addition to all of the previous briefs and petitions that had been filed by the applicants.

Time Now for Oral Arguments Before the Court of Appeals

ON SEPTEMBER 5, 1967, an oral argument was scheduled to be heard. Once again, attorneys for all sides battled it out before a blue light that allotted each of them a certain amount of time to make their case. When all parties were done and all cases presented, the Commission departed and took fifteen months and sixteen days to make their decision. On January 22, 1969, they handed down the decision in the following way: The FCC voted three to one (not even a majority of all seven commissioners) to deny renewal of WHDH's license and award it to BBI. Commissioner Hyde abstained, Cox recused himself, and Rex Lee did not participate because he had been appointed after the case had been argued. Given this final count, BBI did have a majority of the participating commissioners.

WHDH was stunned, but they did have several options they could consider, including:

1. *Seek to reopen the record to present newly discovered evidence with a remand to the Hearing Examiner.*
2. *Petition the Commission to reconsider its decision.*
3. *Appeal directly to the U.S. Court of Appeals.*

Benny asked the Commission for an August 1 deadline to go on the air. With the license awarded now to BBI, they were in a victorious mood so much so that they made an offer in 1969 to Harold Clancy, President of the The Herald Traveler Corporation, to buy all of the non-people assets of WHDH-TV, an offer which received a chilling answer of silence.

Harold Clancy went on the warpath. He was now ready to really dig his heels in, and he used any and all means available to him and to The Herald Traveler Corporation. You must remember, they owned a newspaper, and a newspaper can be a very strong voice to use in a time of argument.

In May of 1969, the FCC turned down WHDH's petition for reconsideration along with those of the others. It was a fast decision from the Commission coming just three months after the petitions were filed. Attorneys for all but BBI began preparing appeals and their objections, which when filed, would lead to another argument, only this time before a panel of three of the court's twelve judges. This case was not going away.

On October 31, 1969, Dean Burch was sworn in as the fifteenth chairman of the FCC. WHDH was now arguing that the decision had been arbitrary, capricious, and contrary to precedent. Benny Gaguine and Don Ward were busy defending BBI's position.

Henry Geller, General Council for the FCC, was chosen to argue the case. On May 26, he went before the Court of Appeals and argued as to why the Commission had taken away the WHDH license. He made a compelling case and hit on all of the key points. Five months later, on November 13th, the Court of Appeals handed down its decision and upheld the FCC order. Henry Geller had swayed the court. This gave WHDH sixty days to go to the Supreme Court to file a Petition for Certiorari, asking the Supreme Court to review the Court of Appeals decision.

Clancy's Blockbuster
Petition Against BBI

IN APRIL OF 1969, Clancy fired off a cannon shot that BBI heard resonating through out all of Boston. From out of nowhere it seemed, WHDH filed a blockbuster petition against BBI, charging among other things that Nate David, a BBI official and stockholder, covered up interest he owned and had not reported in other broadcasting operations. Later in 1971, Nate was sued for misrepresentation, fraud, and violation of Federal security laws, in connection with the sale of six thousand shares of unregistered stock in a company called Synergistics, Inc. One of the charges was that he sold the stock to friends and made a commission on the sale. Not being a registered NASD stockbroker, he was not entitled to receive a commission of any kind from the sale of stock of a registered public company. Ironically, since Nate was a lawyer, he could have just charged a legal fee for the transfer of the stock and avoided the issue of illegal commissions. Nathan was deeply shocked and he really took it hard.

In December of 1970, Harold Clancy did an interview with a reporter for a media magazine telling his side of the story. Spring came and there was still no word on the petition against BBI.

My Arrival in Boston

WHEN I ARRIVED in Boston in June of 1971 to take up the duties of my new job, I was thrown right into the middle of this war zone. Everything issue-wise relating to the case was in a total state of chaos. I felt like bombs were dropping all over the place and where ever you walked, you had to be careful you weren't stepping on a minefield. The pressure on everyone connected with this battle was so heavy that no one knew whether to laugh or to cry. It was not long before I was in the same state—somewhere between laughing and crying; I was not sure which. But there was something magical in the air; We were building a television station from the ground up out of an old Caterpillar tractor warehouse we had optioned in Needham, Massachusetts, which was to be our headquarters. Cement was being poured, equipment was arriving, people were being hired, programming schedules were being designed and rate cards were being put together. I went right to work and held nothing back. Maybe we might pull this dream off after all, I thought. And I was also feeling really good that I actually owned an equity piece of what we were building. At any rate, I had accepted the job and there was no turning back. I had to keep going forward and keep my thoughts more positive than negative.

Meanwhile, the battle in the courts continued. On November 10, 1971, Nate David was indicted and BBI filed petitions for expedition. The SEC filed a number of civil charges against him. Benny sent a letter to the FCC informing them that I was now going to be the new General Manager of the station and not Richard Burdick, who originally had the General Manager title.

WHDH Petition Denied

WITH WHDH'S PETITION NOW denied, Clancy went on the attack more viciously than ever. With a victory somewhat assured by BBI, (well, sort of), all other avenues now seemed to be closed to WHDH. The Commission was the only one that could actually set a termination date for WHDH-TV.

In the meantime, at BBI, we moved forward with the following:

- *BBI leased antenna space on the WBZ tower and purchased a new transmitter*
- *Continued building out the studio in Needham, MA and hiring people*
- *Set in motion our starting date of September 26, 1971 which was feasible if the Commission approved*
- *Ordered all necessary equipment for the studio*
- *We could now negotiate for being an affiliate of CBS. (We didn't know it at the time, but CBS had other plans.)*

Even though we were on shaky ground, we were still spending a lot of money on legal fees, salaries, equipment, and for the most part, it was borrowed money. The Herald Traveler Corporation seemed to have a war chest and of course in owning a newspaper, they had the power of the press on their side. In fact, they *were* the press and they could print just about anything they wanted to about us—and they did—and you can bet that it was always something very nasty and negative about BBI. Every time we read the paper, they were hammering away at us. They even went so far as to state that we were going to be bringing in all these crazy people from Hollywood who would ruin the station. This was a tough group to fight because they had been a part of the Boston landscape for 127 years.

We're Building but There's No Start Date

AS OUR BUILDING progressed and we moved closer to our hoped-for starting date, I hired several good friends and colleagues to come and work with me. These great people gave up their jobs, arrived in Boston, and then found themselves living in an atmosphere of uncertainty. All of them had to put up money to buy their shares of BBI stock. If there was a call for a million dollars, and you owned five percent of that, you had to come up with $50,000. Some people had to bet the bank, or refinance their homes, all on a television permit we seemed to only have a tentative hold on. That was a lot to ask of someone. But I must say the people I chose to join me rallied around and we dug in and started building that station from the ground up. In the meantime, The Herald Traveler Corporation kept up with its gunfire and we aimed back at a more frantic pace.

The Supreme Court refused to review the case and now it was up to the Commission to act. They were the only ones who could set a termination date for WHDH.

WHDH stated that it must be given proper time to wind down its affairs. WHDH was not going off the air just yet—not by any means. They were playing the odds and using whatever delay tactics they could employ. No termination date by the FCC had yet been stipulated which meant that WHDH could continue broadcasting indefinitely. Benny wrote asking the Commission for a termination date and received no answer. In essence, the FCC was saying that WHDH could continue broadcasting until further notice.

Finally Our Call Letters and Our Construction Permit

On July 24, the FCC ruled the following: "WCVB can go on the air any time soon." We had been awarded our call letters, WCVB-TV, and the FCC issued our construction permit. We were, in theory, not moving forward at our own risk anymore. Meanwhile, our cash drain continued.

Broadcast executives from around the country thought the FCC was intent on breaking up their industry. Now local groups who had the funds and determination to oppose renewals of television stations were putting multiple owners on notice that their renewals were vulnerable to challenges. This would have made the total value of all of the stations in question somewhere north of $3 billion and a lot of broadcast executives were keeping a very close eye on what was going on in Boston. Not to mention the fact that I'm sure they were all really shaking in their boots.

BBI requested a September 1971 date to the FCC to go on the air. The court was on summer vacation in July and August and thus we were in an agonizing wait and see position. Benny said to keep building the station so we kept building.

The Supreme Court then denied WHDH's Petition for Creterori (which means a discretionary appeal by the court) in June, and WHDH had petitioned it to reconsider that action in July. BBI had written to the FCC in July, reporting on our state of construction and requesting that it specify a date in September for WHDH-TV to cease operations and for WCVB-TV to commence.

WHDH had petitioned the FCC to reopen the case on spurious grounds, supplementing that petition as to Nate's earlier indictment by the state of Massachusetts for violating security laws and again for the SEC matter. WHDH also petitioned the Court of Appeals to seek permission from the Supreme Court to recall its mandate, so it could remand the case to the FCC. Then, the FCC filed a request with the Court of Appeals asking it to recall its mandate and to remand to the FCC.

At this point in time, Harold Clancy vowed that the day would never come when they would lose WHDH-TV. This was a war that was going to be fought in the gutters of Boston and he was going to personally fight it to the finish. He thought BBI had placed a spy in his organization.

Meanwhile, we were convinced that our phones were tapped. To prove it, we fed phony stories into the phone lines and sure enough, they would pop up in the newspaper and various other places. Clancy assigned a squad of reporters to dig up information on all of us. Our attorneys were telling us not to step out of line under any circumstances.

"Do not talk to anyone. Do not put yourself in a situation that could jeopardize our ability to get that license. Everyone keep your mouths shut, please!" Benny Gaguine would say to us.

Bob, Can You Come
Over to My Hotel Room?

ONE DAY MY secretary received a telephone call from someone who said she was a friend of mine from California who would not give her name. I picked up the phone and said hello.

"Hello Bob," said the sultry female voice on the other end of the line.

"Who is this?" I asked.

"I'm an old friend of yours and I just happen to be in Boston right now in a great hotel room overlooking the Charles River. Can you come over and join me so we can get to know one another all over again and have some fun?"

"What is your name?"

"Well, I want to surprise you when you come over here."

"Why don't you give me your number and I'll call you back."

I took her telephone number and quickly called Benny.

"Benny, I just received a telephone call from a woman who would not identify herself and she's inviting me to join her in a hotel room here in Boston."

"Stay put Bob. You're not going anywhere," he told me.

"No kidding. I'm not going anywhere. I'm sure she's got a photographer hidden in the closet and they're just waiting for me to get over there."

I soon learned that Clancy went so far as to send two guys to California for a month to go to every advertising agency that I had ever been to when I worked in sales at KTTV. He was looking for any dirt on me that he could find. I am happy to say that he never found anything bad about me. Certainly a tough test to pass but I was very happy to pass it. Anything that Clancy could find out about us to prove that we were not qualified to have this license, he was looking for.

The Nate David problem was something that the Commission could not ignore and it became a festering sore for BBI during the proceedings. It seemed certain that the Commission would ask the Court of Appeals for a remand of the case so the Commission could consider what action to take. The rumor was that they were going to freeze BBI's license because of the Nate David problem. There was another rumor going around Washington that not only was the Commission going to ask for remand, they were going to take action looking toward the revocation of BBI's construction permit. When Clancy heard this, he was beaming. Sure enough, in August of 1971, *Television Digest* published an article stating that the FCC was about to freeze BBI's permit, pending resolution of the SEC charges against Nate David, which had been filed at the end of July.

Every day that went by was costing BBI a small fortune in salaries and bank loans. BBI quickly took the position that Nate David was innocent until proven guilty. Benny wrote a letter to the Commission, which probably saved BBI. The letter stated that if BBI was to forfeit all of the investments and time and people that it had put into motion on the basis of pure allegations, this would constitute a denial of due process. He told the Commission that BBI was prepared for its September airdate and that Nate David would take a leave of absence until everything was resolved. The letter was written and delivered and then we heard rumors that the Nixon White House was now directly interested in the outcome of the case. This was easily understood since the *Herald Traveler* was the only Republican newspaper in a heavy Democratic town like Boston.

Over at BBI we were starting to feel the ownership of that coveted television permit slowly slipping away from us. Here we were building a television station from the ground up in a matter of weeks with no real strong ownership of that permit. We could not apply for the license until construction of the station was completed, which was scheduled for some time in September.

Bad News for Us from CBS

THEN MORE BAD news came. CBS pulled out from any affiliation with us, citing their fear that since we had promised the FCC we were going to be producing so much local television, we would certainly end up preempting a lot of their programming. They weren't wrong in thinking that.

Shortly after BBI filed its letter in mid-August, the FCC, rather than freeze our permit as rumored in the *Television Digest* article, requested that the Court of Appeals withdraw its mandate and remand the case in order that the Commission might consider the effect of Nate David's legal problems on BBI's qualifications to hold a license. BBI opposed, citing the finality of the case, noting that Nate had stepped aside and would not participate in BBI's activities until resolution of his litigation. BBI also pointed to the substantial investments and the personnel commitments it had made in reliance upon that permit.

All of this back and forth was working to the advantage of WHDH. The more time that dragged on, the better it was for them. After all, they were still operating the station. They were suddenly feeling so upbeat that they painted their tower a bright new color at a cost of $85,000 and made new sales and marketing presentations. Morale at WHDH was now at an all time high and they were making plans for their fall schedule. This was a really amazing turn of events. They had a blowup on a big screen projector in their ad sales presentation that read: "With all the changes in Boston TV this fall, isn't it nice to have someone you can depend on?" They really thought they had us. Meanwhile, they were running the station, generating revenue, and we were spending our money faster than ever to just stay alive.

We received permission for an equipment test. BBI now had forty-five people on board and we were in advanced stages of construction. Our studio had already been built and our corporate offices were taking shape. Ironically, a positive story about BBI appeared in *Broadcasting Magazine* about the progress we were making.

Sweating Bullets at BBI

AT BBI WE were still sweating bullets. Every day was a race to the end with so much uncertainty going on that I don't even think I slept most nights. Of all of the highs and lows I had experienced since my arrival in Boston, this was the lowest. We were still proceeding at our own risk as far as I was concerned.

Our cash situation was growing desperate. We had a burn rate of almost $300,000 per month, which meant that our four million dollar loan from the bank would soon be gone. Clancy's spy reporters were working harder than ever. Benny and Don continued their barrage of petitions. Benny kept saying to us, "More delays are going to put us out of business."

The Supreme Court Comes to Our Rescue

ON OCTOBER 12, 1971, the Supreme Court denied WHDH's Reconsideration of its June denial of WHDH's Petition for Certiorari. Clancy went around saying, "Such a travesty could not, and would not, be allowed to prevail. The Boston community is behind us and we will continue to fight."

Ironically, there was a collision of WHDH and WCVB test patterns around 2 a.m. one morning. At this point, I'm sure the viewers in Boston had had enough of this ongoing legal case. I know that over at BBI, we sure had had enough.

Finally, the Finality of the FCC's Order

THEN ON DECEMBER 29, 1971, the Court of Appeals refused to remand the case to the FCC. This pointed to the finality of the FCC's order. It also found that the charges against Nate David were not relevant and not directly related to BBI. Both sides made the usual kind of statements and then Benny asked, "Okay, so when do we start broadcasting?" It was now BBI's turn to taste a little victory, at least for the moment anyway. Even if WHDH did an automatic reply, the Supreme Court rarely granted hearings on cases that have previously been turned down. Nate David obtained a postponement of the hearing of his civil case by the SEC.

Many predicted the demise of the *Herald Traveler* newspaper if they lost WHDH-TV. In January of 1972, Harold Clancy admitted that the newspaper could not survive without the profits of WHDH-TV.

Permission Granted to Sign On As WCVB-TV, Channel 5

IN EARLY MARCH of 1972, the Commission voted four to one to put WHDH off the air on March 19th at three a.m. The FCC had finally granted permission for WCVB-TV to sign on as Channel 5 in Boston.

Clancy went out of his mind with rage. The only avenues left for WHDH were to file more petitions, make more charges against BBI people, and to try and maneuver for more delay, if they could find some way to do it. Not surprisingly, WHDH filed new charges against BBI alleging that Edward C. Bursk, who was a BBI stockholder, was involved in questionable deals. It fell on deaf ears with the commissioners. Then the Greater Boston Labor Council filed a petition in favor of WHDH, stating that 2,500 members would now be out of work.

One Last Gasp of Air from Clancy

JUST SIXTEEN DAYS before WCVB was to go on the air, Clancy's legal team filed for their last gasp of air at the Supreme Court: they asked the high tribunal to stop all legal proceedings until the Commission looked into the case once more, and to stay the March 19th switchover date. Their reasoning was the loss of 2,500 jobs at the *Herald Traveler*.

WHDH then hired former Supreme Court Justice Abe Fortas as a consultant who had contacts at the Supreme Court. WHDH had only six days left to live. The Supreme Court was the only ruling body that could now keep them alive. Abe's job was to try and keep the case alive in front of the Supreme Court. He needed to get postponements and he seemed to have the right people connections to possibly get them.

BBI retained Bennett Bosky who had helped with the earlier filings in the Supreme Court. It was agreed that the best BBI course of action was to simply request that the matter be considered by the entire court rather than a single Justice, as was the usual practice for stays prescribed, and to our surprise it worked. Word came back to us that the entire court would consider the petition at some time during that same week at one of its informal daily conferences. There was a very strong tension in the air at that moment. We all felt that victory for BBI was very near. However, the BBI engine needed more fuel in the form of cash from all of us and once again we had to reach into our pockets. Understandably, there was a lot of grumbling. Nobody really wanted to put any more cash in. All we wanted was that elusive FCC license so we could really go to work.

And Now the Waiting Game

THE GOOD NEWS was that the Supreme Court would now be acting. WHDH filed its petition just five days before the switchover date. Benny told the BBI people that in his opinion, the Supreme Court would certainly not wait until the last day to make its decision. We hoped he was right. And so we waited.

Monday passed. No word.

Tuesday passed. No word.

Wednesday passed. No word.

And Thursday passed. Still, no word.

All we did during this very agonizing time was sit around and play cards and shoot the breeze, or climb the walls, or punch the walls. We were all worn out and tired.

"Heard anything?" the same questions echoed in the hallways.

"No, not yet?"

"Let's not think about it for awhile," I used to say to everyone.

"Right, let's just try and relax," people would say under their breath.

Our severe cash bind had now forced us up against the wall. If the vote went against us, bankruptcy was inevitable for the company and for a lot of us individually. We were still roaming the hallways trying to keep our spirits up. And still, no word was forthcoming.

"What happens if we don't hear anything today?" I asked Benny. "This really doesn't look like it's going in our favor, does it?"

Benny had no answers and by evening he was biting his fingernails. The phone suddenly rang and everyone jumped. Don Ward, who was our emissary monitoring the proceedings in Washington, had been calling the court clerk every hour on the hour and all he continued to tell us was, "No word, yet. No word, yet." An hour later, Don called again and told us the clerk wanted Leo Beranek's home phone number, but nobody knew why. Don placed another call to us and said the court clerk told him not to call him anymore.

All we had in front of us were unanswered questions. Had the court adjourned? Why did the clerk want Leo's home phone number? Why did the court clerk tell Don not to call anymore? Lots of questions, but no answers. Now it was Friday, and more questions were being asked. Was the court going to wait until Monday? If so, why? What is it they have to think about over the weekend? What about that great victory party we have planned?

At 5:30, the telephone rang and Leo yanked it off the hook on the first ring. Don Ward told him that the court had adjourned for the day. Adjourned? How could they do that to us? What does it mean? Benny gave us his legal interpretation, "All it really means guys is that we can all go home now. Apparently they're going to consider the case over the weekend." Leo sank back in his chair. We all walked out of his office with our faces dragging on the floor. There were so many unanswered questions. What if we signed on as WCVB-TV on Sunday and then on Monday we had to get off the air? I wanted to put my fist through the nearest wall.

Then mysteriously, as we were still shuffling out of Leo's office the phone rang again. Leo picked it up. It was Don Ward again.

"WE'RE ON THE AIR!" Don shouted.

Leo cried out as loud as he could, "WE'RE ON THE AIR! WE'RE ON THE AIR!" I felt like a truck just hit me and I had to grab hold of something so I wouldn't fall over. There was complete shock and disbelief in the eyes of all of us. Not one of us moved. It felt like a hundred pounds of tension came off my shoulders. I went home and slept for hours.

At 11 p.m. that Saturday night, Harold Clancy appeared on WHDH-TV's news and he thanked the viewers of Boston for their support. He expressed his hope that during the changeover, no viewer would experience any inconvenience. WHDH-TV then put on its final movie, which had the very appropriate title of *Fixed Bayonets*.

Leo Beranek had already mailed our celebration invitations for a victory party at the Marriott Hotel in Newton. The invitations read, "It's Time to Celebrate. BBI has finally realized its impossible dream." We had finally won. Armed police guards were placed around our studio in Needham, in anticipation of a possible bomb being planted by someone who didn't take kindly to the final ruling. And now, after two weeks of taping in preparation for our launch and all of the stress we had been under, we were ready to celebrate.

The BBI victory celebration started at 1 a.m. at the Marriott hotel in Newton. Hundreds of people showed up. We never knew we had so many friends and colleagues. The party went on until about four in the morning. There was a lot of yelling, screaming, and hugging. All of the BBI team was there except Nate David. I felt sorry for Nate and I was hoping that he would someday soon be able to put all his troubles behind him. The fight had taken a great deal out of us, but in victory, we were energized.

On Sunday, March 19, 1972 at 3:05 a.m., WCVB-TV signed on with two words: "Hello world," followed by a brief introduction by Matthew Brown and Leo Beranek and then a thirty-minute program describing BBI's plans for Channel 5. We then left our call letters on the screen until our first broadcasting day began that morning at 6:58 a.m.

Now, of course, we had to make good on our WCVB promises.

We're On the Air

March of 1972

IN MARCH OF 1972, Richard Nixon was celebrating his historic trip to China, *The Godfather* was the hottest movie, and there was a new television station in Boston called WCVB-TV. Now that we had the station we had to make good on our WCVB-TV promises. For starters, BBI had promised the FCC the following:

- *Twenty four-hour broadcast day, five days a week*
- *BBI would editorialize, where WHDH had a policy against it*
- *BBI would preempt affiliated programming at certain times and replace it with local programming*
- *36.3 percent of our 160.5 hour per week schedule would be local and live!*
- *25% of our ownership would go to key employees, with no one owning more than 7 percent*
- *Profits would be minimized*
- *Fewer commercials than the National Association of Broadcaster's code allowed*
- *High integration of ownership into the station's daily operations*
- *No paid political or religious advertising and political candidates would be given free time*
- *BBI would cooperate with nearby schools and other organizations engaged in research and in training personnel for work in the television industry*

Needless to say, all of the above would prove to be a difficult task for any television group under the best of circumstances. This was certainly a tall mandate and we were now going to have to live up to this difficult list of challenges. I really thought that a lot of the original BBI ideas were going to be almost impossible to attain. But this was the job that I signed up for so I was going to give it my best. I can tell you this, if I had been around when those promises were made to the FCC, I would have advised BBI not to make them. They were too ambitious. I was never once asked by anyone at BBI, "Bob, can we do this?" It was always understood that we could.

BBI's executive management team's starting lineup was the following: Judge Matthew Brown, Chairman of the Board; Dr. Leo Beranek, President and CEO; William Poorvu, cofounder, Vice-Chair and Treasurer; Nate David, Executive Vice-President/ General Manager, Creative Services; and Joshua Guberman, Secretary. Richard Burdick had been our first General Manager and Larry Pickard was our first Director of News.

BBI's original shareholders included Stanton DeLand, attorney and Chairman of Harvard's Board of Overseers; Oscar Handlin, American History scholar; Robert Gardner, film maker and anthropologist; Gerald Holton, Harvard professor of physics; John Knowles, senior executive at Massachusetts General Hospital; William Andres, Chairman of Dartmouth's Board of Trustees; Henry Jaffee, television producer; William Poorvu, real estate developer; Charles Maliotis, business executive; Constantine Pertzoff, architect; Nate David, Esq; Alford Rudnick, Esq; Charles Marran, business executive; Jordan Baruch, electrical engineer; Alfred Morse, business executive; and Edward Bursk, publisher. All of the above were a group of Boston citizens whose fundamental mission was to simply bring better television to Boston viewers.

Leo Beranek was an audio expert who had written many noted books on acoustics. He was the cofounder of the consulting firm of Bolt, Beranek and Newman, which was one of the most respected acoustical computer, information, and science and communication companies in the country. Leo became one of my closets friends at WCVB and someone I came to truly admire and respect.

Judge Matthew Brown had served for a time as special justice in the Boston Municipal Court. He was very distinguished and very likeable.

Bill Poorvu was the treasurer and was probably the most active

BBI shareholder who had an office at WCVB. He was one of the original founders of BBI, and as he likes to remember, he hosted the early BBI meetings in the back of his office in Cambridge, since there was no formal BBI office back then. Bill wrote the first BBI business plan and helped steer the company during those early, chaotic years of its existence when it had no money and was in constant battle with the *Herald Traveler*. Bill has a great business and strategic mind.

In many ways, Bill Poorvu was a very important person to WCVB-TV and to me personally. I always made sure that I consulted with him in the early days about many of the important challenges facing us. His insight and thoughts helped shape many of my own ideas and I still look back fondly on the many things we did together as WCVB-TV was growing.

Leo and Bill hired the firm of Harrington, Righter, and Parsons as our first national sales representatives. I then brought in Tom Maney as Vice President and Director of Sales who left his job as general manager of WTTG in Washington to join me in Boston, and Gerry McGavick joined us as Vice President and National Sales Manager. Shortly, Mike Volpe from Los Angeles joined us as Vice President, Local Sales Manager. All three men believed in what we were doing and were very hard workers. They were also very close friends. We also had two salesmen from WHDH and two salesmen from WBZ as part of the team. In addition to our programming schedule, sales proved to be a very tough uphill battle for us. We were considered the cowboys from Hollywood who had taken down the *Herald Traveler* and put 2,500 people out of work.

Gerry McGavick, National Sales Manager, WCVB, writes:
"When Bob, Mike Volpe, Tom Maney, and I started at WCVB, the Boston press called us "The Carpetbaggers," since none of us were native New Englanders. As a sales team we had our tough challenges set out in front of us, but with the help of Bob as General Manager, WCVB, an ABC affiliate, went from nowhere to becoming the Number One station in Boston in terms of revenue and ratings. I was fortunate to have worked for Bob and my former boss John B. Sias who was president of Metro TV Sales, a former division of Metromedia. To me, Bob and John were the all time best television executives I have ever

met. To this very day, I am very happy to have been part of Bob Bennett's success story."

Michael Volpe, Vice President, Sales Manager WCVB, 1972 to 1982, writes:
"Bob was a very visible GM back then and he encouraged the entire sales force to be extremely visible as well. I have always said he was the Vince Lombardi of television. He energized you when he talked to you. He came out on the road a lot with the sales team and the buyers were surprised to see the GM telling them what the station was doing and what kind of programming was being scheduled for the community. We appreciated him being there with us on the firing line. He used to tell buyers that people watched programming, not stations, and WCVB had the best programming and the best place to put their advertising. But it was one tough battle in the early days because no one wanted to pay our rates. Our buyers were telling us what they wanted to pay. They were in fact coming right out and telling us to lower our rates or they wouldn't buy. Nobody believed we could pull off all the programming we were talking about.
In 1973, ABC acquired the Olympics and everything then broke in our favor. The Olympics turned national sales around which in turn boosted local sales, but it was one tough battle back then because Boston saw us as the outsiders. WBZ was our main competitor and it seemed we were always running into those guys. We had a sales staff of seven people, all men, and then we hired three women to work with us. Within one year, all three women had the number 1, 2, and 3 spots in sales. They were very aggressive and focused on selling. WCVB was a great place to work. The camaraderie among the sales people was fantastic and we sold a tremendous amount of advertising. When I look back at it now, I realize it was the best place I ever worked."

Josh McGraw, Local Sales Manager, WCVB-TV, writes:
"My broadcast career spanned 35 years, from 1971 as a floor director at the CBS affiliate in Denver, to 2006 as Regional Vice-President of Clear Channel Television. Of all of the jobs and promotions I have had over the years, landing an account executive position in 1978 at WCVB-TV was and still is the

biggest thrill and sense of accomplishment I have ever had. My competition for the job was virtually the whole country! Even when I was promoted years later to Local Sales Manager in 1981 and then later to Vice-President/Sales Manager at WCVB, while significant and momentous, it can't compare to the emotion and sense of pride I felt when I was first told I had the AE job at WCVB.

Even before I started I sensed that WCVB was special and different. A close friend of mine, Tony Palminteri, (who also later worked at WCVB) told me he remembered WCVB while working in New York at ABC affiliate relations in the mid-1970s. He told me that I was now going to be working at the only television station in America that would preempt the Number 1 network show Happy Days *for a locally-produced program like "Pollution in the Charles River." It seemed like Bob Bennett and WCVB were in the press almost daily. I remember attending several television meetings over the years in Las Vegas, Chicago and Philadelphia. The network owned and operated station salespeople would see my name badge and say, "Oh, WCVB," then bow in sarcastic reverence.*

Even before I met and got to know Bob, his presence and philosophies were felt throughout the station. I remember quite specifically the following at WCVB:
- *If you're not changing, you're not in first place.*
- *Are you doing the same things this year as you did last year? If so, you're losing ground.*
- *Excellence knows no time clock.*
- *Only those who dare to fail greatly can achieve greatly.*
- *Ingenuity, plus courage, plus work, equals miracles.*
- *Enthusiasm is the propelling force necessary for climbing the ladder of success.*
- *Failure is not the worst thing in the world. The very worst is not to have tried at all.*
- *Act as though it was impossible to fail.*
- *It takes courage to push yourself into places you have never been before, to test your limits and to break through barriers.*
- *Accept the challenges so that you may feel the exhilaration of victory.*

In 1979, I was making a sales call with my sales manager, Mike

Volpe. We were pitching the buyer that controlled the largest account in Boston and they were spending about $3 million with us on WCVB alone. In my package of specifically tailored programming, I created for the buyer's account an upcoming buy with several locally produced programs. The buyer quickly informed me that they did not want to buy any locally produced "crap" as she called it. I turned to Mike and I had never seen him so angry before. Mike told her straight out that he never wanted to hear her talk negatively about WCVB's locally produced programming ever again. If she did, he would have a conversation with her media director and the president of the agency and consequences then may be that WCVB would become unavailable for her clients to buy. Part of me was concerned that we may just have just lost our biggest account, but the other part of me was incredibly proud of the stance Mike took, and on that day he demonstrated to me just how important local programming was to the station's position in the Boston market.

Working at WCVB made you feel important because you were part of something very special. Localism became part of your DNA. We not only had to make our mark with buyers, we also had to deal with the rivalry going on with other stations in the Boston market."

Joseph C. Dimino, Vice President/GM, WSBK-TV 38 Boston, (1977-1982), writes:

"There was always some good natured rivalry back then between Channel 5 and Channel 38. Of course, it wasn't always much of a contest in the days before cable. But when it came to sports, WSBK-TV, our little VHF station held its own in Boston, thank you very much. It was our time to shine and I never missed the opportunity to point that out to Bob Bennett whenever I had the chance. Channel 38 had the Red Sox and when they made it to the playoffs in 1975, we were now the focus of attention, which in the past had always seemed to have gone to Bob and his station. So with a great magnanimous gesture, I invited Bob to be my guest at the game.

I had forgotten that ABC was always part of the mix, televising the game nationally while 38 televised it locally. As Bob and I walked into Fenway Park I could finally feel the spotlight of fame shining on me. This was surely TV 38's finest moment. Just then, as we walked into Fenway, the famed announcer for the Red Sox—the beloved Sherm Feller--intoned in his unique voice: "Will Bob Bennett of WCVB please report to the ABC truck." He had done it again! He wouldn't have even been at the game if it weren't for me. I swear to this day that he arranged Sherm to page him as he walked into a standing room only ballpark!

Bob is a very unique person. No matter if you are a CEO or an automobile mechanic, Bob talks and acts with you the same. He's always been this way and he's always interested in people for who they are. One time when our children were young, we were all at Cape Cod together and Bob came to our apartment and saw the kids drawing with crayons on paper. He naturally made a big fuss over the artwork and offered to buy a drawing from my daughter. He gave her $20. You should have seen her eyes light up. For the rest of the vacation, she kept drawing these little squiggly things hoping that she had found a steady art collector."

My family was still living in Westport, CT, and soon joined me in Boston in June of 1971, after the house was sold and school was over. We ended up buying a beautiful home in Wellesley on Carris Ridge Road. We loved the house and it was perfect for entertaining and having weekend guests over. Casey attended Wellesley High School and Kelley was enrolling in Colby Junior College. We arranged one day for Casey's High School class to come in and tour WCVB-TV, and the kids had a great time watching television shows and getting an understanding of what goes into making a television station work. During one of Kelly's years at Colby, she came down with a girlfriend and the two of them were interns in the news department for one month. It was great having her there. After Colby, Kelly went to Boston University and graduated in 1975.

Maria Morales, Bob's secretary, writes:

"I began work at WCVB in 1975 when Bob was General Manager. When I left he was President of Broadcasting for Metromedia. That kind of ascent was amazing. Working with him was a tremendous learning experience. I was in awe of his forward-looking philosophy and every day we worked together seemed to bring new and exciting experiences. In the early days

*of WCVB, Bob was someone who pretty much kept his thoughts
and emotions under wraps. Perhaps it was because he sorted
out situations in his mind before he acted on them.*

*After several years, however, when he knew that he could trust
me with sensitive information, he would open up and tell me
what was on his mind, not in great detail, but more like a hint
of what was on his mind. His enthusiasm and optimism about
all the projects and programs he started or helped grow was
never-ending. Bob was full of ideas and the staff adored him.
His concern was always professionalism first and foremost
and he demanded perfection from his managers. He always
challenged them to explore new ground and new technology
with the engineering department whenever possible. He was
always challenging our sales people to sell more airtime and
they always rose to the task. In fact, everybody working with
us rose to the task at hand under Bob. He wanted to become
number one in the market and he ignited our programming,
sales, engineering, public relations, community outreach, and
everyone to step up to the challenge and we did it: We became
Number One. He was committed to public service programs and
strongly supported the community. It was Bob who introduced
Boston Broadcasters, Inc., to what broadcasting was all about.
He convinced them to take risks with programming and to
always give our viewers the information they really needed.*

*Bob has a big heart and is generous to a fault. He adores his
family, respects his coworkers, and always considered loyalty
a necessity in personal and business relationships; and once
he got behind a project, he always defended it strongly and
convincingly. Once when I was annoyed at an individual who
was being less than polite to me on the telephone, he called
me into his office and said, "Maria, you need to know that
honey will get you more than vinegar. You need to be polite,
regardless...." It is something I have never forgotten.*

*An example of his care, concern and sensitivity, was during
the 1978 blizzard when everyone was staying off the streets.
Our janitor walked from his home in Roxbury through four
feet of snow just to make sure he was at work because of the
commitment he had made to his job. When Bob found out
about it, he made sure to thank him and to acknowledge him*

for his great effort."

Joseph C. Dimino, GM, WSBK-TV 38 Boston (1977–1982), writes:

"I think the first time I really got to know Bob socially and when our friendship really developed was when he invited me to a cookout at his home in Wellesley. It was mostly Channel 5 people, but I knew most of them. Bob had set up a bunch of round tables around the pool and on each table was a bottle of red wine to go with the hamburgers and hot dogs. Now, I'm a bit of a wine follower, which he knew, so when I sat down and read the label on the wine bottle, I was shocked to find that it was a Chateau Lafite-Rothschild. Bob wanted me to believe that he had no idea of the quality of the wine and could care less. Of course, in time I came to find out that he did know the quality of the wine, but he just happened to have a case of Chateau Lafite-Rothschild lying around. He always got a kick out of yanking my chain."

Daniel Berkery, President/GM, WSBK-TV 38 (1983–1995), writes:

"One day, Joe Dimino came in my office and said to me, 'Dan, I want you to meet this guy Bob Bennett who has just come into town from being General Manager of WNEW in New York. He's now GM over at WCVB-TV.' I had already heard of Bob and was somewhat familiar with his track record. When I finally met him what impressed me about him more than anything else was the fact that no matter whom he was talking to in broadcasting, no matter what anyone's position was, a janitor, secretary, a station manager, a station owner, he treated them all with the same respect. He always had time for you and was always around to answer your questions. The people at WCVB-TV loved him. Everyone knew he was a tremendous leader. In the broadcast world I think Bob was a lion. There are not too many lions out there. He came to Boston with this tremendous legacy behind him. He had done things as a GM in Washington and in New York that no one had ever done before. People were in awe of him. Metromedia certainly got a lift from being involved with him."

Life at the Station

MEANWHILE, AT WCVB, our equipment was finally in place. During the time we were waiting (or should I say battling) for the license, we had produced a fair amount of programming that we were now broadcasting. One of those programs was a kid's show called *Jabberwocky*, which was an animation series and one of the first of its kind. Our initial programming schedule had a lot of syndicated programming that we had bought from Metromedia.

As the station GM, I had a lot of early-on decisions to make and I was convinced that WCVB-TV should have one of the best newscasts around. Initially we filled our newsroom with people who had been at WHDH-TV and who already had a great deal of experience working in a news operation. Don Gillis did sports and we made Jack Hynes and John Henning co-anchors of news. I did not want to establish a radically new vision in the newsroom at first, because I wanted to have as smooth a transition as possible.

In our early days, Larry Picard was building our news team. I soon realized that his vision and my vision were not one in the same, and I knew then that I was going to have to make a change, which was tough since Larry was an original BBI person. I moved him out of news and over to another job, and he never got over it. He ended up leaving BBI and walked away with a good deal of money from the sale of his stock. I then hired Jim Thissel to run the WCVB news team. He was well respected in the news business in Boston and he and I worked closely together to build our news team. I always felt that news made your reputation and set the tone for the station. When we first started we did news from six to six thirty and eleven to eleven thirty.

Job applications were coming into the station in the thousands. All kinds of new and enthusiastic faces were showing up all over the place. Our team was pulling together and soon we were not only just a family, we were a proud group of hard working people soon to be making television history. We just didn't know it at the time.

My first real challenge was to find an affiliation with a network. WHDH-TV had been a CBS affiliate and we would have liked to have kept the CBS affiliation. However, CBS had jumped ship because they were scared of the massive amount of local broadcasting that we had promised the FCC. They no doubt envisioned us preempting a big part of their network schedule in favor of our local programming.

That left us with ABC, if ABC wanted us, and we thought they did. We soon found out that ABC was also afraid of the threat of any massive preempting we might do, and they didn't seem to want any part of us. We learned that ABC was considering the purchase of one of the other stations in Boston, and bypassing WCVB-TV. I couldn't let this happen.

The Challenge to
Become an ABC Affiliate

LEO BERANEK AND I went down to New York City to visit ABC and their affiliate committee to try and persuade them to let us be their Boston affiliate. We had to give them our programming schedule and I could see that it scared them. What came out of the meeting was no definitive answer, but we could see that they were not leaning in our favor. I believe that the end result of that meeting only made them more interested in buying a station in Boston if they could find one for sale. The general feeling we believed when we walked out of that meeting was that they believed WCVB-TV would preempt ABC all over the place and negatively affect their ratings.

Our problem was that as an independent station with no network affiliation, we would have had to purchase a lot of programming and that would be very costly. We would also have to have made a deal with the Red Sox and spent millions of dollars to feed our growing programming machine. If we were affiliated with a network like ABC, they would have supplied daytime and late night programming and saved us a lot of programming expenses. Leo and I left there very annoyed that we did not get an automatic endorsement.

When Leo and I arrived back in Boston, we went to the bank to let them know how much money we would need to borrow in the first year as an independent station. While we were at the bank, I got so mad over the whole non-commitment from ABC that I immediately went over to a phone and called my friend Elton Rule who was the President of ABC. I had known Elton when he was a sales manager and general manager of ABC's channel seven in Los Angeles. I had competed against him and knew him well and I considered him a good friend. He was aware that I was in Boston and that I had joined WCVB-TV. I called him and when he got on the phone I was ready for him.

"Elton, let me tell you something." I said to him. "I love you and I love ABC. We would like to be affiliated with ABC because we feel we'd make a great team together. As you know, I've never been a network affiliate. I've been an independent for twenty-five years so I know a little about the independent television world. If you choose not to be affiliated with us, I am going to be the best independent in the whole damn country. We're going to have the Red Sox and lots of syndicated programming. ABC is going to be hard-pressed to beat us. If you don't make us an affiliate, ABC is going to lose. It makes no difference to me. I can go either way. But right now, I'm sitting here at the bank figuring out how much money I'm going to need. If you say no, I will declare my independence with the press today and tell them that I've done everything in my power to bring ABC to channel five in Boston. I will tell them that ABC has chosen not to join us and I wish them well. In effect, I'm declaring my independence right now unless I hear from you in five minutes."

There was silence on the other end of the line.

"Bob, I'll call you back in five minutes," I heard him say.

I returned to Leo who was sitting with the bank executive. Exactly five minutes later the telephone rang. It was Elton.

"You've got a deal, Bob. We're in."

"Elton, I'm delighted. WCVB-TV is going to be the best affiliate ABC has ever had."

I hung up the phone and turned to Leo with a big smile on my face.

It was going to be a lot easier for WCVB-TV to be an ABC affiliate than an independent station. The Boston press was favorable and the trade press was delighted since it was a story of historical significance.

Fred Pierce, Former President of the American Companies and Chairman Emeritus of the AFI, writes:

"I would describe Bob as the consummate professional broadcaster. As GM of WCVB-TV Channel 5 Boston, he initiated a program of localism that was unsurpassed by any measure, while being one of the best ABC-TV affiliates in the U.S. His focus, which was based a lot on local news and public service, catapulted WCVB into being the clear audience leader in the market. Bob's many years on the ABC-TV's Board of Governors further demonstrated his business acumen as well as his creativity in building the cooperative relationship between the ABC-TV Network and the affiliate body he represented. As President of ABC in the late 70s, I personally observed his role in ABC's ascendency to the number one position in audience and advertising revenue.

As the 80s began, ABC needed to diversify and I recommended to the Board that we buy ESPN to utilize our unsold sports inventory rights, particularly during the week. As I recall, Bob was one of the few GMs who thought an ESPN acquisition would strengthen the network and the company over the long term. Needless to say, he and I were right. ESPN was then a losing operation, and today of course is now the leading sports cable network earning well in excess of a billion dollars annually. Over the past fifteen years, Bob and I have served on the Board of Trustees for the American Film Institute (AFI), a graduate school dedicated to teaching the film makers of tomorrow, i.e., directors, producers, writers, and cinematographers of film, television, and Internet. Bob has been extremely supportive of the AFI's activities, both financially and as an active board member of this nonprofit organization. When recently faced with the loss of government financing for the AFI, Bob supported the economic and creative potential of the AFI's 100 Years Countdown of Movies that I proposed as Chairman. This series of eleven specials that ran on CBS-TV contributed $12 million to AFI and stimulated national awareness of the best in classic movies. We have Bob to thank for a lot of this great work."

Joseph C. Dimino, GM, WSBK-TV 38, Boston (1977-1982), writes:
"As GM of Channel 38 in Boston, I was competing with Bob and

he was tough to compete with, but back then the broadcasting community was pretty close. I decided that I would have a surprise 50th birthday party for Bill Flynn who was Vice-President and General Manager of WSBK-TV 38. The party took place at Polcari's restaurant near the old Boston Garden at North Station. I figured it would be a good idea to invite all the movers and shakers in the advertising and broadcast business and I would make this a very dressy affair; I wanted everyone to come in tuxedos. The first person I called was Bob Bennett. Naturally, he said, 'Yes.' I then proceeded to call about thirty people until I came to Jim Coppersmith's number. Jim was running Channel 7, WNAC at the time. To know Jimmy is to love him. In that nasally voice of his he said to me, "Joey, you know a lot of people are not going to come because of your stupid tuxedo idea, since we will all just be getting out of work. Just have us come in our business attire." I decided Jim was right so I called everybody back and told them the tuxedo idea was off and to come in business clothes. I called everyone that is, except Bob Bennett. I just somehow forgot to call him and tell him. On the night of the party, there was a great turnout. And then there was Bob, industry leader, GM of WCVB-TV, trying to explain to everyone why he felt it was necessary to dress in a tuxedo for Bill Flynn's birthday party. Needless to say, he was very gracious and managed, as always, to turn this into some advantage for WCVB. We still laugh about this every time we get together. He never forgets."

WCVB: First and Foremost About People

I LIKE TO believe that WCVB-TV was first and foremost about people, and in my opinion, we had assembled one really great team of professionals—articulate, talented, focused, and hungry to try new things. It is no surprise that WCVB has won so many notable awards and prestigious broadcasting prizes such as regional Emmys, DuPont Awards, Gabriel Awards, and Edward R. Murrow honors. All of these are proudly on display at the station and I have my own fair share hanging in my own home. In many ways, WCVB back then was a mini broadcast network that was there for viewers on the local level. David J. Barrett, president and CEO of Hearst-Argyle once said, "People define great TV stations, and, over the years, WCVB has been blessed with the best of Boston's TV professionals."

In many ways, WCVB has always had a two-faceted approach: a deep commitment to community involvement and a great deal of local programming. I will add one more facet to that approach: people. We had the best and they were totally dedicated to the station. Here are some of the great people who helped make WCVB great.

Paul Rich was Director of Public Relations for Tufts University when we found him. He was a guest speaker at a function for a Time Magazine event when he first heard of an opening at WCVB-TV. Joe Ryan, who was our Vice President of Community and Public Relations, was in the audience that evening and heard Paul speak. He was impressed and went up to Paul to compliment him and to tell him a little about WCVB-TV. Joe explained to him that we were a new station and looking for enthusiastic talented people. Paul thanked him politely and then informed him that he was not really interested in leaving his job at Tufts. Joe did finally convince Paul to at least have lunch and to visit the station. Paul came to the station two or three times for interviews and fact-finding trips and the more he came, met the people, and looked around, the more intrigued he became.

Paul started at WCVB-TV as Director of Public Relations and reported directly to Joe Ryan. Paul's job was essentially to get WCVB-TV in the papers and he did a superb job at it. He fed WCVB-TV news to all of the local and international entertainment writers and kept our name out in front of the pack. To this very day, Paul and I are still very close friends and we work together on a number of different projects.

Paul Rich, Director of Public Relations, WCVB, 1972–1976, writes:
"In June of 1973, I was recruited initially by Joe Ryan, Assistant VP of community services at the station. I had been Director of Public Relations/Publications at Tufts University at the time. My initial interview for the position of Director of Public Relations was arranged by Bob, then General Manager of Channel 5. The interview happened to fall on June 23, 1973, and at that time my father was in dire health and had been transferred to Tufts Medical in Boston that day for what was to be one last desperate operation. I visited with him for most of the day, but took a couple hours off to drive to Needham for the decisive interview with Bob early that evening. The interview went very well—Bob and I hit it off immediately. However, so content was I in my job at Tufts and with all of the ancillary activities on campus that my entire family benefited from (kids at summer camp, wife in academic courses, etc.) that I hesitated to change. But Bob, ever the consummate salesman, convinced me it was the right decision. He went further by saying that there were opportunities I should think about at Channel 5 beyond public relations.

I accepted the job, rushed back to the hospital and got there in time to tell my father, who smiled weakly and said, "Good job!" He passed away one hour later. Needless to say, that was a very emotional swing for me. I dedicated the new job to my dad. Somehow there was bonding that took place between Bob and me that has survived thirty-five-plus years as coworkers and then as business partners. Among the many common interests that Bob and I share is our mutual love of boxing. From that day forward, he never could hear enough stories about my father, who was a successful amateur boxer."

Phil Balboni came to WCVB in August of 1972. He was smart, creative, energetic, and eager to learn. He was hired by Leo as our first Editorial Director and he wrote and assembled editorial pieces, and in some cases, went on screen delivering some of the best editorial segments I have ever seen. In 1978, Phil took over as our Editor of Public Affairs. We met on a regular weekly basis and had some very memorable editorial meetings where we debated issues. Our Editorial and Public Affairs Division was the voice of our station. Phil also proposed a number of programs that were issue-oriented and would give needed information to our viewers. He was involved with documentaries, special programs, and three-hour prime time issue-oriented programs. He created such memorable programs as *Five on Five* and *Calendar*, but he was most instrumental in bringing to my attention an idea he had for a program called *Chronicle*.

Phil Balboni, Director, Editorial and Public Affairs, WCVB-TV (1972-1980), writes:
"Bob always had an open door policy at Channel 5, a reflection of the kind of person and the kind of manager he was: warm, open, willing to listen, a real lover of people and the interplay of ideas. I walked through the door in the fall of 1980 with an admittedly big, brash idea—the creation of a nightly news magazine in the prime access time period, other than news, the most hallowed ground for a local station to program.
I had developed a very trusting relationship with Bob starting from the station's beginning in 1972. While I was by no means one of the most important department heads at Channel 5, I knew Bob and I knew that he respected the quality of my work as Editorial Director and then as head of both the Editorial and Public Affairs Departments where we made creative documentaries and primetime specials. My most

recent innovation before that meeting was a monthly hour-long newsmagazine called Calendar, that we ran in primetime, preempting ABC programming—something very few stations were willing to do, but something Bob Bennett never hesitated to do when he thought it was right for the station and the community. Chronicle was both a creative and a rating success with Natalie Jacobson as host who was partnered with the urbane, sophisticated Curator of the Niemen Foundation for Journalism at Harvard, Jim Thomson, a handsome world traveler whose gravitas made up for his lack of television polish.

I had been thinking hard about the future of the great station we had built. How could we preserve Channel 5's traditions of great community service and innovative local programming and especially in that key 7:30 to 8 p.m. prime access time period? It was clear to me that commercial pressures were growing and that sooner or later the station needed a consistent nightly program that could compete successfully against powerful syndicated fare from big Hollywood studios. Bob read my memo proposing the formation of an unprecedented team of producers, videographers, editors, and reporters, and the launch of a Monday through Friday strip of half-hour newsmagazine programs designed to inform and entertain Bostonians. He smiled and started to kid me in the way that only Bob could, lighthearted but probing and just sharp-elbowed enough to remind you that running a major market television station was serious business and you better have thought this through carefully.

That first conversation with Bob led to many more over the next nine months, culminating in August 1981, when he gave me the final green light to launch what came to be called Chronicle, born on January 20th, 1982. Here it is some thirty-plus years later and Chronicle is still winning its 7:30 time period every night against all competitors. It has become the most respected and the most successful local television program in American broadcasting history.

The record should show that Bob was not an easy sell on this. He made me work as hard as I knew how to back up my projections, financial and otherwise. The battle raged on behind the scenes at the station for many months. The programming department *fought back, quite understandably, not wanting to give up access to this key time period that it controlled for almost a decade. The sales department had to sell ads in this new program and it was unenthusiastic at best, downright hostile at times. And then there was the proposed budget: $1 million a year and some 30 people, which was a great deal of money in 1982. Even for a powerful and highly successful station like WCVB, that was real money, big money, a huge bet on the unknown, a gamble that local programming could win out over increasingly stronger national competition.*

As long as Bob may live, and I hope it is for a very long time to come, he will in my opinion, never show more courage, more devotion to an ideal, than he did in making his final decision to approve Chronicle. He had to stand up to his close colleagues in sales and programming. He had to justify that enormous expense to the Board of Directors of the station. He did it all with grace, style, and good humor that are among the many hallmarks of Bob Bennett, a man of courage and vision and strength."

A Very Special Television Program: *Chronicle*

PHIL BALBONI CAME into my office one day and told me about an idea he had for a new program that would be investigative in nature to be called Chronicle. The more we listened the more we became fascinated by the idea; but we quickly realized that this was not going to be a usual run-of-the-mill production budget and schedule. This was something different and very unique. First of all, it would call for additional people to be hired to produce the show and an annual budget of $1 million. I told Phil I would think about it and we agreed to meet again soon, but I gave him the go-ahead to continue to develop the idea.

In August of 1981, I went in to the board along with Bill Poorvu and proposed the idea of Chronicle to them. I told them I felt strongly that this was something that the station should be doing but there was a real cost to it. I told them that in time, we would recoup this cost. They gave me the go-ahead. Everyone was elated.

Once we had the go-ahead from the board and the budget to put everything in place, Phil and his team went on a research trip across the country and visited with other stations to see what they were doing. He and his production team spent four months in preproduction and then we were set to go. Chronicle was aired in the 7:30 to 8:00 prime time frame, and to our surprise it did not do so well in the ratings. Each show dealt with several compelling issues per segment, so it may have been that viewers were finding the show somewhat confusing.

In 1972, Paul La Camera joined WCVB as Director of Community Relations. Prior to his arrival he was the Director of Communications for the Greater Boston Chamber of Commerce and also worked as a reporter for the Boston Record American and Sunday Advertiser. Paul is a very talented executive who helped the station grow in popularity over the years.

Paul La Camera, Director of Public Affairs, later President and GM, WCVB-TV, writes:

"First and foremost, I believe during my almost three and half decades at WCVB-TV, that Bob Bennett was the greatest general manager in the history of local television. I believed it then...and continue to do so today. And I saw and met some very good ones along the way, including working twelve years with one of the best ever—Jim Coppersmith, Bob's successor and my predecessor.

Boston Broadcasters had the vision of what would soon become the ideal, the paradigm of a local television station. But Bob put it into play...made it happen by inspired leadership. One could never fail in Bob's eyes as long as you were working toward the ideal of WCVB. There was never fear of trying...of experimenting...or even of failure. That culture, to my mind, is the rare byproduct of truly great leadership.

It may be a cliché...but when you met Bob, you left feeling that you had just spent time with the most important person in the business, and that, at the same time, you were his equal. That was his gift. Always reflecting leadership, his inspiration, his vision, his greatness in the most facile and charming of ways... and making you feel equally great about yourself.

I joined WCVB in January of 1972, from the Greater Boston Chamber of Commerce, where I was Director of Communications two months before WCVB's March 19, 1972 launch date, and remained there until September 30, 2005 when I left. During my time at the station, I was Director of Public Affairs, a producer of various local public affairs programs and special projects, Vice President of Community Services, Vice President and Program Director, Vice President and Station Manager, and for the final twelve years, President and General Manager. Those early days of WCVB were literally Mickey Rooney and

Judy Garland "putting on a show." Nothing was beyond Bob's inspiration and our collective imagination…dramas, children's programs, situation comedies, experimental public affairs shows on medicine, science, the elderly, the community etc., documentaries, and, finally, prime-access magazine shows as still exemplified today by the thirty plus year old nightly 'Chronicle.'"

In 1982, Phil went on to become Director of News and Paul La Camera took over as Executive Producer of Chronicle. Paul fiddled a bit with the program structure and changed it to one segment per program. The program then took off in the ratings and it was unstoppable. It beat everything in that time slot and is still on today, giving competitors a "ratings" run for their money. When Hearst brought WCVB-TV some years later, they syndicated Chronicle and it was a hit across the country. It is one of my all-time favorite programs.

Chet Curtis arrived at WCVB in March of 1972, and was one of the last people, if not the last one, who came over from WHDH. He was hired by our News Director Larry Picard and we were glad to have him as he was a great addition to our news team. Chet was energetic, looked great on camera, and when he reported the news, he had a special magic that made viewers relate to him. Some of the other members from our original starting news line up were Jack Hines, news; Don Gillis sports, and Bob Copeland, weather. Prior to WHDH-TV, Chet had worked at WCBS in New York and WTOP in Washington. Chet started out at our station with the 6 a.m. Eye-Opener News, and then did the midday 12:00 to 12:30 news, Monday through Friday, as well as special news segments on the weekends. In 1976, he moved into the 6 p.m. news with all of the professionalism a newsman could have. Along with his co-anchor Natalie Jacobson, whom he married in 1975, they branched out and covered special events such as the Queen Elizabeth visit that had somewhere between twelve to fifteen remotes going at one time. WBZ-TV in Boston was the dominant ratings station for news at that time and we were going head to head with them.

Natalie Jacobson was one of the first females in the country to anchor nightly news. She came to the station in 1972, and she was a terrific on-air news personality. She auditioned for the job over a three-day testing period, where she had to write, think, persuade, and read the news on camera. We hired her and she started work on June 6, 1972 as a reporter. She began doing public service and public affairs material and was soon anchoring the midday news as the first woman in New England history to do so. I fell in love with her style and professionalism. Other stations from large markets tried to hire her away but she always claimed she was "too" Boston to leave.

Natalie Jacobson, Newscaster for WCVB-TV, writes:
"I was driving down a highway one day and my cell phone rang. The voice on the other end was a welcome surprise. "So, how the heck are you? Do you have a man in your life? I want to know if you have someone you want to spend the rest of your life with." It was Bob Bennett. There are a lot of things you can say about Bob Bennett. He's wise, he's fun, he loves to win; he brings out the best in people. But above all, you can really say he genuinely cares about people.

As a young reporter in 1972, happy to finally get a job in news, I was already high on life. Little could I dream just how far the rocket ship would climb, how addicted a group of people could become to soaring the universe in search of excellence. And how much fun it all would be.

When Bob Bennett took the reigns of WCVB-TV, dreams became reality. No programming idea was too silly, no news story too complicated. If it was right for our viewers, Bob would say, "Give it a try." And if your idea failed, you lived to try again. Not only were you "not" berated, Bob urged you to think through what went wrong. Was the idea sound, but the execution off? Or was it the other way around? We learned at least as much from our mistakes as from our successes. And we learned that to "think big" was not only accepted, it was expected. What a gift to a person like me.

Bob asked one day, "Why should Hollywood have the lock on original motion pictures?" So we sent out the word throughout New England, "Got a script? Send it to us." Hundreds of writers poured forth. Bob had promised that WCVB would produce the winning script with top talent and first-rate production. The result was the film Summer Solstice *with Henry Fonda and*

Myna Loy. This was a first in the country for a local television station to do. We also created the sitcom Park Street Under, *which took place in a bar in a subway station, which many believe became the inspiration for the NBC series,* Cheers.

Working at WCVB under the direction of Bob was like living in a candy store of innovation. Anything was possible. We churned out programming the likes of which no station in America had ever attempted then or now to do, not in number and not in quality. We looked around and asked, "What was missing on TV?" We were not content to allow public television to own the children's market with Sesame Street *and the like, so we created our own children's show and we called it* Jabberwocky.

The forced bussing issue was tearing the city of Boston apart. We created the show Sound Off *and filled the studio with ordinary citizens on both sides of the issue. I've always thought that the definition of "passion" was rewritten every time I watched this show. In fact, I think I cried once after hosting a particularly explosive show.*

People needed a real life Dr. Welby, so we created House Call, *with Dr. Timothy Johnson. The reverend-turned-doctor became a household treasure, to this day. Again, the uniqueness of an individual lit the idea lamp. Harvard University had this somewhat "whacky" law professor, Arthur Miller. His students loved learning from him, so how about the rest of society? We created* Miller's Court *and it was scintillating. New England is known for it unique character and geography and our original program* Calendar, *which later became known as* Chronicle, *captured this.*

Boston, the hub of New England, attracted people from all walks of life: writers, chefs, musicians, politicians, and fashion gurus. The here and now of time was captured live every weekday morning on our program Good Morning. *A general manager succeeding Bob agreed to give the name* Good Morning *to ABC, which is now* Good Morning America *and our show became* Good Day.

As far as news goes, there could be no more vibrant newsroom in my opinion than at our tiny space at 5 TV Place. And we captured all of this news live, morning, noon, and night, on our newscasts. From the beginning we became part of the

community. That belonging directed everything we did.
We were guided by the belief that information was the key to
everything in life. In spirited debate, we argued the merits of
any particular story that day. Everyone's opinion mattered. In
the end, the best idea usually won.
I do remember that Bob knew how to keep the newspaper critics
happy. He actually sent roses to a critic who rarely said a nice
thing about us. I was incredulous. "How many people do you
think send her roses, Natalie?" Bob asked me one day. Well, for
one thing, he certainly from there on received good press. Flatter
the enemy. It was a good lesson."

At the time, our co-anchors for the 11 o'clock news were John Hennings and Jack Hynes. Together they were not much in the way of magic and our ratings were not overly strong. I decided to pair Natalie Jacobson with Jack Hynes, which saw an improvement in our ratings, but not by much. I had to find somebody who had some spark early-on to jumpstart our newscast.

In 1971, Tom Ellis was the news anchor on the Westinghouse station in Boston that was dominating the market in news. He was a good-looking Texan who had strong delivery, a great smile, and looked almost like an actor in the way he carried himself on camera. Viewers seemed to like him. I disliked him because he was a competitor of ours. Since he was doing so well in the ratings, he was transferred to New York and he bombed. For whatever reason, New Yorkers did not take a liking to him. I decided to offer Ellis the job at WCVB and he accepted. In 1975, we put him on the air with Natalie and our ratings went through the roof.

Natalie did not like working with Tom. She preferred working with Chet Curtis. But the Ellis/Jacobson team had sparks flying because they were both so competitive on camera. Neither one of them gave an inch. Members of the BBI board were not fans of Tom Ellis. They thought he was too Hollywood in some ways and did not fit the conservative New England image they had in mind. They were happier with Hynes and Henning.

Two and a half years into Tom Ellis's three-year contract, he now had an agent and he demanded more money. I had several meetings with his agent, and then had to leave to go on a trip to California. Before I left I asked his agent for his word that Tom Ellis would not leave his job at WCVB until we reached, or didn't reach, a final agreement. He said to me, "Bob, you have my word."

When I returned from my California trip, I was driving out of the Sumner Tunnel listening to the radio when I heard the following news lead: "Big news in Boston Today—Tom Ellis leaving WCVB-TV Channel 5 for Channel 7."

I was so mad I almost drove the car off the road. I immediately called his agent and demanded an explanation.

"Bob, what can I tell you? It's true," he told me. "But I want you to know I'm no longer representing Tom Ellis. I don't want to have a client who is so disloyal and dishonest, so I've quit."

From there on I hammered away at Ellis's reputation every time I could. I never missed a press conference and always made sure I mentioned what a disloyal person he was and someone who could not be trusted. At Channel 7, much to my happiness, he bombed.

Teaming Chet Curtis up
with Natalie Jacobson

NATALIE JACOBSON HAD magic dust all over her. She was a real natural television personality and it registered on camera, and the viewers loved her. I teamed Chet and Natalie up on the news set and they became an extraordinary news team and our ratings began to soar. Sometime later they were married and they became the first husband-wife news team in New England. Our public relations people capitalized on it and our ratings continued to go higher and higher. Natalie held this co-anchor and then anchor position from 1972 until 2007, when she retired. With Natalie at the news desk, News Center 5 won nearly every broadcasting award out there, including several New England Emmys for best newscast and the top awards from the Associated Press and United Press International. In 2007, Natalie was honored with the Centennial Lifetime Achievements Award for excellence in journalism by Suffolk University. She is the second journalist to ever receive this award.

Natalie Jacobson, Newscaster for WCVB-TV, writes:
"There is no way to remember the halcyon days of news at WCVB-TV without saluting the leadership of Jim Thistle. Thistle was to news what Bennett was to the whole operation. It was Bob who hired Thistle and he let Jim run the shop as only he knew how. This was another example of Bob's leadership. The news department of the Bennett/Thistle days kept us racing. There are many news stories that come to mind, such as the crash

*of World Airways into Boston Harbor, the phony marathon win
of Rose Ruiz, the Blizzard of 1978 which shut down a region of
New England for a week, the elevation of Cardinal Law that
took us to Rome, the unprecedented eight-hour live coverage of
Queen Elizabeth's visit to Boston, the parade of the Tall Ships
and the daylong coverage of the funerals of Tip O'Neill and
Rose Kennedy that allowed us to relive our history with our
viewers. Bob Bennett always stressed a sense of unity within our
station. News, programming, engineering, and sales were all
one team. People like me got to work on news as well as regular
programming. We each became the best we could be. I like to
think our viewers benefited enormously from our creativity.
None of this would have been possible without the leadership
of Bob Bennett."*

By 1978, Chet and Natalie's popularity among viewers continued
to grow so they asked me for more money. They had even hired
an agent to negotiate with me. I told them that I was not a fan of
agents and did not like doing business with them. I told them that if
my negotiations with their agent started going in the wrong direction, this might not help their case. So it came to be that their agent
began negotiating with me and it was not going well. Our conversations would end up in screaming matches in which the table was
being pounded and this guy would threaten me and the station in
all kinds of ways. I held my ground and we finally worked out a
number that was satisfactory, which ended up as both salaries being
combined as one.

But Chet and Natalie made a great husband and wife news team,
and that no one could deny. In 1981, they had a baby girl they
named Lindsay Dawn. It was the biggest news in Boston. The *Herald* ran it on the front page with only these words: "IT'S A GIRL!"
and everyone knew who they were talking about. It was such a big
news item that reporters were sneaking in and getting past hospital
security to take pictures of the baby. The station received over five
thousand gifts for Lindsay Dawn that day which consisted of hundreds of booties, hats, blankets, dolls, etc. The last time there had
been this much attention on television was when Lucy and Ricky
Ricardo had Little Ricky.

Our news ratings under Chet and Natalie continued to go

through the roof. They covered election nights, telethons, and the Boston Symphony Orchestra. Wherever news was, Chet and Natalie from WCVB-TV were there.

Chet Curtis Newscaster, WCVB-TV, writes:
"One thing that I can say about Bob Bennett is that he always encouraged people to come up with ideas and that no idea was every too crazy or too wild if you had thought it out and believed in it. If one of us had an idea that we might think was of value, we brought it to him to see if something could be made of it. He always told us to never be afraid to fail. His door was always open for us to walk in and there were always lively, spirited, and open-ended conversations and debates on new ideas. He always encouraged us to do our best and everyone on our team took his advice and rose to the task. Bob was very inspiring and people always gave them their best."

Maria Morales, Bob's secretary, writes:
"There was a Boston newspaper critic named Monica Collins who did not like WCVB-TV and she wrote many negative articles about us. Bob decided to do something about it and went out of his way to spend some time with her, and before long, she began to cool off and wrote positive things about us. He charmed her with his attention and she loved it. He has that way about him. He could sell ice to Eskimos if he put his mind to it, and truth be told, they would be happy with their purchase."

Paul Rich, then Executive Vice President/CEO BBI Communications (1976–1982), writes:
"True to his word back on June 23, 1976, Bob asked me in 1976 to start thinking about getting in to the sales end of the business. The relationship between he and I solidified during the three years when I was in charge of not only public relations, but also marketing/promotions for the station. He had taught me a lot about the syndication business by including me in on deals he was doing with television syndication salesmen from companies such as Norman Lear's Tandem Communications, 20th Century Fox, etc. So, I began to pick up a lot of information about the business. Consequently, together in 1977, Bob and

I came up with the idea of creating our own syndication company whereby we would license the station's award-winning programs to other stations around the country. We cofounded BBI Communications, Inc., and I was placed in charge of running this new division of Boston Broadcasters, Inc., while still holding down the job as Vice President of Public Relations/ Promotions for the channel. It was the first time in the history of broadcasting that a local television station became the source of creating and producing syndicated programs, not only in the U.S. but on TV stations and networks around the world.

By this time, the station had built up immense credibility with viewers in New England, which was manifested in the ratings, press attention, and old-fashioned "buzz" everywhere you seemed to go in Boston. It was producing and gaining top ratings with primetime dramatic specials, the movie-of-the-week Summer Solstice *(Henry Fonda and Myrna Loy) on ABC Network and a sitcom created at the station and coproduced and codistributed with Norman Lear. The station literally steamrolled everything in its path—all competition locally in the ratings, awards, national press...all the while attracting the attention of the broadcast industry powers in New York and Los Angeles."*

WCVB Programming

WCVB WAS GROWING in revenue and our news and programming people were turning out some of the best, if not *the* best news and original programming around. It was time now to try some new things and we were not at a loss for ideas. It is interesting to note that other WCVB veterans include Bill O'Reilly of Fox News and Keith Olberman of MSNBC.

Before I get into the nuts and bolts of the WCVB-TV television programming schedules between 1972 and 1982, there are some very memorable programs that I believe helped shape the future of WCVB-TV.

The first program worthy of mention is *House Call*. Back then, we knew that medical information or lay medical information would be very helpful to the public, so we began looking for a doctor to host a medical program and we found Dr. Tim Johnson. Dr. John Knowles, a doctor at Massachusetts General and an original BBI shareholder, knew Tim Johnson and made the introduction. Richard Burdick, vice president of the station made the introductory call to Tim, who was fascinated with the idea of medical issues being presented on television. Tim had no formal training in television, like many others, but as soon as we placed him in front of a camera we knew we might have something magical with him.

House Call, in my opinion, was one of the most important programs that WCVB has done to date. We felt that as a television station with an obligation to the public, it was our duty to convey important medical information to our viewers. The show was on Monday through Friday and Tim usually had a specialist on each show from Mass General live for fifteen minutes. They would discuss all kinds of medical issues, and then at the end of the program, the audience would call in with questions about the program's subject matter. It was really a new programming concept. Nobody had ever done anything like this before. Needless to say, from the popularity of the show, Dr. Tim Johnson became a household name in New England. He became the family doctor for thousands of home viewers.

House Call was important to us because we realized that we were touching a nerve among viewers. This generated a great relationship between us and our viewers. The show was so successful that we expanded it by adding a Thursday night 7:30 to 8:00 program for about a year. We then started doing one-hour specials with Tim and we would run them in prime time, preempting ABC's network programming. Every one of those shows received nothing less than a 40 share. This new breakthrough in programming was so interesting that many in the broadcast industry started to wonder what exactly that station in Boston was doing with its programming lineup and how it was achieving such great success.

In my opinion, there was never anything more important on WCVB-TV than Tim Johnson's health program. It was so important to me that I told the senior people at ABC, including Freddy Silverman, that they should hire Tim Johnson for the ABC network. ABC took my advice and hired him. Tim did all kinds of health programming for them, including a once-a-month segment in their popular show, *Nightline*. ABC also had Tim on three nights a week with minute-and-a-half segments in news broadcasts. I went to J. Walter Thompson and convinced them to syndicate these three-minute medical pieces. They sold it all over the country and we got enough money back from that to pay us for all of our production expenses and then some.

Dr. Tim Johnson writes:

"When Bob and his team at WCVB-TV first approached me to do some medical segments, I was very intrigued. Of course, no one at that time knew how popular these segments would be and that I would someday make an actual career out of being a television doctor. I was a little nervous in front of the camera when we first started but I knew that getting out this important

medical information to viewers was of great importance. Bob Bennett was the first one to come up with the idea of medical segments on broadcast television. He saw something way back when that no one else did.

Medical doctors on television talking about life's diseases and the progress being made in medicine are commonplace today. But back then we were real television pioneers. We have Bob to thank for that. I do remember that when we first started our segments, there were no places in the halls of WCVB-TV where I could hide from people who were looking for me so they could ask me questions about their own health. I was happy to give them whatever thoughts I could."

The Great Trip to China

IN 1978, CASEY graduated from the University of Denver and Marjie and I were very proud of him. That same year, Marjie and I joined John Kluge and a host of television executives for a trip to China. I was asked to head up a delegation by the Chinese government to bring over high-ranking broadcast network executives from the U.S. The Chinese Government wanted to impress us with what they were doing in broadcasting and they were also interested in anything they could learn from us. I took with me senior executives from ABC, NBC, and PBS. We all went over on a junket and had a great time. Every time we traveled through a town, the local mayor would come out and meet us for a hand shaking ceremony. I remember we would all have to drink tea with the mayor from little teacups. We did have a chance to see the Great Wall and it was quite an experience.

Since all of the Chinese officials wanted to hear from the head of the delegation, I had to do most of the talking. I received word one day that the Vice-Premier wanted to meet with us in the Great Hall of the People. We didn't believe it at first and then I received a phone call saying, "Get down here quick. He wants to meet you right now." So we all went down to the Great Hall of the People and I thought it was because they just wanted to take our picture. We stood in an area outside of the hall and had our pictures taken and then we began to leave. Someone started shouting: "No, no, turn around and come in. He wants you to come in."

As we made our way into the Great Hall of the People, I pictured Richard Nixon in China talking with an interpreter at his side. As we walked in, I could see just how large and intimidating the room was. By the time we walked in to the center of the room, I was so nervous I couldn't think of my own name. What was I going to say to the Vice-Premier? I didn't have a speech prepared. And I knew all of the people who were with me were hoping they could have a crack at giving some kind of speech to him. We were invited to sit down after a moment of silence and then I was asked to get up and speak. I simply said the following: "This is the biggest moment of our lives, to be here in this beautiful country of yours. When we go home, people will ask us what is was that most impressed us during our trip to China. I think it would be nice if each of my colleagues were to ask a question of the Vice-Premier, so they will all be able to say that they spoke to the Vice-Premier in the Great Hall of the People."

I then introduced each person and asked them to ask their individual questions. We all had a great and memorable time.

Marjie Bennett writes:
"China was quite an experience. It was actually a very hard trip to make because the accommodations back then were not so great. The food was terrible. None of us really knew what we were eating. Everybody on the trip lost weight and one guy had his pants fall down on him because he couldn't hold them up anymore. One time we found a bottle of Coca Cola and we were all so excited. We even found ice cream once. As hard a trip as it was, it was very exciting. Bob and I returned years later and so much had changed for the better."

Ronald Reagan in My Office

IN 1979, RONALD Reagan was running for the presidency of the United States and he and his staff wanted to use my office after his segment on the *Good Day Show*, and after that he wanted to have an interview with the local paper. When I came in the next morning I saw that the door to my office was closed, so I waited until the door opened; and then I went in and was introduced to Mr. Reagan. We shook hands. I then said to him: "You know Governor, there hasn't been that much class sitting behind that desk since I left here last night." I thought I was trying to be light and funny but there was no reaction from him. I thought that was rather strange so I pressed on.

"You know, when I came here to Boston in 1972, the Board asked me what my politics were and I told them that I was a Ronald Reagan Republican and I can bet you I was one of the few Republicans around here at the time," I told him. Once again there was no reaction from him. No laugh. Nothing. I thought it was funny but I was very surprised at his blank face and lack of acknowledgement that I was talking and joking with him. I was now getting very uncomfortable but I was intent on walking out of there with something from Governor Reagan. So I pressed on once again.

"You know Governor, when I was a young man living in California in 1964, and you made your speech for Barry Goldwater, I was so intrigued with what you were saying that I had to pull over and concentrate on your message. Not only at that time did you sell me on Goldwater, but you made me a lifelong Ronald Reagan Republican." Once again I looked directly at him. No reaction. The only thing I could do at this point was thank him for coming and watch him walk out the door.

Later I walked over to his assistant and had a chat with him. "Gee, I seemed to have just struck out with Mr. Reagan. I can't understand it. I talked and joked with him but he never reacted to anything I said."

"Bob, don't take it personal," his staff person said. "First of all, it's very possible that he may not have even heard you. His hearing is not too good. But you know it could also be possible that he didn't like your stories."

I was in shock at what this person had just said to me. I looked at him in a funny kind of way and then said, "Yeah, that's possible...I guess."

"And it's also possible that for some reason, he just didn't like you."

Now I was devastated, but somehow I found a way to laugh it off.

When WCVB-TV originally went on the air in 1972, one of their mandates was that they would not sell political time, but rather they would give it away to candidates. Up until the time when Reagan came in, I was taking Sunday shows and afternoon shows and try-ing to figure ways to generate as much revenue as possible because the Board would not let me sell political time of any kind. Shortly after Reagan left my office that day, his people called up and wanted to buy time on the station for his campaign. I told them that we did not sell time to political groups and they told me that they would not accept that. They wanted to buy time and they were going to figure out a way to do it, so they went to the FCC and made a case that they needed to buy television to succeed in New Hampshire. And lo and behold, the FCC said that we could now go ahead and sell political time. So we opened our doors for political spots and the money was just pouring in. Any spot we had, they bought.

I would, some years later, run into Ronald Reagan again. Some-time around 1989, I received a call from his office and was invited to come over and meet him in his retirement office with Marjie. I was thrilled to go and Marjie and I went over to meet him. When we arrived, there were about twenty-five guards all around him. Mrs. Reagan wanted to keep his mind active so she was constantly invit-ing people over so he could talk and keep his mind going. While we were there, he got up from behind his desk and started showing us all of the pictures around his office. Each picture had a story that went with it and he would tell us that story. At that time, people knew very little about his Alzheimer's disease. Reagan was an eloquent tour guide and would show us a picture of him riding horses with the Queen of England, and then he would suddenly stop and say, "Where was I? What was I talking about?"

As we were going out, I said to him, "You know Mr. Reagan, Marjie and I were married at Forest Lawn Cemetery (and I knew that was where he was married to his first wife) and people would laugh at us all the time over the fact that we were married in a cemetery." He looked at me and said, "I was never married in Forest Lawn. Nancy and I were married in North Hollywood." I knew he had either forgotten his wedding with Jane Wyman, or didn't want to admit it.

A year later I was invited to play golf with him, but I chose not to because I heard that he would ride in his golf cart and say nothing to anyone all day. It was something that I just did not want to do.

Our Own Situation Comedy:
Park Street Under

IN 1980, WE went on the air with a situation comedy called *Park Street Under*. This was a first since no television station had ever produced a sitcom. The going price for off-network syndicated shows was outrageous, so we decided to see if we could produce one ourselves.

Park Street Under is a subway system stop in downtown Boston. The main character in the series was a bartender who was an ex-Boston Red Sox pitcher. There was a barmaid character and the stories would unfold as all of these characters sat around the bar drinking. *Park Street Under* aired on Monday nights at 7:30 and the critics said that it was as good as any situation comedy on any network, and it won the time period.

Not long thereafter, two people left ABC's program development department and went into the programming department at NBC. The following season, *Cheers* came out on the NBC program line up. *Cheers* was a program about an ex-baseball pitcher who worked in a bar in Boston. There was a lead barmaid character with a lot of different types of characters who sat at the bar and drank and told stories. Sound familiar? You would have thought they would have at least changed the ex-pitcher to an ex-football player, or changed the city from Boston to somewhere else, but they didn't and that sure made a lot of us at WCVB-TV very angry. I remember watching the pilot show of *Cheers* and was really shocked as to just how similar it was to our own *Park Street Under*. I wanted to sue and consulted with our attorney who told me that I could do it if I wanted to, but there was just enough changed throughout the show that it would make our legal battle difficult, long, and costly. In the end, I decided not to do it, but it sure put a bitter taste in my mouth.

Norman Lear Comes to Town

NORMAN LEAR CAME to town when we were honoring him at the New England Chapter of the Academy of Television Arts and Sciences. He was the main speaker and that evening he told me how much of a fan he was of WCVB. I then told him about a new show we were doing called *The Baxters*. The show was about a regular family that essentially had the same kind of problems that all typical American families face. The half hour segments dealt with problems of contemporary ethics and changing values. We would tape a show in front of a live audience and ask them to react to the subject matter. We wanted their opinions and then we would take that material and edit them into the show, which then made for what was probably one of the first interactive television shows ever.

Unlike most sitcoms of that time, *The Baxters* was left open-ended and the audience responded enthusiastically with their thoughts about each episode. Stations that carried the show across the country could choose between producing their own locally produced discussion sessions or presenting a national version of the segment. Our first season of *The Baxters* was produced at our studio in Needham and our second season the shows were produced in Toronto and Ontario.

I went into more detail about *The Baxters* with Norman and he told me that it was one of the best ideas he had ever heard. Next year we found ourselves in Los Angeles producing the series with Norman who was now our partner. He supervised the writing and producing and he played the host who surveyed the audience. Norman loved his role. We produced *The Baxters* for four seasons and

226

we tried to syndicate it, but unfortunately we were not able to sell it nationally. I can still say today that WCVB-TV was the first television station in the country to produce a sitcom.

Norman Lear, Television Executive, writes:
"I went nuts the first time I heard about The Baxters *and saw the show. I thought it was the best idea for a show I had heard in a long time. I loved the whole idea of presenting a specific family problem within the show, and then having a live audience react to it and discuss it in detail. The show was in essence giving the audience the opportunity to interact with the host and the cast. I loved it.*

When I was introduced to Bob Bennett, we started talking about the show and I told him that I thought The Baxters *would work on a national level. At the time we had* Mary Hartman, Mary Hartman *and* Fernwood *in production and I could place* The Baxters *into national syndication along with these shows. Bob and his people were interested and we then jointly produced the show, with production shifting to Los Angeles. When in national syndication, we found that the show did better in markets that had a good host, because the host was able to solicit a better question and answer segment as well as ignite more controversy around the issues. As is always the case, a good television host is key to the success of any kind of television program that is produced. I found Bob Bennett to be a first rate television executive and someone who was very excited and committed to* The Baxters. *To me, it's as good as a television idea can get."*

Our Own Movie: *Summer Solstice*

IN 1981, WE produced a movie called *Summer Solstice*. Once again, this was a first for a television station. Nobody had ever heard of a television station, especially one in the fifth largest market in the country, producing a movie. Our WCVB staff got to the point that they felt they could do anything. I kept encouraging them to come up with new ideas and one day one of them came to me and said, "Why don't we do a movie?" I said, "Alright, let's take a look at the idea." We came up with the idea of running a contest and asked people to send us their screenplays. We sent out a notice in the trade press saying that we would give $5,000 to the best original screenplay. The judges would be from universities in the Boston area. The only condition was that whoever sent in their scripts had to live in New England. We wanted a New England effort and we would try to make the movie if we felt it was worthwhile. Originally, we felt we might receive maybe two hundred scripts. To our great surprise, we received over seven hundred and fifty scripts. We sent the judges our top twenty choices. They then came back to us with their top five choices.

Summer Solstice is the longest day of the year and the movie script was about an older couple who dated and found themselves on the beach in New England. Over the course of their relationship, they cheated on one another, broke up, got back together again, and in the end, the woman ends up dying on the beach in his arms. It was a very beautiful and touching story.

At that time Henry Fonda was doing *On Golden Pond* in New Hampshire. I suggested we send the script of *Summer Solstice* up to

Fonda, so I had two guys from the station drive up to New Hampshire and hand deliver it to him.

We then called him to gauge his interest about acting in it. He told me he shouldn't even be doing the film he was doing now because he was so sick, but agreed to look at it since both of my guys had driven all the way to New Hampshire. "Call me tomorrow and I'll tell you my reaction," he told me. We called him the next day and said he was impressed with the script and that if we could get Myrna Loy to play opposite him, he would do it. I remember his last words on that telephone call were: "Don't ask me why I'll do it, but I'll do it." *Summer Solstice* was the last picture Henry Fonda made.

On the day filming began, I was on the beach sitting next to Fonda when the director called to strike the set. There was a great deal of yelling and screaming, with everyone hustling and bustling and picking up and moving things, that Fonda said to me, "What the hell is all that about?" I turned to him and out came the words, "I think that what you are seeing Mr. Fonda is enthusiasm." He looked at me and said, "You know something, you must be right. I haven't seen real enthusiasm in over fifty years."

ABC bought *Summer Solstice* from us, preempted a block of programming and ran it on the ABC network. It won the time period. We spent about $500,000 making it and sold it all over the world, breaking even in syndication, and it surpassed our expectations in revenue from foreign sales.

Highlights From Our Fall
1973 Program Schedule

HERE ARE SOME of the highlights from our fall 1973 Program Schedule:

- *A total of 161.3 hours of broadcast time per week, which was all but 6.7 hours out of the maximum possible.*
- *Broadcasted all night, five days a week.*
- *50.7 hours per week of locally produced programming, including news and repeats.*
- *37.5 hours per week of local news and original programming, not counting repeats.*
- *Produced special-interest programs directed to minorities, the elderly, consumers, children, the deaf, the unemployed, college students, and women.*
- *Aired eight locally produced shows in prime time, five shows Tuesday through Saturday, 7:30–8:00 p.m., and two shows Saturday and Sunday, 7:00–7:30 p.m.*
- *Produced a ninety-minute entertainment/educational show each week day morning, a sports magazine show, a medical show, Candlepin Bowling, a minorities program, a religious program, a New England institutions program, and a New England magazine program. Each of these shows was repeated in the five all-night periods.*
- *Produced 36 local news broadcasts per week, totaling 16 hours and 25 minutes; and in addition, produced a new-type*

show, The Investigators and You, Me, and Joe, a public affairs show.

- *Produced 35 specials totaling about 27 hours between September to August 1973, all of which appeared in the time period between 6:00–11:00 p.m. These specials added about 0.5 hours of local programming per week, bringing the total to about 51 hours per week with repeats and about 38 hours without.*
- *WCVB had the largest news staff with over 125 people, which made it the largest television news group in New England. We also had the most modern equipped studios and transmitting facilities in the nation and we were the first station to broadcast News for the Deaf.*
- *We editorialized on the important problems and issues that faced the Boston community under the guidance of a highly qualified Editorial Board and Editorial Writer.*
- *WCVB-TV was the only station in New England that had the capability to telecast live remote pickups daily. Using a modern PCP-90 video camera and a microwave link between the camera and the studios via Boston's Prudential Building, we had the capability to have incoming live, remote television which provided on-the-scene coverage of breaking news events throughout Greater Boston.*
- *WCVB was Boston's only locally owned television station that was dedicated to serving its communities with informative programs, entertainment, and sports through its own original locally produced programming and the programming of the ABC Television Network.*
- *We were the first local station to produce an "ABC After School Special" called The Cheats.*

Needless to say, the above was a lot of programming coming out of just one television station located in the fifth largest market in the country. By the Fall of 1974, we were broadcasting a total of about 163 hours per week, and without repeats of any kind, about 40 hours of locally produced programming each week—which was once again more than any other station in the country.

We produced the hard-hitting series, *The Investigators*, which probed current topical problems like flight safety at Logan Airport, fire safety in skyscrapers, and drug traffic. We broadcast several issue-oriented public programs such as *You, Me and Joe* and *Campaign '74/Briefing Session*. We were known as the station that produces informative and often controversial programs for groups with special societal concerns and problems. Our 1974 line up included *Third World*, a public affairs program directed at the needs of the minority community in Boston; *Aqui*, a Spanish language program produced by Latin Americans; *Your Place and Mine*, developed and produced by women for women; *Looking Around*, a program designed for the elderly, and *Opportunity Line*, a program that brought job opportunities to those who were out of work. We produced *Jabberwocky*, a locally produced program designed to expand six- to eleven-year-olds' perspective of themselves, which won many national awards including the National Association of Television Program Executives, Action for Children's Television and Hollywood Festival of World Television, and was carried in syndication by fifty television stations representing about 65% of the country's total television market.

In 1974, we produced a number of programs to meet the needs of a wide spectrum of people, *Good Morning*, a live locally produced ninety-minute program that featured information/variety issues and live remotes covering topics that were provocative, educational, stimulating, and substantive; *House Call*, a live program on information medical/health issues; *Five On Sports*, a live sport show that probed the unusual and headline sports happenings; *Music Makers*, a locally produced musical variety show; *New Heaven/New Earth*, celebrating the faiths, goals, and interests of the religious communities; *Outlook New England*, a locally produced public service program; *Screening Room*, a program that provided a showcase for a wide variety of mostly experimental programs that would otherwise have no television exposure; *Sound Off to Management*, in which management personnel would appear in round table format and answer questions from viewers; *Nightshift*, a late night program that offered the opportunity to six New England colleges and universities to present original television programs; *The Earth Works* and *Cozmics*, both science programs; and *Candlepin Bowling*, which was one of our highest rated locally-produced programs. This series consisted of nonprofessional bowlers bowling with candlestick pins, which are unique to New England.

In 1975, in our endeavor to continually be responsive to the problems, needs and interests of our viewers, we combined 23 regular locally produced programs (not including local newscasts), with the offerings of the ABC Network. Each month we produced at least two new specials averaging about 41 minutes in length. We became more committed to the idea that our programming should help our viewers. After some assessment of the problems in the New England Market, we identified the following ten as the most important issues facing our viewers and we directed our programming to it:

- *Consumerism: Inflation and the Cost of Living*
- *Crime and Corrections*
- *Economy and Unemployment*
- *Education and Youth*
- *Energy Crisis*
- *Government and Politics*
- *Health Care*
- *Poverty and Welfare*
- *Social Justice: Minorities, Elderly and Women*
- *Urban Development*

By 1975, we were producing 30 full news broadcasts per week. That year we broadcast two new series, *Briefing Session*, a program about issue-oriented public affairs, and *Sunday Open House*, about regular community issues.

In 1976, we produced 40 specials, and repeated 38 previously produced specials. We also produced a 17-part series called *The Boston Legacy*, that examined Boston's ethnic groups, focusing on their historical, social, and cultural contributions to the city. We produced editorials seven days per week that ran about one minute and thirty seconds in length. Our series *Five All Night*, in the 1:30 a.m. to 6:00 a.m. time frame, featured a ten-minute newscast, one or two recorded shows or a movie and two hours of repeats of WCVB-TV's locally produced programs, with the latest news headlined inserted.

We were the only all-night station in New England and our all night offerings were highly popular. It was estimated that the nightly audience varied between 10,000 and 30,000 homes, depending on the night of the week and the programming being shown. That was no small feat back then.

By 1977, we were broadcasting 163 hours per week, all but five hours short of continuous 24-hour operation. We were broadcasting 54 hours per week of locally produced programs, which included 19 hours a week of news, specials averaging about 45 hours per week; and 13 hours of late night programs. Without repeats, WCVB-TV was broadcasting about 42 hours of locally produced programming each week. We were still Boston's only locally owned television station. In 1977, we produced 32 news broadcasts per week plus about 30 news headline broadcasts in or between programs. In addition we carried six ABC Network full newscasts. We introduced a new series called *Sunday Open House*, that featured segments directed at such issues as education, nutrition, science, and technology. This series became nationally syndicated.

By 1978, without repeats, WCVB-TV broadcasted about 50 hours of locally produced programming each week. We produced 17 local programs that were produced either by the station's programming department or Public Affairs departments. It was recognized nationally that we were producing and airing more locally produced programming than any other network-affiliated station in the country. And we were still the only locally owned station in New England, which only intensified our dedication in serving the needs of our viewers with locally produced news, public affairs, and entertainment programs. We had sixty people working in our news department and now had a large technical unit for electronic newsgathering and live remote coverage of major news events.

We inaugurated a new series entitled *Checkpoint*, which appeared within the 6:00 newscast three nights a week. *Checkpoint* had several reporters presenting investigative feature-length pieces of single topics. These pieces kind of took on the form of mini-documentaries. We also maintained a separate investigative capability within our news department that worked independently on a day-to-day newsgathering and reporting system.

We produced *Park Street Under*, an experiment in local dramatic production that was set in a fictitious café under Boston's famed Park Street subway station. This weekly prime access series offered a satirical look at topical issues.

City Streets was introduced and appeared both biweekly in prime access and weekly on Sunday afternoon. This series was the successor to our long-running *Third World* program that focused on the area's Black, Asian American, and Native American communities.

We introduced *Miller's Court,* a show that probed and hypothesized legal issues with a studio audience. The series was hosted by Harvard Law School professor Arthur Miller and was intended to make the law more understandable to the layman and consumer.

That year, we also had scheduled syndicated series such as *Donahue, The Undersea World of Jacques Cousteau, Animals, Animals, Animals, Tarzan,* and *Lawrence Welk,* among others.

By the fall of 1980, we were now airing more than 60 hours a week of locally-produced programming. This number included 19 hours per week of news, specials that averaged about 75 minutes per week; 9 to 10 hours of original late night programming; along with hours of late night repeats of programs. Without repeats, our broadcast schedule totaled approximately 50 hours of local programming per week. As usual, WCVB-TV originated more locally produced programming than any other network affiliate in the country. We scheduled 30 local news broadcasts of varying lengths, plus about 30 news headlines that appeared in or between programs. In addition, we carried 10 ABC Network full newscasts, *ABC World News Tonight, Nightline, 20/20,* and ABC *Close-Up* documentaries.

By 1980, we were broadcasting 24 hours a day, and Tuesday through Saturday we aired *Five All Night,* in addition to such fare as movies and repeats. *Five All Night* continued to be very popular and offered unique program features such as celebrity visits, performances and informational segments. WCVB was without a doubt a powerhouse of programming.

WCVB was, and still is, a vital aid for charitable organizations by devoting airtime to telethons and fundraising efforts for such groups as The Muscular Dystrophy Association, United Cerebral Palsy, and The Children's Miracle Network.

When WCVB was at full steam, we produced 60 hours of local programming, which was about twice as much as any other ABC affiliate.

To have been able to have produced all this important programming on a continual basis, year in and year out, was truly an amazing feat. It is a testimony to all of the wonderful people who made WCVB-TV great.

Perhaps our first and most difficult challenge to overcome

was arousing interest for WCVB among advertising agencies that seemed to be, for the most part, populated by people who either had a family member or friend who once had worked at the *Herald Traveler*. We knocked on a lot of advertising doors but the reception we got always seemed to be rude and hostile.

We hired the advertising agency of Humphreys, Browning, and McDougal to represent us in the Boston community. We started with this agency and were doing fine with them for about a year, and then suddenly they began to tell us what prices they wanted to pay for advertising on WCVB. It seemed that one of their executives, the buyer for an automobile group, had asked us to submit avails for what we were selling. We were now an ABC affiliate, with a lot of young viewers, which meant we were skewing a very attractive demo for advertisers. The first year, to our surprise, the automobile dealer did not buy us at all. I gulped on that one. The following year, they requested our avails again and we submitted them. Soon thereafter they came back to us and told us at what price they would be willing to pay for our avails. Nobody had ever heard of an advertising agency telling a station what price they should charge. We refused to change anything and they refused to buy us. They wanted to set our pricing and we were not interested in that kind of an arrangement.

I called the agency and told them that that I wanted to meet with the owner and the people in the media department. I assumed somebody over there, probably in the media department, was holding a grudge against us. Something was certainly wrong and I was intent on getting to the bottom of it.

A meeting was set and I said to them in no uncertain terms the following: "Look, you do not set our prices. I set our prices. We have to be competitive in the market place. If we are not competitive we will not have a chance of succeeding. You cannot dictate to us what prices we will sell at. When you buy the *Boston Globe*, they have a price for a full-page ad. You either buy it or you don't. We have to raise our prices every year to stay competitive. Everybody out there adjusts to the market. We're cancelling our contract with you. We're not going to do business with you. You do not have to buy us, but you do not tell us what prices to charge." We walked away from it for six months and it probably cost us about seven hundred and fifty thousand dollars in lost revenue. About six months later, they started buying us and paying our prices. I had proved my point.

By the end of the second year, we were meeting just about all of the promises that BBI had made to the FCC. Around this time I began to realize that the BBI board was really not interested in the high profit that the station was generating, which came as a very big surprise to me. In some ways I don't think they actually believed we were making the kind of money that was coming in. I think they really wanted that FCC license so they could have a platform where they could do good things for the community. It was almost as though they looked at WCVB as a service to the community, and the money came second. Since I was a bottom line kind of guy, I really didn't fit in with them totally. I always thought a real big part of my job was to make that station profitable.

In those days, the FCC would judge every station by the percentage of local programming, the percentage of public affairs, and the percentage of news they were doing. Stations were judged nationally as to how they stood against other stations. They were not judged by quality, but by quantity. I am very proud to say that WCVB, for ten years in a row, was number one in the top three categories: the most news, the most public affairs, and the most local programming. It was an amazing feat.

My Strong Relationship with the BBI Board

MY RELATIONSHIP WITH the BBI Board continued on very good terms and it was always enormously satisfying to me. I never went to them with anything they didn't approve. In my own mind, I never wanted to fail them. They were terrific people and always very supportive. I have always judged myself by the bottom line and the quality of our programming. Still, whenever I would report to the board, they were never totally enthusiastic about all of the money we were making. WCVB's big money came at the end of the second year as our advertising revenues began to soar. I remember clearly that when we had started with ABC they were not a strong network. Two to three years into our ownership, ABC was picking up steam and we were really benefiting from it.

I never once felt that as a team we couldn't make WCVB the best television station in the country. That actually was my goal. I kept taking the pulse of our viewers and creating an atmosphere whereby our programming team could produce the best local programming in the country. I kept surrounding myself with highly creative and intelligent people and made sure that we always kept ideas in the air and challenges in front of us. As time went on, I kept getting more and more enthusiastic. We felt strongly that there wasn't anything we couldn't do.

Meeting with Leonard Goldenson

AROUND THIS TIME, I was in New York at a meeting with Leonard Goldenson, Chairman of the Board of ABC, Elton Rule, President of ABC, and Tony Thomopoulos, President of ABC Entertainment. Somehow, the subject came up about the high cost ABC was paying to produce situation comedies. The numbers were somewhere between seven hundred and fifty thousand dollars to one million dollars per episode. I told Leonard that we were doing a situation comedy in Boston for about fifty thousand dollars an episode. He was not aware of *Park Street Under*, and looked at me and said, "Bob, on the ABC network level, we're paying a great deal of money per episode." He couldn't believe it. He turned to Tony and said, "Tony, do you know what Bob is doing up in Boston? Would you see what and how he's doing it and Bob would you send me copies of that show?"

Needless to say, Tony was not happy about hearing this, since he now had to look at what a mere affiliate station was doing. I sent him several copies and about a week later he called me and said, "I like them, but I just want to tell you they're really not deserving of being on the ABC network level. But how are you doing them at that price?" I told him our budget break down and I never heard from him again. He never sent the shows back to me either.

CNN at this time was getting a lot of press, both positive and negative, and cable was starting to gain a foothold in homes across the country. The idea of twenty-four-hour news intrigued me, so one day I called Ted Turner and introduced myself.

"Ted you don't know me, but I heard about your CNN idea, and while I think you're crazy, I like what you're trying to do. However, I want to tell you something. Twenty-four hour news is going to be very difficult to pull off. You can't do live news from around the world. I just think it's an impossible thing to do. You're going to have to have over eight hundred people to pull something like that off. I've got a hundred and twenty five people running around in my news department just trying to produce three local newscasts a day."

"I think I can do it, Bob."

"I'll tell you what I'll do, Ted. If you ever get your CNN News idea off the ground I'll give you my six o'clock news every day for you to use. You won't have to have a New England base, since we'll supply you with that. The only thing you'll have to pay for is the upgrade of the talent."

"Well why would you do that?"

"Because I believe anybody as crazy as you can use a little help. I respect what you're doing and I want to help you. I happen to believe that a guy like you could use a few friends. I've tried to do a lot of crazy things in my time and I've always needed friends around me to help me. I want to be a friend and help you out."

"What do you want in return?"

"Simple. If you get CNN on the air, then the only thing I want is the exclusive rights to CNN in New England. I'll be willing to pay you something."

"Bob, you can have it for free."

"No, I don't want it for free. I just want to pay a reasonable price and to say that I'm buying CNN."

WCVB-TV is the First Station to Carry CNN

IN THE BOSTON papers, WCVB then announced that we had the ability now to cover any story anywhere in the world and we would be doing it live. We had CNN international, ABC national, and WCVB local, which made us the single most important source for news in New England. We sent Ted our six o'clock news. I then convinced Metromedia to join us, and they then came in with Los Angeles, Washington, D.C, and other markets. All of these things became very important to Ted. He was doing me a favor as well. Soon Ted Turner had seven out of the top ten markets helping him with news for CNN. He was thrilled. I was thrilled. He used whatever parts of our news he wanted and we in turn used whatever parts of CNN's broadcast we needed. Ted then decided to do *Headline News*, which added another dimension to all of the Metromedia stations.

That sealed our relationship, which became a wild one. I went down to Atlanta for the opening and it turned out to be good for me, because I could then say to the people in Boston that if there is anything going on in news anywhere in the world, we've got it covered with WCVB-TV, ABC News, and now CNN. ABC never said a word to me about it.

I soon received word that Reese Schonfeld, who worked with Ted Turner in the launching of CNN, had said that I was the bravest guy in the world to be the first one to take CNN.

Reese Schonfeld, Television and News Executive, writes:
"The first thing we needed at CNN was national distribution so I called three people I thought could help us, John Corporon, Bob Bennett, and Marty Haag. Corporon was the news director at WPIX New York, Bennett the General Manager of WCVB in Boston, and Haag the news director at WFAA. WPIX was the ITNA flagship station in New York. WCVB-TV and WFAA were ABC affiliates, and dominated news in their markets. Both stations had worked closely with ITNA. Each of them was very news smart. They understood that CNN would mean, among other things, a twenty-four-hour news services that they could tape or use live in their news programs. I offered them exclusive rights to CNN. They accepted immediately. Corporon, as an independent, had no problem publicly acknowledging his role as CNN's corresponding station. Haag wanted to keep it quiet. He was only a news director, not a General Manager. Bennett, who owned a piece of his station, could afford to be less discreet. When Advertising Age called to ask how CNN was going to get national coverage, I told the reporter about our corresponding stations, independents, and network affiliates. She believed independents might help us out, but not network affiliates. Not only was WCVB an ABC affiliate, but Bob Bennett was President of the ABC Network Affiliate Association. I suggested she call Bob.
*Bob told her that WCVB would indeed be a corresponding station. She asked, 'How can you do that? You're President of the ABC Affiliates.' Bob said, 'I can do that because ABC doesn't run my f---ing station.' The reporter printed the quote minus the 'f---ing,' and it was as if CNN had hung out a neon sign. Once Bob went public, other network affiliates were quick to follow."** *

(*Excerpt from his book, Ted and Me Against The World, *Reese Schonfeld)*

Over time, WCVB-TV turned out to be the pride and joy of ABC. One interesting story about Ted Turner is that when WCVB-TV first aired CNN, it was working out great for us. Turner was thrilled with his relationship with us. I called him and told him that I wanted to work out the same deal with the other Metromedia stations in Washington, New York, and Los Angeles. If I was able to pull this off, this would be a big deal for CNN. Fortunately, John Kluge thought it was a great idea too.

Sometime later, Westinghouse joined ABC in launching a new twenty-four-seven news network to be called the Satellite News Network to compete with CNN. John Kluge and Metromedia were invited to join them as partners. The Satellite News Network was designed to compete directly with CNN and CNN's *Headline News*. When John joined this new network, he thought that he was going to be an equal partner with them. They had other plans. When they had their press conference, John was invited and assumed that he was going to be a major part of it. To his surprise, up on the dais was seated Leonard Goldenson, among others, and there was no chair for John Kluge. He was not even invited up on the stage to speak. He was mad and so was I. With ABC and Westinghouse getting together, Ted Turner had reason to be nervous: a new competitor was being launched to compete with CNN. This was just about the time that I had come back to Metromedia and John was about to sell the company. John came to me and said, "We've got to cancel CNN, Bob."

I was very surprised he said that to me and my retort was: "I'm not going to do that John. I'm going to cancel ABC and Westinghouse."

"Why are you saying that, Bob?" he asked me.

"First of all, to embarrass you, John. You thought you were going to be a full partner and all they wanted was the right to be able to say that Metromedia was involved with them. From the beginning, John, they really didn't want you as a partner. They were using you to get into our markets. If we're going to cancel anyone it should be ABC and Westinghouse, not CNN."

In the meantime they had started their network and they were spending more money than they thought they were going to have to. Ted, in turn, also had to ramp up his spending to compete with them. Ted flew into Logan airport and then took a helicopter down to Cape Cod and landed on the beach, near where I have a summer place. He had with him Bob Wussler, Executive Vice President of CNN, and they arrived on my doorstep.

"Bob, we're here to ask you to please not cancel CNN."

"I have no plans to cancel CNN, Ted," I told him. "If I cancel the Westinghouse and ABC news network they will go under. They will not make it. It's a union issue. The unions in New York, Chicago, Los Angeles, and other markets we're in won't let their people do news for us and for someone else at the same time. If I do cancel them, I have to make sure that you will never take CNN from my station and that you won't increase the price.

"You've got a deal, Bob," he said as he enthusiastically shook my hand.

We cancelled ABC and Westinghouse and they backed off. They were already on the air and they just cancelled their news service. When I was back in Boston I announced that WCVB was keeping CNN. About a week later, ABC and Westinghouse dissolved their competitive twenty-four-hour news channel idea. I believe my decision to keep CNN had a lot to do with keeping it on the air.

Needless to say, this had cemented my relationship with Ted Turner, and then one day I received a call from Bob Wussler who told me that Ted wanted me to come down to Atlanta as his guest. Ted wants to recreate MGM as it was in 1939. He was infatuated with *Gone With the Wind*. I agreed to come down for the weekend. Wussler met me at the airport and we went over to the baseball stadium, watched a game, talked, and then went to the airport where we flew from Atlanta to South Carolina.

Ted's place was approximately 15,000 acres. There was a long driveway with trees on both sides that created a kind of tunnel effect, and at the end of tunnel he had recreated what seemed to me was Tara. You will remember the opening scene of the movie when Thomas Mitchell jumps over the fence. It looked exactly the same. It's been said by many that Ted Turner, in his own mind, thought he was Rhett Butler and that he had recreated what looked like Tara. We get to the end of the drive, Ted stopped the car, the dogs came running up jumping all over the place, and I looked up to see Hattie McDonald descending the stairs. I couldn't believe it. It was an exact look alike. I was near hysterics.

"What's so funny, Bob?" he asked me.

"Nothing, Ted. I'm just looking around. Beautiful place you have here."

Wussler and I exchanged glances. Ted had no sense of humor.

I was shown around and then I went to my room. We had dinner. Wussler was in the other room with Ted's wife, and Ted and I were alone. Ted was doing the most of the talking because he was trying to sell me on becoming Chairman of the Board of a company that wanted to recreate MGM in 1939. I did not want to do that. I told him I was a broadcaster, not a motion picture guy. "Get someone who understands that business Ted," I told him. "I don't trust anybody else Bob. I trust you," he said to me.

"Did you see my *Sixty Minutes* interview Bob?" he asked me.

I had seen it, but for some reason I told him that I hadn't, so we went into the other room and watched it. Before he put it on he put on *Gone With the Wind*, and we saw the tunnel effect of the trees with the house and Thomas Mitchell jumping over the fence and Ted turned to me and said, "What does that remind you of Bob?"

"Well, it looks like your place here, Ted."

"It does, doesn't it? Who do you see me as?"

"Ted, you're Ashley Wilkes, aren't you?"

Annoyed, he said to me: "No, Bob. No. I'm Rhett Butler." He turned away in disgust.

"But Ted, you don't look like Rhett at all," I told him.

In the other room I caught a glimpse of Bob Wussler who was holding his side as he was laughing.

A year or two went by and Ted wanted to go ahead with the MGM golden age idea, and he bought MGM from Kirk Kerkorian. Ted overpaid for it. All he really needed was the library, not the studio.

Reese Schonfeld writes:

"Bob came down to visit Ted Tuner at his plantation. I wasn't present, but the story comes directly from Bob. On the night of a visitor's arrival, Turner had the habit of asking his visitor to watch a tape of Gone With the Wind. *When he asked Bob to watch it, he agreed. Bob was silent until about ten minutes into the film, and then he said, "Ted, I know you must hear this all the time, but the resemblance is so amazing that I can't help myself. Every time he walks across the screen I think it's you. I wanna say, "Ted! Ted!" Bob paused, Ted beamed, and then Bob said, "Ted, you're...Ashley Wilkes!" All weekend long, Bob called Ted "Ashley." If Bob Bennett wasn't afraid to confront ABC, he certainly wasn't afraid to rib Ted Turner."**

(*Excerpt from his Book, Ted and Me Against the World, *by Reese Schonfeld)*

Leonard Goldenson Offers Me
the Job of President of ABC

ONE DAY, I received a call from Leonard Goldenson who told me that he wanted me to be President of ABC. Elton Rule was retiring. I told Elton that I was honored, but I wasn't quite ready to make a move. However, I'd be happy to explore the idea with him. Shortly thereafter, I was in a dinner meeting with Leonard and Elton in New York City.

"Leonard, in thinking about me for the position of President of ABC," I said to him, "I think there is something you should know about me first. If I take the job as President of ABC, the first thing I will do is fire Roone Arledge."

Elton almost fell off his chair. There had been some feuding in the past between him and Roone, so I could see he was in agreement with my idea. Roone also wanted Elton's job. Leonard was surprised about my statement, but he pressed on.

"Why would you want to fire Roone Arledge?" Leonard asked me.

"Well for one thing, it's my understanding that, if you ask Arledge to come to a meeting, he may or may not come at all. If he could fit it into his schedule, you might see him, maybe. I don't want that kind of a guy on my team. And in my opinion, he should never have bought baseball for ABC at a time when no one wants it."

I could see I had Leonard's full attention.

At this point, I think Goldenson was really confused and surprised. I told him that he better think about all of this before he hired me. We went along this way for another six months, but I never took the job.

Dick O'Leary writes:
"Back in the 70s, ABC and all of its fiefdom—Entertainment, News, Sports, ESPN, Cable Channels, Television stations, Radio stations and networks, scenic attractions, et al—were getting a little long in the tooth at the ABC Corporate level, which was that of Chairman/CEO and President/COO. I knew that Leonard Goldenson was looking around for a President of the company and the three logical contenders internally were Fred Silverman, Roone Arledge, and me. Leonard appeared to be looking for an entrepreneurial warrior type more so than someone who had been successful in the field or operators of television divisions. Corporate executives are best cast from those who have a substantial "Management" ingredient, and that was not Fred, Roone, or me. But Leonard Goldenson, Chairman & CEO, and Elton Rule, President and COO, knew Bob and had concluded that he, uniquely, had a Top Management quotient and that his makeup was historically as somewhat of a TV entrepreneur and warrior. I thought so as well.

Bob was offered the opportunity to come to ABC as President of Broadcasting, with the belief that someday he might become ABC Corporate President/COO and ultimately CEO of ABC. I wholeheartedly agreed. The discussions were of course confidential at the time, and no one else in the company except Goldenson and Rule were involved in talks with Bob. Bob did not accept the offer and I am sorry that he did not—not for my sake, because I was quietly considering retiring to Sunny California after a decade of life in the Big Apple, and the whole idea of being the equivalent of the "Joint Chiefs of Staff" never entered my mind. I preferred being on the line where I belonged, not in the corporate suites, which were foreign to me. But I sure would have loved to have Bob as my boss.

Years later, when Elton Rule retired, the subsequent corporate execs presided over the sharp decline of ABC's fortunes and were forced to sell the company to Cap Cities Television. As good of corporate managers as they were at Cap Cities, they were not able to totally stem the decline. ABC was then sold to Disney.

I am personally convinced that had Bob Bennett accepted the ABC offer, his leadership would have resulted in ABC owning Disney, if he had so chosen."

John Ross, Friend of Bob, writes:

"Bob Bennett and I have been close friends for over 50 years, during which time we have enjoyed many, many personal, social, and business encounters.

In early 1977, I was in Boston staying with Bob and Marjie, trying to solicit radio stations to carry a twenty-four hour Radiothon to benefit Leukemia Research and hoping to use Bob's contacts. During breakfast, Marjie suggested that maybe Bob could arrange some WCVB time for the Leukemia Society. Bob thought it was a good idea. He agreed to do it and offered to clear four hours on a Sunday. As a result of Marjie's idea, and the subsequent help of Bob, "4 Hours for Life," a special Televent, was eventually seen on over one hundred television stations during a ten-year period, raising over $50 million to help in the fight against Leukemia. He saw the opportunity to help and he rose to the task."

Time to Think About Selling WCVB

IN 1981, THE BBI Board started to think about selling WCVB. Many of them, who were around sixty-five years of age when we received the license, were now seventy-five and older and were starting to think about their estate planning needs. WCVB-TV was their biggest asset. I did not want to sell it at that time, but they asked me what I thought we might get for it if we sold it. I told them that my best guess was about two hundred million dollars. They were shocked and had to look me in the eye to see if I was joking. At the end of the meeting Bill Poorvu came up to me.

"Bob, can I make a suggestion to you?" he said. "You shouldn't throw around numbers like two hundred million dollars to the Board. You're scaring everybody. These guys think you've lost your mind. They all respect you, but don't you think you're two hundred million dollar number is a bit off the wall? Why are you even making up a number like that?"

"Because, Bill, I believe that's the price we can get for WCVB."

William J. Poorvu writes:
"At the request of many of our older directors who, by that time, had been with us for almost twenty years and wanted some liquidity, Bob and I were assigned to figure out a strategy to sell the station. We recommended a limited private search to the few broadcasters whom we thought were not only financially qualified, but who could be counted on to continue our commitment to local programming. At that point in time in the early 1980s, most people were still receiving their news from

broadcast television. We agreed that when we received what we considered to be an acceptable bid, we would bring it to the board for their approval."

Now Who Do I Know
Who Would Love to Buy WCVB-TV?

NOBODY REALLY SAW the value that was inherent in WCVB at the time. I felt that I did and I secretly knew who was looking for a station to buy. It was my old friend John Kluge, of course. His prior statement made some years back to me was still echoing in my mind: "Bob, if they ever make that station in Boston into something, I just want you to know that I'll be the first one in line to buy it." How could I ever forget those words?

I picked up the telephone and called John. I always wanted to have something that he really wanted and now I had that something: WCVB-TV. It was actually a good time to think about selling WCVB, since a lot of media companies were looking for stations to buy. Television stations were money machines. Anyone who had a good station was happy because it was most likely generating a lot of revenue. A station in Philadelphia had just sold for a record seventy million dollars. That was unheard of money back then. I felt that I knew the market as well or better than any other broadcaster—and I knew that our Boston station was unique and would command higher dollars.

Bill Poorvu and I contacted all of the groups looking for stations to buy and invited them to make a bid for WCVB. Bill and I met with each one of them. They would fly into Boston and we'd discuss the station and possible terms that might be acceptable. We gave them all a deadline for their bids. I then told John to be in Boston on the day that all of the final bids were due. He was very pleased to be a part of the bidding and asked me if he could be the last bidder. I told him yes, but I could not give him any special consideration. He checked into the Ritz Carlton Hotel and Bill and I met with him in the bar. In the meantime, we had received all of the bids. In the lobby, John was holding his piece of paper in his hands. I walked over to him.

"John, there's a lot of money going after this station," I said to him. "Don't come up short and miss out. If I'm not mistaken, it's going to take over two hundred million to make this work."

A Sheet of Paper with the Magic Number

JOHN LISTENED TO what I said, and then excused himself and walked out the front door of the hotel. He returned about three minutes later and handed me a sheet of paper. I opened it and read the number two hundred and twenty million. I showed it to Bill, who I could see was getting wobbly at the knees once he looked it over.

The deal was done. I had told the BBI board that we could get two hundred million for WCVB and we just sealed the deal for two hundred and twenty million dollars. But I must tell you, John Kluge was a very smart man. He was no fool. He later ended up doubling his money on the station when he sold it to Hearst.

William J. Poorvu writes:
"Bob and I decided on a sealed bid auction and after some discussions, the Day of Judgment came. In the end it had come down to three companies, all of whom had submitted to us their bids. One of them was John Kluge, who controlled Metromedia and was Bob's former boss. The one caveat we had with John was that he had asked to present his bid in person at the close of bidding. We met John at the Ritz Hotel, then on Arlington Street in Boston in the late afternoon. Bob and I sat on one side of the table with John opposite us. After some pleasantries, John offered us a cashier's check for $1 million and a handwritten bid for $220 million, which was at that time the highest price ever paid for a single station. He was the clear winner. I suddenly felt Bob's hand gripping my leg. Obviously, this was an emotional

*time for both of us. We somewhat casually, or what we thought
was casually, thanked John and told him he had won. I decided
as a gesture of confidence, or perhaps in a fit of euphoria, to
return the check by saying that his word was good enough for
us. Our lawyers could work out the formal agreements. The
meeting soon ended, and I limped off to meet my wife at a
Bastille Day party of which I have absolutely no memory. What
I do remember, however, is Bob's prediction that he made to me
several months earlier at the start of the bidding process—John
Kluge was our man."*

The BBI Board could not believe what they were hearing when Bill
and I returned to the station and told them.

"We just sold the station," I told them.

"For how much?" they asked.

"For two hundred and twenty million dollars," Bill and I said.

"How much did you just say?" they all asked incredulously.

The board was really at a loss for words. That much money? That
was impossible. All they ever really wanted to do was just give back
good television to the Boston community. They just got richer doing
it than they ever thought possible. The sale of WCVB for two hundred and twenty million dollars made television history and made
millionaires out of forty-five people. I was one of them. My own
gamble had paid off. I had hit my home run. The press went wild.
Two hundred and twenty million dollars for a television station was
unprecedented. Television history was made.

Paul Rich, Executive Vice President/CEO BBI Communications, Inc., writes:

*"Bob and I were together at the Ritz Carlton Hotel in Boston on
the night the station was formally sold. He and I were alone in the
bar reviewing the public relations impact of the announcement.
Boston had what Bob often termed a 'love affair' with Channel
5 (and the feeling was mutual). He and the other leaders of BBI
were concerned that a giant, national public company such as
Metromedia would disturb the relationship between the channel
and its viewers. Frankly, Metromedia was better known for its
commercial achievements in the industry and not so much for its
community relations, as was WCVB. I always believed that the*

key to the deal was Bob Bennett. Metromedia CEO John Kluge, who had followed Bob's career after he successfully resuscitated Metromedia's WNEW-TV in New York, seemed determined to recruit Bob to head his entertainment empire. At that time, Bob was in the top tier of broadcasting's power brokers. It seemed every network and major independent in America (including Ted Turner) was courting him to become their CEO.

As Bob and I chatted in the bar, the other principals in the deal were meeting elsewhere in the Ritz Carlton. It was late, and Bob was quite drained from the long day of discussions that took place. I had been summoned by Bob to attend this meeting at the last minute (so tight was the security); I had to use cocktail napkins to write down the procedures we should follow in making the announcement. We would write a draft news release that would be especially sensitive to the fact there would be no change in the station's commitment to local programming and the community, announce details of what the new ownership would mean to the staff, and simultaneously arrange a press conference the next morning at the station.

What struck me more than anything else during these critical few hours was that Bob and the Board made the final decision with such calmness, poise, and recall of details. In previous months, Bob had met regularly with other potential buyers, including ABC Network and Cap Cities Broadcasting—both of which he was not only very close to, but had also considered him as a candidate for a top executive position in their companies. So Bob was under considerable pressure to advise the Board on what was the better of the options—not only the purchase price, but also the effect of the channel's loyal viewers and the extraordinary staff and, curiously, the longer term. Bob had earlier in the year been talking with the Board about the possibility of the station becoming the flagship/centerpiece of a station group. In fact, I know that at the time there was a leading investment banker with offices in Boston and New York who said that with Bob's name alone, he could easily raise $1 billion to fund a group of five or six leading stations around the country."

After the euphoria wore off and everyone came down to earth, I realized that the staff was not happy about the sale and they came in to talk to me about it. They were upset that our WCVB family was being broken up and unsure about their jobs at the station under the new management. I assured them that I was going to be around and that I was going to stay with the station, even though it would be under a different title and position. John had offered me the job of President of Metromedia Broadcasting and I accepted. I did everything I could to calm the staff but I don't think they ever got over it, at least not in the early days of the transfer of ownership.

Riding My Bicycle Backwards

AROUND THIS TIME, I told the staff that I could ride a bicycle backwards and no one believed me. As a kid in Altoona, I had learned to ride a bike backwards. After much trying and lots of scratches and black and blues, I was one of about six proud kids in Altoona who could ride around town on his bicycle backwards. Once you know how to do it, I suppose you never forget something like that. So I used to joke around with the sales department that I could ride a bike backwards and no one believed me.

"I can ride a bike backwards," I would say as I walked through the different departments.

"Oh come on, Bob, you can't do that," they would say to me.

"No, I'm telling you, I can ride a bike backwards."

"I'll bet you fifty dollars you can't do it," was a challenge thrown out at me by one of our salesmen. This went on for months and I kept collecting bets until it was as high as $350. Everyone continued to egg me on, but I kept the bidding going until one day I announced: "Tomorrow is the day. I'm bringing my bike in and you will all be able to see me ride it backwards."

"Right, Bob. Sure thing. We can't wait," came the grumbling.

The following day, I brought a bike in and asked everyone to meet me in the back of the building at a designated time. The entire news department came out along with others and soon there were over a hundred people standing there ridiculing me. No one believed I could do it. It didn't matter. I knew I could. So I walked the bike around to the very back of the building where no one could see me, and waited out of sight for about three minutes. I knew they were all out there watching and waiting and hoping I'd make a fool out of myself. Then I drove out, backwards, just like I told them. Everyone was laughing, screaming, and applauding. I made a circle, turned around and made a big deal about collecting the money in front of them.

That evening, I was at home watching the end of our eleven o'clock newscast, and all of a sudden Natalie Jacobson said, "You may not have met our General Manager Bob Bennett, but he is quite a nice guy and for a long time has been claiming that he could ride a bicycle backwards. Of course, no one here at WCVB believed him. So we'd like you now to take a look."

And then all of a sudden they went to a video of me riding my bike backwards to the tune of "Rain Drops Keep Falling on My Head." They ended the news with me riding my bike into the distance. I had no idea that a camera had been rolling that day, and Marjie and I just sat there laughing.

Josh McGraw, Local Sales Manager, WCVB, writes:

"Everyone knew that Bob was a hustler. He was known as the Bobby Riggs of broadcasting and he would always play games with the sales department and challenge us in many different ways with little games such as tossing the rubber ball into the trash can to see who could get it in the most. He was always daring everyone and one day he got into a betting contest with Tony Palminteri, who at that time was one of WCVB's Account Executives. Bob was ahead and offered Tony a chance for double or nothing. Bob would turn his back and throw the ball over his shoulder. Tony took the bet. Bob won. Bob wanted to give Tony another opportunity to win his money back and asked Tony if he ever pitched quarters. Tony reminded Bob that he grew up in Queens, N.Y., and started pitching pennies when he was just a little boy. They began pitching pennies and once again Bob was beating Tony. Then Bob offered Tony a double or nothing bet that he could beat Tony by throwing the quarter off his shoulder without looking. Once again, Bob won. And Tony was fuming, so Bob now told Tony that he would like to bet him that he can ride a bike backwards. Tony looked at him like he was from another planet. Bob said that because the risk of serious injury to him was high, the stakes needed to be high. He

then challenged the whole sales team that he could ride a bike backwards and everyone began putting up money that he could pull this off. At what seemed like weeks of procrastination from Bob, he finally set the day that he would perform this miracle. Meanwhile, all of us thought that he was crazy.

By now, word of the backwards-bike-riding stunt had traveled through the station and everyone was aware of it, and the Good Day *show decided to carry the event live. Bob brought a bike on the designated day and rode it in the normal seated position, but seemed to be having some trouble keeping his balance. He then disappeared from view behind a building and about a minute later he reappeared riding the bike backwards. We were all astonished. But the story doesn't end here. About a month or so later, Bob came to the spring NEBA party and in front of a group, he bet Tony that he could walk the length of the rooftop pool on his hands right along the pool's edge. Tony was so psyched out and dispirited that he didn't take on the bet, and I didn't blame him."*

The Search for My Successor

WITH THE STATION now being sold, I had to find a successor. I had three people in mind. One was John Conomikes from the ABC station in Pittsburgh, who was a terrific guy; Ward Huey from Dallas with the ABC station there; and Joe Dimino, who was at the time with the Storer station in Cleveland. All three of these executives were fabulous broadcasters. John had worked at the ABC station for almost his entire professional career. He was working under a person who was not going to retire for about another year when I offered him the job. He accepted and then went back to the Board to tell them he was going to resign. They told him he wasn't going anywhere and then quickly moved his boss out and put him right in as the President of Hearst Broadcasting. This was a great deal for John and a big loss for me.

I then went to Ward Huey who was in a similar situation, working for a person who had been there for years. Ward was waiting for him to retire. He accepted my job offer and then went back to resign. They told him, "No way." They moved the other guy out and put Ward in his place.

Joe Dimino was a very strong contender in my mind for the position, but logistics did not work out. Joe is one of the most talented and creative television executives I have ever met. To this day, he and I have remained very close friends, stay in contact on a frequent basis, and see one another just about every summer on Cape Cod.

John Conomikes, friend, writes:
"Bob and I first met in 1975 in California at an ABC Board of

Governors meeting. We had dinner together and soon realized that our pasts were very similar: we both grew up in Pittsburgh, both our parents had moved away from Pittsburgh, we both went to Taylor Alderdice School, and we both went to Staunton Military Academy—Bob being five years ahead of me. We also shared similar likes and dislikes on a number of things. What are the odds of being at a dinner with a complete stranger and finding that his background is just about identical to yours?

When Bob was going back to Metromedia after the sale of WCVB, Bob wanted me to run the Metromedia TV stations, but for personal reasons I turned the job down. Hearst ended up buying WCVB-TV in 1984.

To me, Bob is the ultimate local television executive. He loves the business and somehow he found a way to do a tremendous amount of local programming and news that touched a strong nerve with his viewers. Everything he did was successful. He's a very bright guy who has always wanted to do the right thing for the station and for the community. He's feisty, competitive, honest, and fair, but he can be tough. If I was ever in a foxhole in the middle of a battle, I would want him in there with me. People said he was out of his mind to do the program Chronicle, *but he proved them wrong. In television, no one has done it the way he has."*

I thought now that since WCVB was going to be a Metromedia station, maybe someone who knew his way around Metromedia might be a good candidate. I suddenly thought of Jim Coppersmith. Jim had been a general manager at WNAC in Boston and was now President of Hubbard Broadcasting. He was well liked, well respected and he was an ex-Metromedia guy. Jim had run WNEW in New York, and was one of the sales managers in New York and LA. He had a lot of real television experience and I thought he would be the ideal guy. He had a great sense of humor and was always very professional. He knew the Boston market and he knew Metromedia. I chose him as the GM for WCVB and it worked out very well. I am very happy that I am still great friends with Jim today.

Jim Coppersmith, President & GM of WCVB-TV (1982-1994), writes:

"Working with Bob Bennett on a daily basis was interesting, exciting, and an adventure in an amalgam of work, joy, and competitiveness like I have never seen before. There was always a two-way loyalty between us and there never was an ounce of phoniness. He gave you loyalty and he expected it back in the same full measure. He once said to me, 'If I have to choose between loyalty and talent in someone I am hiring, I will go with loyalty every time.' Bob has Bill Clinton's charisma and Ronald Reagan's ethics. His sense of humor is great and his ethics are impeccable. He is a Master Salesman, a gifted leader, and an executive par excellence. He has the rare ability of making a person feel that he or she is truly important to him and that is simply because everyone is important to him. It does not matter if you are the hall porter or the President of the United States. Everyone is looked in the eyes, listened to, appreciated, and recognized; he is very generous in that regard.

Bob is to local television what Bill Paley, David Sarnoff, and Leonard Goldenson were to Network Television and what Ted Turner is to cable television. When he handed over the reins of WCVB-TV to me in Boston, the station was broadcasting over fifty hours a week of local programming—news, sports, children's shows, sitcoms, magazine shows, a made for television movie for the ABC Network, the Boston Marathon, After School Specials, legal shows, medical shows, and specials on every conceivable subject. We were rebels. We once preempted a World Series game to spend the night covering a hotly contested Boston Mayoral Race. We drove ABC crazy, but we always asked ourselves, What would Bob do? *And we tried to do it.*

Many people have said that while I ran WCVB, I was always in Bob's shadow. That was partly true because I chose to believe, as did many others, that he was my inspiration. He was and is my true friend and will always be my true friend. He did cast a very long and important shadow. He was a legend back then, and the success he made of WCVB cast his shadow out for miles. Bob spread a lot of sunshine."

We soon realized that as the new General Manager, it was not going to be an easy job for him to run WCVB his way, since the old General Manager, me, was still around. I offered him whatever advice I

could and he was a hands-on excellent station manager. As I think
about it now, I was having my own set of problems at this time,
dealing with the idea of adjusting to the fact that WCVB was no
longer my baby. I still had control of it under my new title at Metromedia, but it was no longer day-to-day. I soon realized that I really
loved running a television station more than running a group of
television stations. From that standpoint, it was a bit difficult for
me to accept. But I was very proud of what we had done at WCVB
and to this day have never stopped talking about our accomplishments. WCVB was an unusual situation. We had the odds stacked
up against us when we started and we achieved far in excess of what
anyone of us had ever dreamed.

For the people who had been with WCVB and were now working
for Metromedia, there was a lot of uncertainty and in some cases,
bitterness. They had lost their station to a big entertainment media
conglomerate and here I was, still sitting in there with them. Some
thought the excitement we once knew was now gone. It took a while
for that feeling to end and for a new camaraderie to be established
at the station.

Around this time, Marjie and I bought a condominium in the
Ritz Tower in Boston, right next to the Public Gardens. We loved
it. It was within walking distance to just about everything and we
moved in with great enthusiasm.

Now I had a new job, President of Metromedia Broadcasting
Group.

Honorable Bruce Selya, a friend, writes:

*"I first met Bob over thirty years ago when I was a practicing
lawyer and he was at the zenith of his career, moving from
WCVB to Metromedia. We had an immediate affinity because
both of us were highly competitive, but not much for pomp and
ceremony. Bob is the sort of fellow that in his leisure prefers
jogging suits to more fashionable gear. We spent a good deal
of time walking, talking, and critiquing current events back
then. We also became doubles partners in tennis. Neither one
of us was a very good player, but it didn't take me too long
to understand that Bob hated to lose at anything. Our most
frequent opponents were two fellows our age who were much
more proficient at tennis than we were. But they rarely beat us*

because Bob was so fiercely competitive and fearful of losing that we would eventually take over each match—I must admit, with some goading from me.

Our friendship continued when I became a Federal Judge in 1982. Bob was, at that time, particularly fascinated by a string of organized crime cases that I was called upon to handle. I could regale him for hours on end with stories of the Mafia and la Cosa Nostra, and he in turn would regale me with stories of show business. Bob was fascinated with a mobster by the name of Frank "Bobo" Marrapese. I believe that the most appreciated gift I ever gave him was a mug shot of Bobo, which he displayed in his office for several years. Bob was always a fascinating character to me in terms of the fact that he was like the lantern around which the moths circle. People from the entertainment world frequently came to our remote corner of Cape Cod, where my family and Bob's family have summer places, to pay homage to Bob and his wife Marjie.

Bob was instrumental as a friend in helping to guide me through two very serious times in my life. The first was when I received a diagnosis that I had a series of progressive eye diseases that would eventually impair my vision to a very great extent. It's difficult to imagine who among your friends you can bring yourself to talk to about such a critical lifecycle event as the threatened loss of vision. Though I have been blessed with many friends, I found that Bob was someone with whom I could discuss the subject frankly and honestly. Bob would not allow me to feel sorry for myself. His attitude was comprised of two components: first, that I should never forget how fortunate I had been to have had useful vision for long enough in my life to accomplish what I had accomplished, and secondly; as long as ways existed to defy or circumvent this impairment, that he was confident that I would have the will to find those ways. That was very good advice and strong counsel. I have found that although my vision did get as bad as was forecasted, perhaps even worse, I am still able to work productively, and I think my overall attitude is good. I do not feel the least bit sorry for myself. That is due in part to Bob and to other friends like him who have helped to keep me on the straight and narrow.

The second instance where Bob has had a profound influence on *my life, and in this case, may have actually saved it, began one time when Bob and I were out for one of our usual walks near his home in Newport Beach. We were walking across a bridge and I mentioned to him that I was having mild gastrointestinal problems. He noted that I seemed to be breathing rather heavily and he didn't like my pale color. He asked me if I had seen a doctor about the problem. I told him that I had not. He made me promise that before I left California, in fact immediately, I would call my doctor in Rhode Island and schedule an appointment for when I returned. When I arrived back in Rhode Island, I went to see my GI and he promptly called in a cardiologist. Within a few days, I was undergoing open-heart surgery. I have only Bob to thank for his perspicacity and refusal to take no for an answer. He made me make that phone call and I received immediate medical care, luckily before any cardiac event had occurred. Now, thirteen years later, I can honestly say that the walk with Bob was one of the most fortuitous events that occurred in my life."*

Back at Metromedia Again

My Two Conditions to Taking the Job

PRIOR TO MY accepting the job as President of Metromedia Broadcasting, I told John Kluge that there were two conditions that would have to be placed in my contract in order for me to sign on: (1) that I be able to stay in Boston and (2) that I would be the spokesperson for Metromedia. He agreed to both. I didn't want to go to New York because John had a reputation of riding his New York people really hard. I did not want to be in the position of fielding 5 a.m. telephone calls from John Kluge every morning. One Metromedia executive actually dropped dead at a train station from stress.

Part of my new job description was that of being the spokesman for Metromedia. John was not a good public speaker and did not have a great relationship with the press. He was hoping that I would step in and court them.

In 1982 and 1983, as President of Metromedia Broadcasting, I was in New York often for Board meetings and frequently met with sales reps and made calls with them when needed. I also spent time with John in his office, going over Metromedia's strategy.

In 1982, John Kluge was married in St. Patrick's Cathedral on Fifth Avenue in New York City, and it was a big affair with white ties and tails for the men. At this time John was, according to *Forbes Magazine*, the wealthiest man in America. Over one hundred people were invited, and as we were getting out of the limousines outside of the church the day of the wedding, our fancy formal clothes attracted a lot of attention. In no time at all there were about five hundred people who came in off the street to see who the celebrity was who was getting married.

The Cardinal conducted the ceremony and I remember saying to John that day: "John, if you are married by the Cardinal in St. Patrick's Cathedral, believe me, 'you are married.' Make sure you read my lips: M.A.R.R.I.E.D. Don't even think about getting divorced. Ever!"

Ironically, John did get divorced some time later. However, not long after his wedding, he and his wife were looking to adopt a baby. I remember saying to him: "John, every kid who is up for adoption should be saying to you, "Pick me! Pick me!"

He did adopt a boy and there were three Godfathers in attendance: Frank Sinatra, the King of Greece or Yugoslavia (I don't remember exactly if it was the King of Greece), and me.

While still based in Boston, Paul Rich and I were commuting back and forth to Los Angeles where we were doing a lot of new production. In addition to my duties as President of Metromedia Broadcast Group, I was also Chairman of Metromedia's New Program Group. At this time Kelly had graduated from Boston College and was now working at the William Morris Agency in Los Angeles. Casey finished up his last year at the University of Denver and then moved out to California. He worked at various production companies shooting advertising for ad agencies, and then together we started Bennett Productions in Los Alamitos, Ca. Marjie and I rented a condominium in Sierra Towers on Sunset Boulevard that was owned by the owner of Mann's Theatre. Sometime thereafter, we moved to the Diplomat condominium on Westwood Blvd.

Paul Rich, Executive vice President/CEO of BBI Communications, Inc., writes:
"The idea of moving to California had been talked about for several months in late 1984, with everyone at the station. The order then came down from Metromedia headquarters just before Christmas of 1984 that I would have to move to Los Angeles. Up to this point, Bob was trying his best to build Metromedia East in order to keep Boston as the company's headquarters, and had been commuting on a regular basis between offices in Boston and Los Angeles, since by that time BBI Communications had morphed into Metromedia Producers

under the chairmanship of Bob's longtime friend Chuck Young, former head of Metromedia's KTTV-TV L.A. I had gone from licensing worldwide the Channel 5 shows such as House Call with Dr. Tim Johnson, Update on Law with Harvard Law School Professor Arthur Miller, The Baxters, This Is America and various primetime specials, to now selling network blockbusters such as Dynasty, Charlie's Angels, Starsky & Hutch, and others. Quite a leap, to say the least. I thank Bob for that. He often said to me: "Reach for more than you can grasp... and you'll be okay." This was a scary reach for me. But with his strong backing and confidence I somehow managed.

Meanwhile, in Boston, Bob had ordered the construction of a new state-of-the-art sound stage that was capable of attracting well-known TV producers and expanding WCVB's commitment to local programs. In fact, Marcy Carsey, formerly a resident of Weymouth, MA, who had been a friend of mine since her days dating back to the creation of Mork & Mindy and other hit sitcoms on ABC, was then in the formative stage of developing The Bill Cosby Show with her own production company. She was looking for a financial partner and studio where she could shoot the series either in Boston or New York to accommodate Cosby's commute from his home in central Massachusetts. She thought long and hard about using WCVB's new facility, but ultimately Cosby preferred a studio in New York City, and of course, he, Marcy, and her partner Tom Werner went on to NBC network fame and fortune.

These were very exciting times and in many ways fraught with emotion and challenges. Just before my move to Los Angeles, my wife Dolly and I just finished building our "dream house"—a five bedroom French Country home just a few minutes away from WCVB. So when I told her on Christmas Eve 1984, that we had to make a final decision that week, we faced the dilemma of leaving the only place where we had ever lived to move to completely new environs. We were, however, comforted with Bob's support and knowing that he and Marjie would also be moving west, and we began to warm up to the idea. We moved in 1985, and our children transferred to LA schools.

Six months later, to everyone's surprise, we learned that John Kluge sold the company to Rupert Murdoch. It took me a year to find another job, this time as head of the television division at the Dino DeLaurentis Company, DEG. I am happy to say we never looked back nor regretted the move. Today, Bob and I are close and still work together."

Rona Barrett writes:
"I started at KABC in 1966, and, in 1968, went on all Channel 5 owned and operated stations. In 1969, I became the first syndicated entertainment columnist for Metromedia appearing on all their owned and operated stations plus an additional 100 other stations across the country. In 1974, I did the first one-hour special starring four of America's hottest female personalities for CBS, and in 1975, started Good Morning America. Bob was the General Manager of many of the stations which carried my specials when they were syndicated, and the most important thing that I can say about him is that he was never afraid to stand up for women's rights. He was one of less than a handful of television executives who understood what I was attempting to do in bringing entertainment news to television. He supported me and congratulated me every inch of the way up my ladder of success.

When my first TV special for CBS aired on the network and eventually went to syndication, Bob was the first executive to buy my special for his station. I never worried about being myself when I sat across a table from him. I always knew that if I asked Bob Bennett a question, he would never mislead me. We became very good friends way back in the late '60s and have remained friends all these years. He was one of the best television executives and leaders in an industry that no longer rewards people for good work and loyalty."

The new Metromedia address was at Sunset and Van Ness in Los Angeles, which ironically was the building I had started my television career in. In many ways it was like going home for me. Paul and I continued doing new production and strengthened our syndication business. Paul was now Executive Vice President in charge of World Wide Distribution. One of the first programs we did in syndication at the time was the *Rona Barrett Show*.

Bob Wood, former president of CBS, who was very well respected and an old friend of mine, was at this time running Metromedia's Producer's Group (MPG). When I came out to Los Angeles, Wood had already hired about twenty-five producers who, for the most part, were working out of their homes. Most of these producers, I came to find out, had never sold anything for Metromedia. I was not happy about this. They were a drag on Metromedia.

Kluge thought highly of Bob Wood because Bob was one of the most respected broadcasters in the business. Unfortunately, I was going to have to fire him. Wood was making about $250,000 a year and was housed at our Van Ness address. When I worked at that building for KTTV way back when, he was already a salesman with some years ahead of me in experience. Bob and I went back that far.

Just prior to my arrival in Los Angeles, Bob and his team had gone to a National Association of Television Program Executives (NATPE) conference, armed with six game shows to sell. Unfortunately, they came back with no sales. That was unacceptable. I guess these salesmen could not sell. I had no choice but to fire him and to reduce the size of the producer sales force. Bob had been spending a fortune on projects that weren't working. After making my case about Wood strong enough to John, he knew it was time for Bob Wood to go.

After our conversation he turned to me and said: "I want you to fire Bob Wood."

"Why don't you do it yourself, John?"

"No, I want you to do it."

John hated firing anyone. He always wanted someone else to handle the details. I knew I was going to be the one to fire Bob. I was actually looking forward to it. It was time to clean up a lot of dead weight.

I was also faced with a unique situation with a man named John Mitchell, who was at that time, the President of the Academy of Television Arts and Sciences. Mitchell was working for Metromedia as a consultant to the tune of about $300,000 a year. His sole job seemed to be to make sure that when John Kluge came out to Los Angeles from New York, he had a celebrity to dine with. Mitchell knew a lot of celebrities and John Kluge liked to be around celebrities. I didn't like Mitchell for a lot of reasons and he did not like me.

As President of Metromedia Broadcasting, I had the responsibility of managing the seven television stations and thirteen radio stations, as well as the Metromedia Producers Corporation, which was our major producing group.

The Idea of a Fourth Network

WE WERE EXPLORING the idea of establishing ourselves as the Fourth Network. In many ways we were really the same as the other networks in so much that we had top coverage across the country and we would soon be making our own original programming. I felt strongly that we should be considered as a strong media buy for advertisers. Metromedia had seven stations in the top ten markets and we should have been a strong consideration by advertisers when their media plans were laid out.

I wanted advertisers to consider us a real buy so I wrote a letter to the Chairman of Proctor & Gamble selling him on the many reasons P&G should buy us. It turned out that John Mitchell was also a consultant to them at the time, and ironically, was in the office of the Chairman on the very day the CEO of P&G received my letter. I was told later that the conversation went something like this: "John, aren't you a consultant to Metromedia?" the Chairman asked.

"Yes, I am," Mitchell responded.

"Well, I just received a letter from Bob Bennett telling me all of the reasons we should be advertising with his organization. What's your opinion on this?"

"Don't pay any attention to Bob Bennett. He doesn't know what he's doing. He's a jerk."

What John Mitchell did not know at the time of this conversation was that a friend of mine was in the room and reported to me later what Mitchell had said.

I was mad and I immediately went to John Kluge.

"John, I want to get rid of Mitchell."

"Why, what's wrong?"

"This is really the very first time that Mitchell could really help us, and instead he chose to hurt us."

I explained to John what happened at the meeting with P&G's Chairman.

"Fire him," Kluge barked at me. "Get rid of him!"

I couldn't wait to fire Mitchell, so I called him up immediately.

"Come on over to my office, John. I want to meet with you."

"Why, what's up, Bob?" he asked.

"Just come on over. We need to talk."

Mitchell came to my office for the meeting.

"I just want to tell you, John, this is going to be a short meeting. Your services are no longer required here. You're fired!"

"Did you talk to Kluge about this?" he asked me defiantly.

"Yes, I did."

"Then who's making this decision?"

"I am, and I'm happy to be making it."

Mitchell went out the door and I never saw him again.

The next confrontation that came my way was that of Silverback and Lazarus, which was the group that handled all of the foreign syndication of Metromedia Producers Group programming. Their office was in Los Angeles and their sales were a very big disappointment to us. They were known for spending big dollars on lavish parties that seemed to produce little or no results. They would go over to the Cannes Film Festival and throw the biggest parties possible. I decided on my own, that they should go, so I fired them. I think they knew it was coming. I fired them and then a few days later I read in *Variety* a lead article that stated, "Silverback and Lazarus sue Bob Bennett for one hundred million dollars." I said to John Kluge: "I hope you're going to help me on this John, because I can't handle a hundred million dollars."

John was, as usual, very supportive of everything I ever wanted to do. He never questioned me or doubted me. I was very fortunate to have a man like him around me. I always felt that the two of us made a great team.

Issues with *The Merv Griffin Show*

THE MERV GRIFFIN *Show* was running 9 to 10 p.m., preceding the news on all of the Metromedia stations. Merv had been around a long time and as far as I was concerned, he was one of the best interviewers in the business. For many reasons a show's ratings can fall, and Merv's show was having problems. As his ratings fell, this had an adverse effect on the lead into my news. The news to me was critical so I could not stand by and just watch the problem evolve. I had to fix it so I decided that I was going to take Merv out of primetime and put him some place else. Al Krivin was very involved with Merv, and after his retirement from Metromedia, he became a consultant to Merv Griffin Productions. However, before Al retired, he gave Merv a five-year renewal in prime time for five years. When confronted by this renewal, I said, "No way. That is not going to happen." So I contacted their office and the storm that came back was unbelievable. It was just like a hurricane. They were hurling every reason and excuse (and insult) they could think of at me. "You can't do this; and you can't do that and remember Bob, Al Krivin signed the contract so that's the way we're going to do it. Everything stays the same!" Things turned very nasty.

I told them, "I don't care who signed the contract; it's killing me in primetime and it's bringing down the beginning of our news cast." This caused a series of meetings, so I went over by myself to Griffin's office for a meeting and there were the chairman of the board of William Morris and Krivin, and on the phone was Melvin Belli who was representing Merv.

When I got there they were adamant and so was I. I told them,

"I'm sorry, but I can't do this anymore. I'll put you on a five o'clock and you'll get as big a number there as you will at nine because the competition is weaker. Trust me on this."

"We can't get celebrities on at five o'clock," they barked back at me.

I stood my ground and told them, "You'll get celebrities any time you ask them to come."

It turned out to be a screaming match between us. I told them that this was the way it was going to be and I left. I then moved the show to five o'clock and the show doubled its ratings and he got every celebrity he ever wanted on the show. This was a parting shot from Al Krivin to me, only I wasn't going to stand for it. It was a nightmare for me but I did it. Ironically, after that incident I became close friends with the head of the William Morris Agency who was in the meeting and who thought I handled myself very well. We made it a point back then to have lunch on a regular basis and to exchange ideas.

In 1983, I was in Hawaii finishing up on a round of ABC affiliate meetings. At that time I was the Chairman of the ABC Board of Affiliates and I was going to extend the Hawaii trip to enjoy more vacation time with my family. I suddenly received a call from John Kluge.

"Bob, get back here as fast as you can."

"Why John, what's the rush?"

"I'm sending a plane for you. Just get on it and get back here right away," he barked into the phone.

I could see something important was up but I had no clue as to what. I boarded the plane and flew back to New York City and walked right into his office.

"John, what the hell is so important that I had to drop everything and come here?"

"Somebody bought the company."

"Who bought the company?" I asked him, holding back the surprise in my voice.

"We did," John said.

"We did? Who *is* we?"

"Me, Stuart Subotnick, George Duncan, and you."

"Really? And what did we pay for it?"

"$1.3 billion," he said with ice in his eyes.

I almost fell off my chair. I looked at him and said, "John, I don't know how to tell you this, but I can't come up with my end of the deal."

John then told me we were going to go out and sell Metromedia to investors. Drexel Burnham were our investment bankers and soon we were on the road with them doing the road show. Occasionally, John would come out with us, but mostly it was Stuart Subotnick, a guy from Drexel, and me. Stuart Subotnick is a very talented and gifted business executive and a very warm individual. I always enjoyed discussing ideas with him and I really enjoyed our time together on the road. When John would join us, he would introduce me, and I would tell our audience all about the history of Metromedia. I would explain to them how we were going to use the success of WCVB-TV as an example of the success we were planning to have in the future. In essence, we were going to use the WCVB-TV success formula with all of our other stations.

Stuart Subotnick, then CFO, Metromedia, Inc., writes:

"Prior to Bob's return to Metromedia in 1982, I primarily knew him by reputation. He was known as a very likable leader who understood the TV business, was creative, smart, loyal, and approached problems with oftentimes unique solutions. I also knew that John had great respect for him and felt that his move to Boston was a negative for Metromedia, but a very positive move for his future in the TV business.

In 1982, John was the CEO and George Duncan viewed himself as the Company's Number 2 Executive, although TV and production and outdoor reported directly to John. In 1982, John was informed that WCVB would be sold to the highest bidder. John knew the bidding would be tough, but was determined to acquire another Channel 5 in a major market. He asked our Legal Department to prepare a bid and leave the offering price blank for him to fill in. He went to Boston hoping to get a read from the sellers, to determine our ultimate bid. Although the indications were that the number had to be at least $200 million, to be sure, he wrote a bid for $220 million and won the station. In fact, it was Cap Cities, who underbid in the mid-$190-million range. John was thrilled to succeed in acquiring WCVB. John was likewise excited to be able to work with Bob

Bennett again.

The problem that now faced John was how to bring Bob back into the Company and deal with George Duncan's operational expectations. John's answer was to create an Office of the President, which included himself, Bob Bennett, George Duncan and a CFO (me). His intent, which succeeded, was to keep the operational leaders off balance as to who would succeed him.

Bob, who did not focus on politics, was extraordinarily successful under this arrangement. Bob not only brought the TV and production operations to new heights, but also began to lay the foundation for his ultimate dream, the creation of a fourth network.

During this almost three-year period, Bob was always under pressure from George, who resented the new competitor. Bob would often question the motives behind certain statements made by George. Bob couldn't care less about politics. His focus was on creating the best TV and production group in the country and, again, the fourth network.

In 1984, the four of us, as equity holders, took Metromedia, Inc., a public company, private. In order to refinance the bank debt incurred to acquire all of the Company's assets, we decided to sell high-yield bonds to the public and to pay back all of the bank debt. In order to accomplish this, we went on a road trip across the country to tell our story to potential investors about the bonds (known as a dog-and-pony-show).

On one visit in the Midwest, we were kept waiting by the principal of the investment firm for about half an hour. When he finally arrived, he stated that he disliked television and never watched it. At that juncture, John abruptly rose from his seat and after a few expletive remarks, started to leave the room. Bob turned white and ran to try to stop John. The investor, who was shaken by John's action, said that he may not like to watch television, but that didn't mean he didn't invest in television companies. With that Bob got John to return to the meeting. This individual's investment fund became one of our major bondholders.

Although the political sniping continued throughout the road trip, Bob ignored it and told a great story about our TV stations and the supportive production company. He put forth the prospect of our unique asset position for creating a fourth network. Our seven stations were in top U.S. markets and we had a production company capable of creating network product. He also explained how much more nimble we were as an entity. We could acquire or create product at economic levels the three existing networks couldn't match. Our stations on their own were throwing off cash flow in excess of $100 million in 1984.

The bond offering was wildly successful and, by the end of 1984, all of the bank debt was paid in full. In less than six months, we had refinanced the entire bank debt incurred to buy all of Metromedia's assets.

In 1985, John contracted with Rupert Murdoch to sell all of the TV stations and the production company for $2 billion. Although the price and the multiple paid for the assets were historic at the time, one could always hear Bob muttering for years about his fourth network idea and how he was rounding third, heading for home, when his wheels were pulled out from under him.

Bob put together and ran a great organization. Without his performance and credibility, we would never have been able to buy Metromedia's assets. These same attributes were the reason the investors bought our bonds to repay the bank debt.

In my book, Bob Bennett had a vision and the guts to try to bring it to reality. He was also a straight shooter in a land of smoke and mirrors. He was so unusual that if he made a mistake, he said so, or if he didn't understand something, he'd ask. That was very unusual at the time.

Sometimes we made presentations to two people; sometimes there were a hundred people in a big auditorium. We had a very convincing story and we did raise the money we were looking for. One Canadian group told John right in front of me that they would invest $50 million on one condition: "You give Bob Bennett a ten year contract." John was getting older and they felt someone younger was needed to drive Metromedia into the future. I was heartened that they believed in Bob so much, but also knew that John Kluge was the real man behind Metromedia."

On one occasion, Stuart and I flew into Milwaukee for the last presentation of the day. I was tired and cranky and we had to wait a half-hour for these people to show up. They finally walked into the room and I began my presentation and within five minutes, I noticed that a guy in the front row was getting a little fidgety. Finally he raised his arm and said, "I don't own a television set, Mr. Bennett."

The constant strain of the trip had been wearing me down and I was very tired and really just wanted to get out of the room and go home. I turned and looked directly at the man who had raised his arm and said, "Oh, you don't have a television set? You know, that's too bad. Then I guess you never saw a man walk on the moon did you?"

The man was startled by my response and I could see that he was somewhat embarrassed and looking for something to say. "Well, I have a friend so I can walk over to his house," he managed to blurt out.

I really couldn't take it any more. I wasn't through with him yet. "You know something—maybe you ought to spend more time at your friend's house. You'll be amazed what the world is coming to."

When the presentation was over I went over to Stu.

"What are we wasting our time with this group for?" I asked.

"These people represent a lot of money, Bob," he said to me.

"Yeah, well after what I just said to the guy in the front row, we ain't never going to see a dime from these people."

A week later Stu called me.

"Hey Bob, remember the group from Milwaukee?"

"Yeah, I guess I shouldn't have blown up at that guy."

"Yeah, well they're in for thirty million dollars."

I was shocked.

"Thirty million dollars, Stu? Are you sure? I'm beginning to think I should be rude to everybody."

Sometimes you just never know.

The Fourth Television Network:
The New Program Group

THE IDEA OF building and launching a fourth network initially grew out of the necessity to lower programming acquisition costs for syndicated programming. As independent stations we were continually getting hit with high costs that were continuing to sky-rocket. The cost of buying programming for independent stations, such as situation comedies, was so expensive that something had to be done to ease the pain. The more a show was a hit on network television, the more we independents had to pay for it. The networks figured that if they had what looked like a hit show during its first year, there was a good likelihood that it would continue until at least three seasons were produced. There was no guarantee of this of course, but they would try and sell us on the future viability of a show being a hit. In essence, they would flat out tell us that if we wanted to buy a certain show, we had to pay their price or else. Their prices were already sky high, but we needed programming. Needless to say, we independents could see the writing on the wall.

As stations in need of a constant and reliable source of programming, we needed at least seventy-five programs per series in order to strip it. As independent stations, there was no doubt in our minds—we were in for big trouble.

At Metromedia, we were looking specifically for something like a *M.A.S.H.*, which we could show weekly. We needed programming badly for the 4:30, 5:00, 5:30, and 6:00 time slots. I told Kluge that it would be more cost-effective for us to buy Fox than to just buy one of their shows. We did buy *M.A.S.H.*, and it was stripped for the Metromedia stations Monday through Friday. The show was a major hit for us and we were making a great deal of money from it. With *M.A.S.H.* as an asset, we finally gave the other network affiliates some competition in the ratings in the early fringe time period. When Fox found out just how much money we were really making from *M.A.S.H.*, they were not going to renew it at the same cost. They wanted to once again raise the price. Bob Morin was the head of syndication at Fox and a reasonably good friend of mine. I went to him to plead my case.

"No way, Bob. I can't do it," he said somewhat maliciously to me. "You want *M.A.S.H.*, the price is higher now."

"Are you telling me we have no room for negotiation on this?" I asked him.

"That's right, Bob. We have no room for negotiation on this. I'm going to get you on this one," he said with a big mean smile on his face.

So much for reasonably good friends, I thought to myself.

All of this scared me. We had seven television stations and thirteen radio stations. I knew just how much those television syndication costs were escalating, and they were not about to stop. Metromedia could not go on buying syndicated programs from others under the current system. We could go broke in the process. I was sure of it. We had to figure out a way to do it ourselves. Somehow we had to change the system.

It was time now to launch the Fourth Network.

The idea of a Fourth Network was a radically new idea at the time; but one born out of dire need to reduce high syndication costs. We proceeded to sketch our idea out. The thought came that we might commingle Metromedia's stations with other station groups to see if we could get enough coverage across the country to be considered a strong media buy for advertisers, and hence, the idea for The Fourth Network. After all, we did have all of the makings of a fourth network: we had top coverage in markets across the country and we were making our own programming. Why not, we said to ourselves. Why not give it a try?

If we were going to pull this off, we needed to find partners who had the same problem as we did—those who did not want to pay the escalating prices for syndicated shows, and who could also put up money for production.

I went to John Conomikes at Hearst, Joe Dimino at Storer, and then visited with Taft and Gannett. The Metromedia station group at the time consisted of five stations and one ABC affiliate, WCVB-TV in Boston. All together our Metromedia stations represented about 25% of the country. If somehow a consortium of station groups could join together to fight off the enemy, we might have something.

Hearst, Storer, Gannet, and Taft were all receptive to the idea and we quickly realized that together, we would have coverage in about 65% of the country. Conceivably, we would now have the strength and ability to look and act like a fourth network. Certainly, advertisers should be considering a buy that reached that high a percentage of the country. We all bought into the idea and we began to think about what programming we could produce. We called ourselves The New Program Group.

Costs were divided up among us for production, and were based on what percentage of the market each group owned. If we had any conflicts, whereby certain groups had stations in the same market, we would alternate; first one would pay their share and then the other.

Strength was gathering among us. I told all of our partners the following: "Look, we all have to realize that the idea of us finding a hit show is going to be very slim. We may have to produce ten shows before we have anything that might even look remotely good. And if we have something that looks like a hit in the beginning, it's going to have to last for at least seventy-five episodes in order for us to be able to strip it. The odds are against us; but I don't see any way around this. If we hit on one or two good shows—it will be extremely advantageous to us. We might get lucky. We might not."

Everyone took a deep breath and then said, "Okay, let's go forward and build the Fourth Network."

The first show that we jointly produced for our new network was a late night show that would compete with Johnny Carson. We may not have been thinking that we were going to put a real strong dent in Johnny's ratings, but we were looking to see if we could find someone who had star power and someone viewers might tune in to see. We found out that there was one host, who, whenever he sat in for Johnny Carson, would produce equally high ratings, or even higher, than what *The Tonight Show* was getting with Johnny hosting the show. That person was Jerry Lewis, who at that moment in time was not involved in any entertainment projects. I approached Jerry and he agreed to try it, so we put together *The Jerry Lewis Show*, which was designed as a late night show, Monday through Friday. My goal was to try and sell it all over the country. Jerry knew everybody in the entertainment business and it seemed that everyone in the business, whether living in Los Angeles or in town just visiting, wanted to be on his show.

Opening night for his show was big, with lights, limos, celebrities, and lots of press. We did the show live in a building on Sunset Blvd., which was not far, ironically, from the CBS building where I started my career as an usher. It was a big night for me and one in which I took note of all my own accomplishments since I had left that job as an usher a long time ago.

To our great surprise, *The Jerry Lewis Show* lasted one week. We never announced it as a full-time show, so we were in essence testing it out on a one-week basis only. On the first night of the show, we beat Carson, and from there on as the week nights progressed, we received a five rating, a four, a three, and then it went down to nothing.

We then produced a program called *On Stage America*, which was an entertainment variety program highlighting various acts. It lasted a total of twenty-six weeks, but in week thirteen I went to ABC and told them I was going to preempt their regularly scheduled baseball (this would have been our WCVB-TV station in Boston) and put in place of it *On Stage America*. It turned out to be the highest rated show that night and it had the largest audience share combined that evening.

ABC was not happy with me preempting their programming; but I told them that if they learned anything from *On Stage America*, it was to do it themselves. Today there is a similar program to *On Stage America* that is very popular and high in the ratings—that program is called *American Idol*.

Freddy Silverman came to my office one day with an idea for a program to be hosted by a young, talented man named Alan Thicke. He had a tape on Alan so he played it for me. I liked it. Alan was bright, articulate, and had great possibility as a late night talk show host. I agreed to produce *Thicke of the Night* in Los Angeles and add it to our Fourth Network programming line up. I was very enthusiastic about the show and called all of my colleagues and we ended up clearing a great deal of the country. The press soon picked up that we were trying to beat Johnny Carson, and then for reasons unknown to us, everything about the show seemed to turn negative. Our goal was really not to beat Carson, but to see only if we could just get a piece of those ratings. *Thicke of the Night* lasted for one year and cost about $100,000 a week to produce.

Fred Silverman, Television Executive, writes:

"I first met Bob sometime in the early 80s at an ABC Affiliate meeting. I later left ABC and went to NBC and we stayed in touch. When I heard he was looking for programming I approached him on a show I was developing called Thicke of the Night, *which was a late night talk show hosted by Canadian personality Alan Thicke. I showed Bob the tape and he liked what he saw and he said to me, "Fine, let's do it." At the time we had an overall deal with MGM to syndicate the show nationally. We produced the show in Los Angeles and it was a ninety-minute format scheduled for five nights a week, which was a very ambitious idea at the time. Working with Bob was great. He was always supportive, easy to get along with, full of ideas, and very enthusiastic about the show. Bob seemed to always have a special feel for television and he always seemed to know what he was looking for or what he wanted.*

The problem with Thicke of the Night *was that Alan was funny in Canada, but somehow could not seem to strike a nerve with the U.S. audience. The show suffered for it. Our first show took us eighteen hours to edit and I suppose right there and then that should have been some kind of sign as to what was to come. The show was originally developed for John Ritter, and Alan was brought in as a producer. John took on another show, so I mentioned to Alan that since he had done a similar show in Canada, maybe he should do this one.*

Back then we were overly ambitious and the critics were all saying that we were trying to take on Johnny Carson, which was not our intent. As the ratings for the show were going down, we changed the format to sixty minutes instead of ninety minutes and simplified the production to get away from more of Alan's standup comedy to a regular talk show type format. The show did get better. We moved the time frame around in certain markets but overall it never did what we had hoped it would do. In some ways, I think it was a show ahead of its time. Bob had a lot of patience with the show. Other executives in his position would have jumped out the window. He was always as supportive as he could be."

Metromedia Stock Hits a High of $585 a Share

AT THIS POINT in time, the price for a share of Metromedia stock on the New York Stock Exchange was $585, and it then split one for ten. It was the highest per share price on the Exchange of any company. Needless to say, we were all very pleased. Since I joined Metromedia as President of Metromedia Broadcasting, the stock had risen from $104 to the $585 number. I had reason to be proud of myself, and all of the team at Metromedia, who had worked so hard toward building a great company.

Around this time, John Kluge went to Washington to meet with the FCC. When he came back to New York he had a meeting with George, Stu, and me. John was very excited about a new idea that some guy he met in Washington had told him about—the new and upcoming technology of cellular telephones. John knew nothing about it. Neither did we. However, in thirty days, we had attorneys working around the clock to apply for licenses in various markets across the country. We were able to acquire licenses in New York, Washington, Chicago, Boston, and Philadelphia for a total investment of about $750 million. This was a very hefty price tag for an investment we all knew next to nothing about. Some years later, John ended up selling the cellular telephone business for somewhere between $4 and $5 billion dollars. As I mentioned before, John Kluge was a very smart man.

When He Takes the Cigar Out of His Mouth, You Ask, "How Much?" and Then You Shake His Hand

FRANK BENNACK WAS the Chairman of the Board of the Hearst Corporation at the time, and was very interested in buying WCVB-TV from Metromedia. John agreed and asked me to look into it. I then had a meeting with John Conomike who was then President of Hearst Broadcasting and one of my closest friends. I met with John and their CFO about their interest in buying WCVB. The meeting was going well, but I had an important point on the sales price that I wanted to make to John and his CFO. I delivered my important point in no uncertain terms.

"Guys, this is going to be simple. The price for WCVB-TV is $450 million. I know for certain that John Kluge will not take a penny less than that. John paid $220 million for that station five years ago so the price of $450 million is etched firmly in his mind. He's not going to budge on it. Trust me. My suggestion to all of you is that if you want it, on the final meeting with Kluge, he'll be there with a cigar in his mouth. Frank Bennack should ask John how much he wants for the station. When John says $450 million, I heartily suggest that you tell Frank to reach out his hand and shake John's hand, right there and then. I'm telling you guys; John Kluge won't take a penny less than $450 million."

They were astonished at what I was saying. As I was heading for the door, I stopped and reiterated it one more time. "Remember, if you want WCVB-TV, that's the price and that's the way to get it. Tell Frank to reach out and grab John Kluge's hand as fast as he can and shake it. You'll have your deal then."

I walked out the door and went back to John's office. I knew that no television station had ever sold for as high as $450 million. I was on thin ice here but I was going on my gut feeling. If we could pull this off, it was really going to be a first.

John looked up from his desk.

"Listen John, this is how it is going to go down. When Frank Bennack asks you how much you want for the station, you take the cigar out of your mouth and just say to him, $450 million. Make sure you say that and nothing else. I have a feeling Frank Bennack's hand is going to reach out and shake yours and we're going to have a deal."

John looked at me and nodded his head in the affirmative.

Television History Was About to Be Made — Again

WHEN THE MEETING finally took place at our corporate apartment at the Waldorf in New York, those present were John Kluge, Frank Bennack, John Conomike, Hearst's CFO, and me. I kept looking over at John Conomikes and he was doing the same back to me. There was a great silent tension in the room and then Frank Bennack finally spoke.

"John, how much do you want for WCVB-TV?"

Kluge looked him in the eye, took the cigar out of his mouth, and said, "Four hundred and fifty million dollars."

The room went silent and I then saw Frank's hand come up to meet Kluge's hand in mid air. They shook and television history was made. I was elated. We than had a press conference and Frank told the press that this was the quickest sale of his life. Kluge was very pleased. After the sale went through, I had a meeting with Frank.

"Frank," I said to him. "WCVB-TV is the most unusual television station that you will ever encounter. WCVB is unique, has its own culture, and a history of success unlike any other station ever. You can go through WCVB and make all kinds of budget cuts, let a lot of people go and change the programming all around, but if you do, the viewers in Boston will turn on you and turn you off. I recommend you make no changes at WCVB. It's a station that's working and making a lot of money."

Frank agreed and promised he would not really change things at the station.

In 1985, I started Bennett Productions in Los Alamitos, California, and my son Casey moved in to run things.

John Meets Rupert

AROUND THIS TIME, John Kluge met Rupert Murdoch at a television conference, and in that meeting Murdoch expressed his interest in buying Metromedia. John pursued it and for some reason kept the sale a secret from me. I think that he was worried that if I knew about it, I would be devastated. When I actually found out about it, I was not very pleased.

In 1986, Fox bought Metromedia for $2 billion, and I was for the first time in a very long time, out of a job. My only solace was the remuneration for the amount of stock I held in Metromedia.

As I look back on John Kluge's career, his success seems to have been built on one very specific mission: to buy a license in a major market at a reasonable price, wait for the market to evolve, and then sell at a high multiple. It has apparently worked just about every time for him, and he built one of the most successful media companies in the world. I like to think that I, and many others who worked there, helped John build Metromedia into the great success story that it was.

Roger Brown, roommate from Staunton, writes:
"One day, Bob's secretary, Maria Morales, called me and told me that Bob was a little depressed because he was not informed in advance by upper management that Metromedia was going to go private and asked if I would call him to try and cheer him up. I called him and suggested that with the sixty million (a number I made up at the time) he was making from the transaction, that he would never miss sending me over a

million or two. As was typical style for him, and in keeping with the way we were highly competitive, he told me that the number wasn't sixty million, it was a hundred million (now he was making the number up) and that a hundred million just doesn't go that far nowadays. Thus he would be unable to send me over any money. When Bob went into retirement, my wife Lea and I were with him and Marjie in California on their boat The Celebration. *I will never forget the dialogue between Lea and Bob that day:*

"Bob, I thought we were going to go out deep-sea fishing today."
"We are," was his answer. "When the crew gets one hooked, they'll call us."

Honorable Bruce Selya, friend, writes:
"Bryant University figured prominently in perhaps the most memorable day I ever spent with Bob and Marjie. The Bryant Board voted, on my nomination, to give Bob an honorary Doctor of Business Administration degree, which of course, considering his history in the business world, he eminently deserved.

When commencement day came, we stood side-by-side on the dais in front of an audience of roughly 10,000 people, and the flowery but accurate account of his many accomplishments, was read. As I personally presented to him his honorary degree, tears began to swell up in his eyes and run down his cheeks. It's a side of Bob that very few people have ever seen, but for me bespeaks the humanity that so characterizes him."

In 1987, to my surprise and great honor, I received an honorary Doctor of Business Administration from Bryant University. Receiving this honorary degree had a very profound affect on me and is something that I will never forget.

Back at our Fourth Network, the *Small Wonder* program was achieving some success. We had produced twenty-two shows and needed to strategize more as to how we might get it to seventy-five shows. I decided to call in all of the station group partners to talk about it. I also decided to invite Barry Diller, who was at Fox, to come to the meeting.

"Barry, I'd like you come to a meeting about *Small Wonder.*
"Okay, I'll come. When is it?"

"It's going to be at 9:30 on Tuesday morning," I told him.

"Well, I can't get there until 10:30," he said.

"Well then you're going to miss an hour and a half of the meeting. I can't ask all of these people to fly in from all around the country and then wait around for you to show up. The meeting starts at nine sharp."

"Yeah, yeah, I'll see what I can do," he said.

The meeting did start at nine-thirty and Barry did not show up until ten thirty. He walked in, sat down, and appeared to be rather grumpy and uninterested. At this point I asked the group to put up more money to do forty-four new shows. Barry looked at me and said, "You can't ask for forty-four new shows. What's the matter with you? That's impossible. Thirteen shows maybe, but not forty-four more."

"Well Barry, thirteen more doesn't help us. Forty-four does. We've got to get up to seventy-five to be strippable."

"Look, let me tell you something, the show is lousy and it's a piece of crap. You should pull the plug on it."

With that remark, he stormed out of the room.

The group did give me the go-ahead to do an additional forty-four shows and *Small Wonder* turned out to be an enormous success. The following year I ran into Barry at the NAPTE convention. We exchanged greetings and then I could not wait to say to him: "You know Barry, that piece of crap show *Small Wonder* you told us to pull the plug on? It's now the highest rated show on your L.A. station."

He looked at me and muttered: "Yeah, I know," and kept walking.

Who Me? Play Golf for the Rest of My Life?

METROMEDIA HAD NOW been sold to Fox and I decided I was going to play golf for the rest of my life. I did it for three days straight in a row and then woke up on the fourth day and said, "Do I really have to play golf again today?"

Honorable Bruce Selya, friend, writes:

"I was out visiting Bob once in California when he told me he wanted to let me in on his West Coast Secret. I couldn't imagine at the time what he meant. He revealed to me that he had acquired a Rolls Royce Cornice, which he kept in the garage of his Wilshire Boulevard condominium. He told me he only used it for special occasions that fit the California lifestyle. I was sworn to secrecy that I would not tell his East Coast friends that he had succumbed to that sort of materialism.

Around this time, Bob was on the board of the Annual Dinner of the American Film Institute and he had invited me to Los Angeles to attend the dinner. I of course was happy to come; the only problem was that he did not tell me that it was a black tie event. I had no tux to wear and told him I was on my way to a tux rental store to get one. He would not hear of it. He pointed out that he had an extra tux that was a little snug for him that he thought would fit me. I tried it on and it did, to my surprise, fit well. The centerpiece was a black velvet tuxedo jacket and I imagine you can picture the rest of the attire from there on, but nevertheless, it would have to do for the evening's event. The dinner was a huge success. Anything that Bob ever agreed to undertake and chair was always a huge success. I will long remember the people and the warmth that I received that evening. It wasn't because I was a famous federal judge; it was because I was a friend of Bob and Marjie."

Ted Turner Comes Calling Again

SOMETIME IN 1987, Ted Turner called me. He had just bought MGM Studios, which included an enormous library. Kirk Kerkorian sold the library to Turner at an unheard of multiple for that time, but Ted wanted it so bad he paid the steep asking price. Ted had his heart set on owning the rights to *Gone With the Wind*, which was one of the gems in the MGM library. Ted wanted me to be Chairman of the Board of MGM Studios and I told him I'd have to think about it.

"Why me Ted?" I asked him one day. "I don't know anything about the motion picture business. I'm a broadcaster."

"I don't trust those jerks out there."

"Okay," I told him. "I'll give it some thought."

Alan Ladd, Jr. was then running MGM Studios, and he had a contract which stipulated that he was to report only to the chairman of the board, who was Ted. Ted was trying to put me in the middle and have Laddie, as he was often called, report to me. We had a meeting and I could see that Laddie was not going to be easy to get along with. He was going out of his way to be rough and impolite. Turner asked the two of us to work out the details and then left the room. Laddie and I were now stuck with one another, each of us looking back at the other over the table. He had this irritating ability to make his voice go lower and lower as he spoke, until I was asking him to repeat himself. I felt he was doing this on purpose to annoy me.

We then went to lunch to further explore additional ideas. As we were eating and talking I soon realized that I had been trying to sell myself to him, and that I should not be doing that. Why did I have to sell myself to Alan Ladd? That didn't make any sense to me. I looked him straight in the eye and said, "Listen to me Alan, I want you to understand something. I don't even know if I want this job, but if I do take it, you will report and answer to me, and on that there is no room for negotiation. So let there be no question in your mind about who will be in charge."

I then got up and left and went to the Bel Air Country Club to meet my friend Art Anderson. Art's best friend, a doctor, was also there. I told Art about the Turner offer and he called his friend over to our table.

"Let me ask you a question Doc," Art said. "This is my friend Bob Bennett, and Ted Turner has just offered him the job of running MGM. Now we might say that Bob is in reasonably good health, but he is fifty-nine years old, maybe twenty pounds overweight, and he's smoking more than he should be. What do you think about him taking on what will probably be one of the most stressful jobs in the entertainment industry?" The doctor looked me over and matter-of-factly said, "You'll be dead in six months." With that, I got up, went to a phone, called Ted Turner, and told him I was not interested in the job.

New World Entertainment

HARRY SLOAN AND Larry Kuppin were two entertainment executives based in Los Angeles. They were looking to buy stations to hold and then resell in the future. They approached me and asked me if I could find stations for them to buy. They gave me a salary and I went out and looked, but at first did not find anything I thought was a good deal. I then recommended they buy KHJ in Los Angeles, but at the last minute they couldn't make up their minds and soon Disney came in and bought it. Sometime thereafter, Ron Perelman, Chairman of Revlon, had purchased New World Pictures, and decided he now wanted to sell the company. New World Pictures contained a library, which consisted of about three hundred low budget films. Harry and Larry asked me if I wanted to be their partner and buy the library along with them. I agreed to join in. Perelman wanted $12 million and we all put in $4 million each. What no one seemed to understand was that the library had a lot of receivables and our investment was paid back to us in about one year. Harry then announced that he wanted to sell it and convinced us all to sell our percentages as well. However, I decided to buy both of them out and own the library myself.

In 1991, I bought out Harry and Larry and now, as New World Entertainment, we bought out Ron Perelman and changed the name of the company to Trans Atlantic Entertainment. I became Chairman of the company and in February of 1992, Paul Rich became President.

The first week after the purchase of the company, I was sitting in my office when several Trans Atlantic executives walked in.

"We're going to be going to the Cannes Film Festival, Bob," one of them said to me.

"Good. Have a nice trip," I told him.

"No, we don't think you understand. We need product."

"Product?" I asked.

"Product, as in new films. We need new films, you know, new product, to show off in Cannes. We can't use last year's product. We need something fresh so we can sell it and tie it in with rest of our film library."

I sat back in my seat and took a deep breath and started gritting my teeth.

"Okay, who's going to make the new movies?" I asked.

"Well, we are, of course."

"And how many movies do you think we should be making?"

"At least three, Bob. At least three."

I was not prepared to start making movies, especially three all at once and under such short notice. What I had learned when I was young was that you always make movies with other people's money, and now, I was going to break that golden rule and make three movies all at the same time, all with my own money. Oh boy, what had I gotten myself into?

We did do the three movies: *Hell Raiser*, *Children of the Corn*, and *Death Ring*, with average budgets ranging from $1.5 million to $4.5 million. However, during this production period, it seemed that every time I turned around, there was a request for $100,000 or $250,000 or more. I used to cringe every time somebody walked into my office. It got so bad I wanted to hide under my desk. Fortunately though, those three movies turned out to be very successful.

Paul Rich had done a great job selling the New World Library to the foreign market, and in those days, the foreign market had no trouble buying low budget films. We were also able to do sequels. We were making very good money back then, but we were getting the sense that it was becoming more difficult to sell to the foreign market.

One day, from out of the blue, two guys came into my office from Chicago and told me they were interested in buying Trans Atlantic. I was really not that interested in selling and gave them what I thought was a very high number as a sales price. I figured they would leave, think about it, and never come back. However, two days later they came back and told me they would buy at the price I had given them. That price was $20 million. Interestingly, I was told earlier by Larry and Harry that I'd be lucky to get maybe $5 million some day for that library.

Gerry Hribal, friend, writes:
"I do have one funny story about Bob. In 1994, I was his golf partner at the Bel Air Country Club for a Member's Guest Tournament. I had socialized with him a few times at the clubhouse, but I didn't know at the time just how competitive a person Bob was. Bob and I were a two-man team. At the end of the first day, we returned to the clubhouse, looked up at the overhead screens and saw that we were leading everyone. Bob was elated seeing his name up there and it was an evening of great joy and celebration.
On day two, the pressure mounted. We went out and played a great game once again, and when we returned to the clubhouse, we found out we were once again leading the pack. Bob was once again elated to see his name on the overhead screen ahead of everyone else. We could see us winning the gold money clip and our names on the winning trophy. We turned our attention to day three which started out with full optimism and the thought to bring home the gold.
We played solid for the first twelve holes and were elated. It was the thirteenth hole, however, that caused us trouble. It's a par three now, and I get up and hit the ball on the green. Bob follows me and hits the ball in front of the bunker. I could see him cringe. He goes down to the bunker and after five whacks at trying to get the ball out, he can't do it. I hear swearing going on. "This is bad," I think to myself. "With this bad hole, our chances of winning are going away." I look down at Bob and I see the veins of his neck coming out. His face is red and he's screaming out words I can't repeat here. I yelled down to him, "Bob, take it easy, let's regroup. Let's take a deep breath." That thirteenth hole killed us. We finished 5th place out of 100 teams. I think we won a piece of crystal. Bob was seething. He did not want to lose. His wanting to win out there was everything."

Reunion Dinner for Metromedia

AT THE NAPTE Convention in Las Vegas in 2000, Metromedia decided to have a Metromedia reunion dinner. About a hundred people showed up. That evening, I was sitting next to John Kluge, and I whispered in a joking way into his ear the following: "John, there are a hundred people here tonight who are celebrating the great success we have had at Metromedia. These are the same people who helped you become the richest man in America. Whatever success you've had, you had it because of the hard work and determination of the people in this room. Why don't you do something nice for them? As a surprise, why don't you announce that you are going to give each and everyone of them $1 million dollars? That's only about $100 million dollars. That's nothing to you."

John looked at me and then found some words in his mouth.

"Are you serious Bob? You're out of your mind."

"No, I'm not John. I think it is a great gesture and it shows them just how much you appreciate each and everyone of them."

"You give it to them, Bob," he stiffly said to me.

"Are you sure you won't do it, John?"

"Of course I won't do it."

"No?"

"NO!"

"Well, if you won't do that, will you at least pick up the dinner tab?"

John looked at me with daggers in his eyes.

"No, Bob, I won't do that either."

The $98,000 Dinner Tab

AND SPEAKING OF dinner tabs, I was on the Board of the UCLA Medical Center for about four or five years and was, to whatever extent I could be, involved in the fight against cancer. A friend of mine named Ed White told me that there was going to be a major fundraising dinner. The theme behind the dinner was to have different celebrities cooking their favorite recipes at various tables, and each guest would go around sampling different dishes. Sammy Davis was the entertainer that evening and he did a wonderful job. Ed then said to me that they were looking for someone to pick up the dinner tab, so that all the donations could go directly toward the fight against cancer. I thought about it, and then realized that it would be an honor to do it. So I agreed and picked up the dinner tab for about 1,800 people at a cost of about $98,000. I was happy to have done it, as I knew the money went toward a very great cause.

In 1991, our friend Sue Ellen Volpe, who is a real estate agent, invited us to look at a house that was for sale on the water in Newport Beach, CA. We had always vacationed there during the summer and loved it. Our offer for the house was accepted and shortly thereafter we moved in. At the time, we had a sixty-seven foot boat which we kept in Marina Del Rey, and soon it was sitting at our dock in Newport Beach.

Bennett Productions continued and, by 2005, we were producing the *Hawaiian Tropic Beauty Pageant* and *Bikini Destinations*, both syndicated in over one hundred and forty countries. We also produced over eighty-five hours of the television series, *The Extremists*.

Returning to My Roots and the
Art of Reflection

The Kid from Altoona Returns to Altoona

IN 2002, I decided to return to Altoona to visit the places where it had all started for me. The last time I was in Altoona was fifteen years prior. I had mixed emotions when I boarded the plane from Los Angeles to Pittsburgh, but I was determined to go back and see my old house and any old friends who might still be around. As we climbed into the air I began to feel elated. I was now returning to my first home and going through my head were hundreds of youthful memories of my mother, my grandfather, my grandmother, friends, school, and anything else I could think of. My excitement grew when we landed in Pittsburgh. My spirits were at an all time high as I drove into Altoona. But as I drove around old Altoona, I could see that the life I once knew was gone. After all, I left Altoona as a boy in 1940.

The Altoona of today is no longer the thriving manufacturing and railroad center it was when I was a boy. Gone are the freight cars, passenger cars, and railroad equipment that made Altoona one of the country's great railroad towns. No longer do railroad construction yards stretch on forever, and no longer is the smell of railroading in the air.

The Altoona of today is trying to recover from years of industrial decline and what people like to call decentralization. Altoona is now the home of the Altoona Curve baseball team of the Double A Eastern League, which is the Double A affiliate of the Pittsburgh Pirates. The seventy-eight-year-old Altoona Symphony Building still stands proudly, and the famous Horseshoe Curve, the Mishler

Theatre, the Cathedral of the Most Blessed Sacrament, and the Jaffa Shrine Center are all solid reminders of Altoona's past.

The Railroad Mechanic's Library, built in 1853, was then known as the first industrial library in the nation. It is still there and is now known as the Altoona Public Library. Ivy Side Park, which once boasted the largest swimming pool in the world, is now a parking lot owned by Penn State. I remember swimming in that pool many times when I was a boy.

The downtown area is still the cultural and commercial center of Altoona, and much of it is listed in the national registry of historic places. Many of the older districts still consist of a mixture of row homes and individual homes that once served as the addresses of many a railroad worker. Altoona is now the corporate home to Sheetz, a fast growing convenience regional chain store.

Despite the fact that many historic buildings still stand from my time and before, sadly, many of them are now gone, including the famed Logan House Hotel. Altoona's fire department, I understand, is the largest career fire department between Harrisburg and Pittsburgh. The Horseshoe Curve, a curved section of track built into the mountainside and owned by the Pennsylvania Railroad, has now become a tourist attraction and listed as a National Historic Landmark. The Horseshoe Curve is known as the Eighth Wonder of the Modern World. The Alleghenies proved to be the biggest obstacle for the Pennsylvania Railroad, and the way this area of track was designed and laid down was a truly remarkable feat of engineering. It was constructed entirely by men with picks, shovels, horses, and drags. It opened to traffic on February 15, 1854.

Built in 1920, "Leap-The-Dips" is the world's oldest roller coaster. Located in Lakemont Park, "Leap-The-Dips" is the only "side friction" roller coaster left in North America. The ride is 1,452 feet long and 41 feet high, and received a full restoration for its reopening on May 31, 1999. It is a figure-eight coaster where its cars travel on wood instead of steel rails for most of the ride.

Altoona is still a city divided into many sections. Those sections are known as: Downtown, Dutch Hill, East End, Pleasant Valley region, Plank Road Shopping Center, Juniata, Logantown, Lakemont, Fairview, Eldorado, the Fifth Ward, and Industrial Park.

As I was driving, I was reliving my past in a city that was in many ways trying to hold on to its past. The real history of Altoona is trains. It has a train history that, in my opinion, no other city in America can equal.

Soon, I was out of my car and walking the streets. Up close, I could not help but be surprised as to just how small the houses and the streets were. Of course, I was much smaller myself back then. I used to think I had the biggest and greatest house on the street. Upon seeing my old house for the first time in many years, I wasn't so sure. I was expecting to see it in the same shiny condition it was in when I lived there. I was sadly mistaken. In fact, I was in deep shock. Here was the house I grew up in and it did not look anything like what I reminisced about. It was no longer the stately home I once remembered. It had fallen into great disrepair with the wooden railing, that had once stretched elegantly across the entire length of the front of the house, now sagging and rotted. I actually wanted to cry. The thought came to mind that I should buy the house and restore it to its old grandeur.

I looked up my old friend Royden Piper, whom I stayed in touch with over the years. There are only a handful of people left in Altoona, including Bud and Janet Shaffer and Patsy Good, that I knew from my early days in Altoona. Royden Piper was one of them and someone I could rely on for the latest in Altoona news. Sadly, Royden passed away in 2008 and with him went a light that had burned brightly in my life. But on the day I was with him back in Altoona, he was full of energy and intent on showing me around.

"Bob, you and I are going to take a ride over the Railroader's Memorial Museum," Royden enthusiastically said to me.

"Where's that?" I asked.

"Right here in Altoona. It's filled with pictures, freight trains, and railroad equipment. All the things we remember being around when we were kids. You'll find it very interesting."

"Okay. Let's go," I told him.

The Altoona Railroader's
Memorial Museum

WHEN WE ARRIVED at the museum, we walked up the pathway to the front door and I noticed that there was a plaque on the doorway with a picture of a Master Mechanic. I found this intriguing since my grandfather Harry Bennett was the Master Mechanic for the railroad between 1900 and 1921. I stopped and studied the plaque. It was a picture of the man who followed my grandfather as the railroad's Master Mechanic. If anyone should be on that plaque, I thought, it should be my grandfather. I decided to investigate and meet with the museum's curator.

I walked in and introduced myself.

"Hello, my name is Bob Bennett and my grandfather was Harry Bennett who was the railroad's Master Mechanic between 1900 and 1921. I'd like to make a contribution of $30,000 to the museum if you'll consider having a picture of my grandfather put up there. Can it be done?"

"Of course Mr. Bennett," he said to me. "But we do have a greater need to complete the Round House. Let me show you what we have under construction."

We walked out to the Round House, which is a large circle where train engines coming from different directions lead into a circle, and then can be swung around to be placed on a different track going out in different directions. They were rebuilding this historical landmark and needed money to fund it.

"How much do you need to finish it? I asked.

"Well, the State of Pennsylvania is putting some money in, but we're short about $250,000," he said.

I thought the matter over. My grandfather, as I mentioned earlier, was a very strong figure in my life. To this day I still think of him often.

"I'll give you the money if you'll name the round house after my grandfather."

"Consider it done, Mr. Bennett. It will be a great honor."

All of the local newspapers picked up the story. Local boy Bob Bennett makes good out there in the world and comes back to Altoona to donate money in his grandfather's memory. This is what stories of importance in Altoona were made of. I was very happy and honored to do it.

As I mentioned, there are still a handful of old friends back in Altoona that I stay in touch with. To them I believe I represented a person who left Altoona, went to Hollywood, became something in the world of television, and went on to be the President of Metromedia Broadcasting. I was, in their eyes, the local boy who made good. Every year I send presents and cards and make a strong effort to stay in touch with all of my Altoona friends. They are wonderful down-to-earth people and I'm very proud to know them. I really do cherish these lifelong relationships of mine.

One evening I invited all of them for a nice dinner at a local hotel and about fifteen of them came. The party was great with lots of pictures and memories. I really felt great.

Bud Shaffer, a friend, writes:

"Wherever Bob's career took him, he always remembered his Altoona and Juniata friends. Many times throughout his career he came back to town and got us all together for dinner. Those were great evenings of sharing old stories and hearing about Bob's business adventures. Bob has remained a very dear friend to all of us and we cherish our memories and our friendship. When he was growing up in Altoona, I don't think the thought had ever crossed his mind that one day he would be a very successful television person."

I returned again to Altoona in October, 2012, for the dedication of the Round House and the Learning Center. At the Learning Center,

Penn State is offering a Bachelors Degree program where graduate students are prepared to go into the management functions at railroads and railroad related industries. I was shocked at how big the Round House actually was, as it could accommodate up to twelve steam engines. In my mind, this is going to be one of Altoona's biggest tourist attractions and perhaps the largest in the region. It was a great thrill for me to be part of all this and to be able to attach my grandfather and my grandmother's names to it. While there, the current Master Mechanic took me to his office, which used to be the office of my grandfather. I was mesmerized by it all and, as I stood there, I could actually feel my grandfather's presence. It is very difficult for me to be able to express my feelings as to what it really felt like for me to revisit and relive that part of his life.

Scrambling in
The Early Days of Television

THE TELEVISION WORLD today is not the television world that I knew and worked in. Back then, people and relationships meant a great deal more than they do now. In my time you could compete against someone at another station, and that competition could be forceful, a fight to the finish. But with that same person you fought against and competed against, you could also be good friends outside of the office. Today, with all the corporate secrecy, the non-compete agreements, and the prevalent cutthroat, kill-the-enemy attitudes, people have to walk a fine line from morning until night. Make sure you're not seen having a drink with your competitor; you might not have your job the next morning.

Today, the bottom line is that king and executives better make sure the king shines. In the Golden Age of Television that I knew, there was a sense of team playing. Now, media companies are giant conglomerates that you can get lost in. Everybody works for the pumping up of the price of the stock and the whole idea about quality programming that really means something to viewers—seems to be an ancient idea left over from an ancient world.

I think that the networks today are being eaten alive by cable and cable is being eaten alive by the Internet, and everyone is in search of some magical platform that will deliver seamless product to millions. There is a mad dash today to keep up with technology and in some ways to stay ahead of it, if that is even possible. All media seems to be melting into one platform that keeps changing at a very fast pace. This platform is instantaneous and one that viewers expect to be free and on demand. This makes it difficult for media companies to keep revenue going when viewers expect entertainment and information to be free.

With the Internet today, live and archived video, e-mail, instant messaging, social networking, weather reports, stock market updates, late-breaking live news, satellite maps, buying a pizza, buying a car, and booking a cruise or airplane reservation are only a click away. And of course we now have the ability to receive video on our handheld cell phones. While all of this is an enormous opportunity to place product in the hands of many, it is also putting enormous pressure on media groups and advertisers to push as much product as possible through this new emerging communication pipeline as quickly as possible.

I'm glad I was in the television business when I was. It was exciting and there was never a working day in my life that I did not enjoy and appreciate it. In many ways I was at the right place at the right time. The BBI philosophy, which was intelligent television for viewers, was unique. They were more concerned about doing something for the good of the community than continually assessing and reassessing the bottom line.

I don't believe we will ever see that kind of idea again in the world of television. I would not even know how to advise young people today who are thinking about careers in broadcasting and communications. My world is gone. Their world has a vast horizon with no end in sight. It is the video computer electronic age that will govern our future and determine how each and every one of us will experience what is now known as new media.

In my day, we could pause and create programming because the technology pretty much stayed the same. There was not really much technology movement back then. Today it is moving at lightning speed. Today's communication world does not stand still long enough to assess itself, let alone be able to successfully program it. Today we can make our own short TV shows or short movies and minutes later; place them on YouTube for millions to see as stored video. It's unbelievable. It was not too long ago that the idea of video over the Internet was more of a dream, with frames per second starting low and then growing until we now have today real-time Internet video anytime we want it, and for free.

Technology is pushing forward at a much faster rate than most of us can comprehend. Today children five years and younger have already learned how to navigate the Internet. My generation grew up with the typewriter. We used to fiddle with carbon paper to make copies. I still remember using White Out to correct typing errors. Now you just press delete.

The electronic world of the Internet is foreign to us, but I suppose we're learning to come to grips with it. We did not grow up with it. In fact, with all of the marvelous things it does, one can wonder how society ever got along without it. The whole idea of sending an instantaneous message electronically that arrives seconds later on the other side of the world, as opposed to having to send it by mail, is in itself a modern marvel. And today, e-mailing someone is considered old hat. People are text messaging, sending videos, video chatting, and embracing the new world of technology.

This is a very different world than the world I knew. Technology seemed to have been standing still in my day, as we were busy producing programming and trying to fill program schedules. Nothing much changed from year to year. You produced programming and sometimes you went live, but everything was based on a programming schedule that was pre-prepared and available to people as a guide. Going live back in those days meant using new technology at its best.

In the very early days of television, we scrambled. It was a new medium and as a new medium nobody really had their arms around it. No one really knew where it was going. We didn't have much to work with in the way of resources, but what we didn't have we invented. Live remotes in the late forties and early fifties were astounding feats of technology. We really believed back then that we were part of a communications miracle and I suppose we were. No one got paid very much back then but we had fun. The excitement disappeared when television became organized, systemized, efficiency-intense, and mass oriented. When I saw it all going that way I became discouraged. One of the major reasons I signed on to WCVB-TV was because it promised something different. It was like television the way it was for all of us in the early days in Los Angeles when we scrambled and we accomplished.

I often wonder why I was so lucky throughout my career and why I was able to succeed the way I did. I was lucky insomuch that magic dust seemed to have always been falling on me for any number of reasons. Professionally, I believe I was able to succeed because I always had good people around me who were dedicated to working hard and had a great deal of pride in their jobs. For those people I feel I was able to always bring out the best in them and to offer them an environment whereby they could achieve their highest goals. I succeeded because I was able to convince people that they were even better at what they were doing than what they themselves believed they could do. I tried to create a working atmosphere for people so they would first like their job, and secondly like the people they were working with. I also feel that I have always been a good listener. I love to listen to people.

I could not be more honored, and more blessed, than to have Marjie as my wife for the past sixty-two years. She has been my biggest cheerleader, my greatest fan, and someone who is very proud of my accomplishments. We are a great team together. When she wakes every morning she asks herself, "What is it I can do for Bob today?" and I when I wake I ask myself, "What is it today that I can do for Marjie that will make her day a great day?" We are very devoted to one another and our marriage has always been one that moves forward as a team. She is my best friend. I love her dearly. We share so many things in common and she is always very appreciative of everything she has. She never really asks for anything; but I find that I go out of my way to please her by getting her things that do make her happy.

Marjie Bennett writes:
"Bob is a great father, a great provider, and a great husband. He has done so much in his life and has given us so many wonderful things to be thankful for. As he was making his way in the world nobody ever gave him anything. He did it all himself. Once he got the job at KTTV, the rest is history. When we got married, I loaned him $100 to buy a suit. He has repaid me in more ways than I ever imagined."

My daughter, Kelly, is very special—and someone I love dearly. We are very close, and I am proud of all her accomplishments as a woman, a person, and as a caring human being who has a careful eye for the safety of animals. Today she is a benefactor for the safety of animals at the Los Angeles Zoo.

When she was younger, she would always sit in the window waiting for me to come home, and when I arrived home she would come out and greet me with a great big hug and kiss. Kelly is very bright and a great pleasure to be around. I make sure I call her every day to tell her how much I love her. I want her to know that I am always there for her as her father and as her friend. I could not have had a better daughter.

Kelly Bennett writes:

"I hope I can express myself as well as I'd like to when it comes to my dad. I don't know if I can find the words to do justice to who he is as a person. I've always been so proud of him, and I feel lucky to be his daughter. I know that I couldn't imagine having a better father. He is always there for me to offer his help and advice and wisdom. He has been supportive, encouraging, and a real cheerleader throughout my life.

I believe that the reasons the various television stations my dad managed became so successful and respected is because he has a way of inspiring the people who work for him. He motivated them to do their best and always went out of the way to be friendly and to remember as many of their names as possible—from the security guards on up. I really think one of his greatest qualities is the way he has of making people believe he is genuinely interested in them. He is always asking questions and listens to what is shared with him. And he is warm and very likable, which makes people feel comfortable and happy. As a consequence, I would imagine, they are more dedicated to their work. He is always interacting with people and I find it fascinating watching him. It is a great talent that he has. He is very curious about just about everything. He is a great storyteller and can tell a story like nobody I have ever met. I wish I had inherited more of his wit and humor.

My parents have such a wonderful partnership and share so much love and history together. My son is eighteen now and I always tell him he has a pretty smart grandpa."

My son, Casey, is a strong-willed and creative person who never ceases to amaze me with his talent and accomplishments. I am very proud of everything he has done in the television world and in my book he is one of the greatest cinematographers working today in Los Angeles. When I look at what he puts up on the screen, I am in awe. His work has been on all three broadcast networks, ESPN, and other cable groups. All of this he started from his garage. He has come a great distance since those early days and I am very proud of him as my son, and as a television professional.

Casey Bennett writes:
"My father is a very tough act to follow. I have learned so much from him as a person and as a television and film producer. He has always been there for me and we have always had the best of times together. He has taught me a great deal about just about everything and has always gone out of his way to encourage me to pursue my own dreams. I can only hope he is as proud of me as I am of him. He is the greatest person for creating opportunities and he has always been there for me as a father and as a friend. I'm the luckiest guy in the world to be his son."

Honorable Bruce Selya, a friend, writes:
"I have never heard Bob Bennett ever speak in a boastful way about what he has accomplished in the world of broadcasting. To the contrary, it was Bob who said to me on one occasion as we were discussing a mutual friend who was a successful television executive in Rhode Island, that much of anyone's success in the television industry came down to a question of timing and circumstance, and that virtually everyone who had entered the industry in the 1950s and had worked their way up through the system would have achieved some success in some way. It was this continual kind of unassuming posture that always typified Bob."

Bill Fine, Current President and General Manager, WCVB-TV, writes:
"One of my favorite Bob Bennett stories involves WCVB's Tenth Anniversary. In 1982, Good Morning America *asked affiliates to send tapes of viewers saying* Good Morning America *from around the country. ABC had agreed to air one such message*

from WCVB on the day of our tenth anniversary. A few days before, every WCVB employee was brought into the studio to tape our GMA message. The script called for Bob to say, 'Hi, I'm Bob Bennett and today we are celebrating our tenth anniversary at WCVB-TV in Boston,' at which point the shot would change to the entire staff finishing the greeting with a very robust, 'Good Morning America!' Our research director, Bill Mockbee, had carefully arranged everyone into position and determined that the camera would pick up every face of the hundreds gathered. Some were sitting, others were on risers, and everyone received a precise instruction from Bill on exactly where to be and not to move 'under penalty of death.' Bill, a very lovable man, was dead serious. He wanted everything perfect for 'when Mr. Bennett arrives,' as he kept saying to us.

All of us enjoyed the scene and were ready for our big moment on national television. Bill's plan was then to call Bob and have him come down as soon as everything was ready to roll. We enthusiastically practiced our line, a full-throated 'Good Morning America!' and we waited for Bob's arrival. During the entire two minutes that followed, no one dared move. Bill was circling us all like a hawk. So far his plan was working, until of course right up until the moment Bob walked into the studio. Everyone sitting just jumped to their feet; everyone standing shifted to get a better view, and the entire room broke out in a spontaneous standing ovation that lasted minutes. Bill Mockbee was apologetic, but since he had worked with Bob for many years, he wasn't really surprised and simply sat down rubbing his head with a look of resignation. At that time, I had only worked at the station for two months and was well aware that Bob Bennett was a nationally respected broadcaster. I just didn't know 'how much' of a nationally respected broadcaster he was. I also learned that day how loved he was by everyone at WCVB and how much of a leader he was, who everyone was willing to follow."

Some Magic Dust Must Have
Been Sprinkled On Me

I HAVE MANY great memories of the people and events that have made up my life. I can honestly say that I have never had a day in my life that I did not enjoy. I always had fun doing what I did, and if I had to do it all over again I would, and I would do it with the same sense of energy and enthusiasm. I have been rewarded many times over and for that I am grateful.

My life has been quite a journey filled with exciting people and marked by accomplishments that are now in the history books. All of this for me was built around the business of television.

Whatever way video is distributed and whatever platform it is viewed from, it'll always be television to me.

As I think about it, I believe a lot of my success had to do with my relationship with my mother, who was very close to me. Many of the things she taught me have shaped not only how I view the world, but how I interact with it. As mentioned before in this book, the most important thing that she ever told me was:

"Bob, whenever you are talking with someone, make sure you make that person believe that what they are saying to you is of great interest and importance to you. Make them feel that they are the most important person in the world."

I have followed that advice all my life, and it has worked.

Acknowledgments

IN NO PARTICULAR order, we are deeply indebted to and wish to thank all of the people who have contributed to the factual information in this book, and to those who have contributed their thoughts and memories.

A note of special thanks goes to Paul Rich for the taped interviews he conducted with Bob of his early years, to Kelly Bennett for making sure that the contents of those tapes were typed and bound in one book called *Bob's Book*, and to Donald E. Ward, Esq., who added insight, personal experience, and legal accuracy, toward helping me understand the long and bitter battle between the *Herald Traveler* and Boston Broadcasters, Inc., for the fight for a broadcast license that continued to be elusive.

A further note of thanks goes to all who helped with this book: Marjie Bennett, Casey Bennett, Kelly Bennett, John W. Kluge, Bud Shaffer, Mitzi McCall, Charlie Brill, Roger Brown, Patsy Good, Jack Duffield, Dale Sheets, Dick O'Leary, Chuck Velona, John Vrba, Arnie Mills, Joe Seidman, Barry Bergsman, Arthur Anderson, Andy Orckershausen, John Ross, Barbara Howar, Maury Povich, Leo Bernanek, William J. Poorvu, Stuart Subotnick, Gerry McGavick, Michael Volpe, Josh McGraw, Joseph C. Dimino, Maria Morales, Daniel Berkery, Fred Pierce, Paul Rich, Phil Balboni, Paul La Camera, Natalie Jacobson, Chet Curtis, Dr. Tim Johnson, Norman Lear, Reese Schonfeld, John Conomikes, James Coppersmith, Honorable Bruce Selya, Rona Barrett, Fred Silverman, Gerry Hribal, Bill Fine and Richard Hindlian, Esq. A special thanks to our editors Alice Sullivan and Penny Landau and our publishers David Dunham and Joel Dunham and their team at Dunham Books.

About the Authors

ROBERT M. BENNETT is a broadcasting visionary who has helped make local television what it is today. He began his career as a salesman at KTTV-TV in Los Angeles and then joined Metromedia where he was general manager for WTTG in Washington, D.C., and general manager for WNEW-TV in New York. Through a chance telephone call from a broadcasting group in Boston, he became the general manager of WCVB-TV, which, under his guidance, became the number one ABC affiliate in the country. WCVB-TV has won over 300 awards including the coveted George Foster Peabody Award. In 1982, Metromedia purchased WCVB-TV, which has long been recognized for its realization of unprecedented local broadcasting. The price tag that Metromedia paid was an unprecedented $220 million. In 1986, the Hearst Corporation purchased the station for $450 million. Today, almost four decades later, WCVB-TV continues to be a major success story.

From 1982 to 1985, he was President of Metromedia Broadcasting, the largest division of Metromedia, Inc., which in turn was one of the largest communication companies in the world. Under his leadership, Metromedia Broadcasting developed into the largest and most aggressive group operator in the country, winning Emmys for the best programs and for the production of a number of television shows. He was the first person to try and launch the Fourth Network, while he was at Metromedia.

He was founding president of the New England chapter of the National Academy of Television Arts and Sciences, and was Chairman of the Board of Governors of the ABC Television Network Affiliates Association. He was a member of the Emerson College Board of Trustees and for ten years was President of the Muscular Dystrophy Association, for two years its Chairman of the Board, and now MDA's Chairman of the Executive Committee.

Mr. Bennett was also the founder and Chairman of the Board, of Trans Atlantic Entertainment and Bennett Productions. In 2003, Mr. Bennett, along with a select group of television leaders, was inducted into the National Television Academy's Hall of Fame.

www.bobbennett.tv

DENNIS RICHARD is a playwright and the author of over 45 plays. His most recent plays include "Oswald—The Actual Interrogation," "The Bobby Fischer Game," and "Diagram for Murder." He has been involved in the media business and is a member of the Dramatist Guild and the Academy of Television Arts and Sciences.